EDUCATION, MIGRATION AND FAMILY RELATIONS BETWEEN CHINA AND THE UK: THE TRANSNATIONAL ONE-CHILD GENERATION

EDUCATION, MIGRATION AND FAMILY RELATIONS BETWEEN CHINA AND THE UK: THE TRANSNATIONAL ONE-CHILD GENERATION

BY

DR MENGWEI TU

Department of Sociology
East China University of Science and Technology
Shanghai
China

emerald
PUBLISHING

United Kingdom – North America – Japan – India – Malaysia – China

Emerald Publishing Limited
Howard House, Wagon Lane, Bingley BD16 1WA, UK

First edition 2018

Reprints and permissions service
Contact: permissions@emeraldinsight.com

British Library Cataloguing in Publication Data
A catalogue record for this book is available from the British Library

ISBN: 978-1-78714-673-0 (Print)
ISBN: 978-1-78714-672-3 (Online)
ISBN: 978-1-78743-005-1 (Epub)
ISBN: 978-1-78754-865-7 (Paperback)

INVESTOR IN PEOPLE

To the parents of the one-child generation
who supported their child's dream, including mine.

Contents

Acknowledgements

This book is written a year after the completion of my PhD. Most of the material in the book is drawn from my PhD research conducted in England from 2013 to 2014. My life has changed during the writing of the book. I moved from England to China. I left my beloved quiet sweet Canterbury and started an academic post in Shanghai. Having lived in England for seven and a half years, the sudden return to and intense integration into a rapidly-developing China brought excitement and challenge. These border-crossing changes constantly remind me of the difficulties my research participants experienced when they first arrived in England as well as when some of them travelled back and forth between China and the UK in response to career pursuit and family responsibilities.

As I continue to analyse and edit the material, the support and kindness I received during the fieldwork period became vivid during each writing day. I still remember the first time I approached a potential participant for my research, asking her to go out of her way to central London, to spend two hours with no financial return and, more importantly, to tell a stranger about her past, her family, her fear and her hopes. Each time a participant said 'yes' to my interview request, I felt a great sense of responsibility to guard her or his story.

The consent form at each interview gave participants the right to decline questions they did not feel comfortable with, and withdraw at any stage of the research. But no one declined to answer any question, even some of the very difficult questions which may have been considered 'rude' in daily exchanges. Some participants went beyond their role to offer me help and encouragement. For example, Bolin let me stay in her house for two nights so I could do a few interviews in the surrounding area; twice I was late for interview appointment by almost an hour because of delayed trains, Wenbin and Liwen waited patiently for me; Ran's parents took me to a restaurant for a meal after the interview so I did not have to leave during the peak traffic hour with an empty stomach. I thank my participants for their trust and willingness to share part of their lives with me, without whom this book would have been impossible.

My two supervisors at Kent, Professor Miri Song and Dr Joy Zhang, had been my guides when I first entered the field of sociological research. Miri is an inspirational woman and her influence on me goes beyond her role as a PhD supervisor. I am also fortunate to have known Joy, another inspirational and intelligent woman who set a great example of how to tell international audiences the 'stuff' about China. I am grateful to have had Dr Johanna Waters and Professor Adam Burgess as my PhD examiners and their valuable suggestions helped to improve the book. Johanna's on-going work in education-motivated migration continues to benefit me. I would also like to thank Kristina Göransson for letting me use a diagram inspired by her book; and for her interest in my work.

Writing a book while looking for a job can be sometimes frustrating. As most writers would appreciate, a long quiet writing period is heaven. Since my return to China in early 2017 my parents put me up for several months so that I could stay in my former bedroom. It was also the room where I wrote the dissertation for my Bachelor's degree, eight years earlier. I am grateful that the Department of Sociology at the East China University of Science and Technology opened its door to me. This book benefited from the support of "The Fundamental Research Funds for the Central Universities". The Head of School, Xuesong He, and the Head of Department, Hua Wang, were so understanding that they gave me enough time and flexibility to complete the book.

I cannot thank my friends and family enough for their unconditional love. I have, for many years, relied on Michael's intellectual and emotional support. I was very lucky to have people who cared about me and the project, so the writing process was less lonely. I would like to express my gratitude to Daniel, Titu and Suhasini, Yvette, Lili, Miaodan, Tony, Yan, Cora, Yang, Shanaj and Moon, Judy, Sarah, Jinger, Michael and Margaret, Paul, Merlin and Gilbert, Jan, Carmel, Shirley, Stacey, Kasia, Eva, Veronika and Virginia and Martin.

Finally, I am indebted to my editors, Philippa and Rachel at Emerald for their professionalism and prompt response to my various inquiries. I am grateful for the anonymous reviewer's comments on the book proposal. I also appreciate the permission from John Wiley and Sons, Springer and Taylor & Francis for me to reproduce some of their published material.

Prologue

Birmingham, UK, 7 June 2014

'You are more than welcome to stay in my place. I'm making five-spices-slow-cooked beef tonight, the Chinese way!' Bolin, in her late thirties, led me to her kitchen as she started cooking: I make Chinese food most of the time, even after having lived here for 11 years. Fortunately my husband has a Chinese stomach, and my sons like my cooking, too. I will never get used to British food!

Food is usually a topic which opens conversation in China. Here in Bolin's Birmingham home, we quickly agreed upon the superiority of Chinese cooking over British cooking; this (perhaps biased) opinion is shared among most of the 33 Chinese migrants I interviewed in various parts of England.

'So, are you used to other aspects of the British life now?'

"Well, I'd say yes. My husband is English, my children have become just like any other British children. So I'll have to adapt. I know many Chinese friends who do not want to change their lifestyle, but I think if you decide to settle in a place, you'd better change yourself to suit the local life—makes life easier".

Suddenly the front door opened and Bolin's two sons rushed in, followed by Bolin's sister-in-law, a young woman with few words who quickly disappeared from the kitchen. The boys were aged 7 and 8, they briefly exchanged school news with their mother in English and then were told to go and get changed. One of them gave me a curious look, smiled and said 'A-yi! (Auntie)' before skipping out.

Bolin laughed: "See, that's the only Chinese word they remember now. My parents looked after them for 5 years, they could speak more Chinese when they were little. Look at them, they are completely British now, there is hardly any Chineseness in them. I tried to teach them Chinese, but they don't use the language, they forget quickly".

'Where are your parents now?'

'They went back to Shanghai a couple of years ago, after the boys started schooling. It was difficult to renew their visa. Also, the British lifestyle doesn't agree with them, especially the food and the weather. Eventually they want to retire in a more familiar environment. They miss the boys so badly though, they looked after them since they were born, but I doubt if the boys will remember their Chinese grandparents in the future. I'm the only child. My parents can only see their child and grandchildren on a computer screen these days. Sometimes I feel I haven't been a good daughter to them. Ai...' Chinese people often sigh with a long 'Ai' when they do not know what to say but still want to express their feeling of disappointment, helplessness, confusion or anger: perhaps a combination of them all. 'Ai' is an ambiguous expression, it can be used at the beginning of a sentence to set the tone of what the person is about to say; in the middle of a sentence to indicate a change of meaning (like 'but'); or at the end of a sentence to politely end a topic, which seems to bring a negative emotion to the conversation. I tried to cheer Bolin up by mentioning her sons: 'Your boys are lovely, are they enjoying their school?'

'Yes, they are doing well in school.' Bolin's cheerfulness came back: 'Especially the younger one, I really want him to become a lawyer. I was a lawyer in China before I came to study in England. I gave up my career as lawyer, but I hope my son will become one, a better one. Well, who knows what they will become in the future?' Bolin had been a lawyer in China for three years before she decided to do a Master's degree in Birmingham. She was planning to return and work in an international law firm in Shanghai after the degree. 'I was naïve, I thought if I could study abroad for a year, my plans will be realised. But life changes faster than plans.'

Upon her graduation, Bolin found great difficulty in readjusting to her life back in China. Her second attempt to leave China was more of a lifestyle choice.

Later that night, after an extensive 3-hour interview, I asked Bolin if there was any possibility that she may return to China in the future.

After my sons grow up, if my parents become ill and need my care, I will move to China for as long as they need. I will quit my job if it comes to that. However, I need enough savings to be able to do that, and I can't leave my sons when they are so young. That's why I'm working hard to pay off the mortgage and to prepare for anything that may happen to my parents.

'Do your parents want you to return?'

'Yes and no. It's very complicated. My parents said they would support my decision. I have always been their centre, I took it for granted that my parents would always be there for me, all I need to do is to tell them my decision.'

Shanghai, China, 27 September 2014

When I met Bolin's parents in Shanghai three months later, they told me that they had hoped for their daughter's return until the birth of their grandchildren. 'I wish I had another child, so I can keep one near me, then I don't need to worry that much about whether Bolin stays in England or not. Ai...'

Bolin's mother turned away to hide her tears. Bolin's father changed the topic to supper: 'Do you like dumplings? We have many dumplings ready in the freezer. They are not supermarket dumplings, we handmade them with fresh vegetables and pork. Let's boil some—quick and tasty!' He explained to me during supper that they usually make a hundred dumplings to freeze and eat a dozen of them each day: 'We don't bother with a lot of cooking these days. It's just the two of us, not much appetite. We like dumplings anyway.'

Bolin's parents live in a 3-bedroom flat located in a pleasant area of Shanghai. The flat was once owned by Bolin's paternal grandparents. As we were having dumplings, the former owners' portraits, which were hanging on the wall near the dinner table, became a blur in the hot steam. Bolin's father bore many similarities to the man in the portrait: 'My father was a soldier. He was strict, but open-minded. I was also strict with my daughter. I finished high school on June 1, 1966. Four days later the Cultural Revolution began, I couldn't go to university, so when my daughter was born, I swore I'd raise her to the highest standard.'

Bolin has been the pride of her parents since she was a child. I listened to the achievements she made, from winning a writing prize in her primary school to securing a place in one of the top universities in China. I also heard her parent's critical remarks about the sometimes lack of obedience from Bolin to the older generation, as well as their disappointment of not being near their daughter and grandchildren. 'We are most likely to end up in an old people's home here,' declared Bolin's father, who was in his late sixties, 'It's just not feasible that we move to England.' Bolin's mother agreed: 'We can still look after each other, and we have some relatives here. I'm sure they can give us a hand when needed. But everybody is getting old, what would one of us do if the other one dies first? These are the questions for the future. We have no answer now.'

Introduction

This book is written nearly four decades after China's implementation of the one-child policy in 1979. The policy permitted families in China to have only one child with few exceptions applied to some rural residents and the ethnic minority population. As a result, 65% of the nation's post-1980s generation comprises the only-child cohort (Lin & Sun, 2010). Bolin was born in 1975. Her family was one of the earliest cohorts affected by the policy. Bolin's mother was pregnant in 1978, but she chose to abort the second child because 'there was simply no time to look after another baby'. Both the mother and her husband were working full time; the extended family members were either living too far away or were too busy with their own work and offspring. When the policy was implemented in 1979, a second child was no longer an option.

Since the late 1970s, a small-family culture has been replacing the traditional big-family culture, especially in Chinese cities. Families became geographically dispersed, and the nuclear three-member-one-child-family quickly became the norm. The 2010 Chinese Census showed an average household size of 3.1 people.[1] In the early 2000s, Shanghai's only-child percentage exceeded 80% of all children (Bao, 2012). When talking to one-child migrants and their parents, it was clear that for many urban families, having only one child was the given, while having more than one child was the exception. It is worth noting that such a belief had different levels of pervasiveness in rural and semi-rural areas for a number of socio-economic reasons. Nevertheless, the dominating norm of the one-child family remained unchallenged until a nationwide shift from the one-child policy to a 'two-children' policy in October 2015, ironically, where women were *encouraged* to have a second child in response to a rapidly ageing population. The new policy allowed couples, who were formerly restricted to having only one child, to have a maximum of two children.

Education, Migration and Family Relations between China and the UK:
The Transnational One-Child Generation, 1–21
doi:10.1108/978-1-78714-672-320181002

Between the implementation of the two population-control policies, China experienced dramatic changes in its economy, environment and international relations. Wealth generation and redistribution led to a new round of social stratification – a process that was previously based on the political background in Mao's era. In a short period of three decades China was transformed 'from being one of the most egalitarian countries to being one of the most unequal' (Biao & Shen, 2009, p. 516). For families caught up among these unprecedented changes the debate of whether to (and somehow bypass the policy) have a second child quickly moved on to the focus of securing a better future for the only child in a highly competitive society – a society that was alien to parents during their upbringing. The competition for educational resources has been a central theme for Chinese families across the social spectrum. The pursuit of children's success in education at great parental sacrifice is perhaps familiar to readers who have come across writings about parenting in East Asian societies or among East Asian ethnic groups.

However, as the education resource diversified, the former clear objective of 'a good state school, and then a good university' was challenged by other options such as private education and overseas education.

The education landscape for the one-child Chinese families experienced drastic changes especially with regard to cross-border education. The reopening of the Chinese border in 1978 also marked the first state-led study-abroad programme. Although in the early years, study abroad was largely state-sponsored and limited to a select few; this feature attached legitimacy and privilege to overseas education (predominately to major Western countries). Hence, study abroad quickly became a magnet that attracted the rising middle-class in China who were the beneficiaries of the wealth redistribution in the 1980s and 1990s.

The outflow of self-funded students was striking in its vast number and rapidly increasing rate. Among students who went abroad annually, the percentage of self-funded students rose from 65% in 1996 to 89% in 2001 (Li, H., 2010) and 92.5% in 2011 (Wang & Guo, 2012). By that time China had become the biggest international student-sending country, and 82.5% of students were funded by their parents (Wang & Guo, 2012). World-leading education providers, such as the UK, witnessed a sharp increase in the number of students from China since the turn of the century. By 2012 Chinese students made up a third of non-EU students in British universities.

The rapid increase of Chinese students from the late 1990s coincided with the coming of age of the one-child generation. It is difficult to separate the one-child identity from the 21st century Chinese migration. The one-child generation refers to the people who were born around or after the implementation of the one-child policy in 1979 until shortly before the relaxation of the policy in 2015. Children born a few years before 2015 may have a sibling or remain an only-child depending on the parental *voluntary* decision.

However, the earlier cohorts remain the only generation that was born and grew up when a *compulsory* one-child limit was in place. This generation includes people who were born before 1979 but remained an only-child as a result of the policy (like Bolin), as well as those who were born after 1979 but had sibling(s). Regardless of being an only-child or not, people who were born between 1979 and 2015 are affected by the one-child policy. However, 'generation' is an ambiguous term. The rough designation of the 'one-child generation' based on the year of the individual's birth does not necessarily reflect a shared experience: childhood in the 1980s hardly resembles childhood in the 2000s.

In this book the 'one-child generation' consists mainly of people born in the 1980s (with slight extensions to the late 1970s and early 1990s). The post-1980s children were the earlier cohort produced by the policy which has been the focus of media and academic attention. From the 1980s into the early years of the 21st century, the one-child generation has been predominately perceived as a 'problem' by the media and by the general public. In the 1980s, as the first cohort of the one-child generation started their schooling, the dominant discourse of the one-child policy shifted, both in China and in the West, to the 'danger' of the 'spoiled' one-child generation. The only-child cohort was commonly labelled as 'little emperors'. The 'selfishness' found among them was referred to as the 'little emperor syndrome'as if it was a disease.[2] In 1987, the Chinese state made a film titled *Little Emperors of China* with the then leading Chinese actors addressing the claimed problems of the 'spoiled' one-child generation.

As the one-child generation was still in the relatively early stages of their lives when the film (and other coverage about the cohort) came to the public's attention, the active agency of these individuals was easily overlooked. The young age of the one-child generation made it impossible to carry out satisfactory studies in the previous decades. Today when we are well into the second decade of the 21st century, the earlier cohort of the one-child generation, in their twenties and thirties, have started taking the central role in the society. The (possibly) misunderstood and under-researched life experiences of the adult one-child generation deserve an up-to-date investigation.

As the one-child generation reaches adulthood and even parenthood, a more diverse profile emerges. Their activities go beyond not only the social boundary of home and schools but also the physical boundary of national borders. Overseas education has been viewed largely as parental investment on a better future for their only child. In this book we will go beyond the child's education and look at the evolvement of the Chinese family system as we make inquiries into the one-child generation migrants' motivation to study abroad, analyse their decision to remain in the UK, and observe how the family dynamic changes as the one-child migrants become parents themselves. The adult one-child experience in this book is a continuation of the existing understanding about the post-1980s children and a way to talk back to the previous literature which focused on this generation.

The One-Child Generation in the World of Migration

It is time to reveal my identity: I belong to the one-child generation. My upbringing was not in any way extraordinary. I grew up in a southeastern coastal city in China. My parents worked as professionals and I had a fairly well-provided childhood. Following the completion of my undergraduate course, I moved to the UK for a Master's degree in Nottingham in 2009. After my graduation I applied for a post-student work (PSW) visa, which allowed me to stay in the UK for two years to work. I found a job at an international trade company, which imported goods from China to be sold in the lower-end market in the UK. The company was founded by a one-child Chinese migrant from Shanghai while he was doing a PhD course at Exeter in the early 2000s. I met several other Chinese staff who were in the same situation as me: having completed a Master's degree at a British university and who held a temporary work visa. Our ages ranged from the early twenties to mid-thirties. Not knowing exactly where our lives were going, we were a little anxious about the temporary nature of our migration status, but at the same time hopeful about our future in the UK.

A shared background quickly encouraged us to learn about each other's stories. What struck me was that under the seemingly similar migration pattern, our upbringing, motivation to study abroad, and outlook in this country were very different. I met Qiaolin (female, 36), from a city in Western China, Qianqian (female, 27), from Beijing and Bao (female, 31), from Shanghai. Qiaolin and Qianqian both had siblings while Bao was an only-child. Qiaolin was born in 1978, and having an older sister she escaped the restriction of the one-child policy. Qianqian was born in 1987 and had an older brother; her parents had to pay a large fine for her birth. Qianqian was sent away to live with her aunt when she was five because her parents, who had their own business, had no time to look after two children. Bao, however, said she wanted to escape the attention and pressure given by her parents; the study abroad was her way to protest against her 'over-protective' parents.

In October 2011, when we had our last dinner together, Qiaolin was starting a family with her British partner. Bao was given financial help from her parents and was looking for a property to buy. Qianqian had just started her job with the company, and I was applying for a PhD course. When I went to visit them for my research two years later Qiaolin had a one-year-old daughter. She and her partner were trying for a second baby. Bao had moved to her new house and was under great pressure from her parents to get married. Qianqian was disappointed by her career potential in the UK; she was contemplating moving back to Beijing.

As my fellow one-child generation migrants and I continue our separate lives and navigate our future routes, I start to re-think the century-old questions that have been asked by many migration study scholars:

> Why do people migrate?
> What happens to people after their migration?
> What is the impact of migration?

More than a hundred years after E. G. Ravenstein's early attempt to generate 'the laws of migration' (1889, 1885), it has been claimed that we are now in 'the age of migration' (Castles & Miller, 2009) where few countries are indifferent to the opportunities and challenges of international migration, and more individuals are on the move than before. While the number of low-skilled migrants in OECD[3] countries increased by 12% during the first decade of the 21st century, the highly skilled or educated migrants increased by 70% (OECD, 2013).

Migrants have been viewed primarily as skill-bearers to be exploited for the host country's economy, and hence the common divide of 'high-skill' and 'low-skill' migrants in research and migration policies. However, a migrant's life is multidimensional. Apart from being a worker, the individual is also a son or daughter, (maybe) a spouse or parent, possibly a property owner, who perhaps owns a business, and who is likely to be a member of several social networks. Furthermore, people are not *born* a migrant, they *become* a migrant at a certain point in their life. The earlier part of their lives before leaving home inevitably shapes their migration decisions and their experiences after migration. There is no uniformity to migration.

In today's migration studies field few scholars are prepared to make a claim on a set of generalized 'laws' of migration, unlike the classical migration theorists in the 20th century (e.g. Massey et al., 1998, Stark, 1991, 1984). Migration research has moved away from system building to more specialized divisions, for example, region (e.g. intra-EU migration), legal status (e.g. refugee studies) and motivation (e.g. education-motivated migration).

The concept of migration generates different emphases depending on the perspective of the researcher: migration can be treated as a *result* following a cluster of factors; a *process* which leads to certain consequences, or a *field* which contains interacting agencies and networks at all levels. These approaches to the concept of migration allow us to open different windows and gain some insight into the various aspects of the moving population.

However, just as few countries are immune to the impact of international migration, few fields can satisfy inquiries about migration without borrowing from other fields. The increasing presence of international students further complicates our understanding of migration as well as the role of education in individual (physical and social) mobility. When Qiaolin, Qianqian and Bao made their decisions to have children, to change jobs and to buy property, to what extent did their former international student experience shape their post-student decisions? Furthermore, for one-child migrants like Bao, how is their migration journey different from non-one-child migrants like Qiaolin and Qianqian, and how is their relationship with parents different from the only children who live much closer to their parents in China?

Defining Study Abroad and Migration

Are international students migrants? This question has been the focus of discussion since the then British Prime Minister David Cameron announced the 'migration cap' in 2010 (Prince, 2010). He proposed to reduce the number of net migration to the UK from 'hundreds of thousands' and keep it under 'tens of thousands'. Students were included in the net migration count. The number of net migrants in 2010 was 256,000 and has failed to decline significantly, with the most recent count in 2016 being 248,000.[4] Since the 'migration cap' is a political goal and was used to target the 'less popular' foreigners such as low-skill workers, then why are international students included in the net migration count?

According to the United Nations Department of Economic and Social Affairs, the definition of an international migrant is stated as follows:

> While there is no formal legal definition of an international migrant, most experts agree that an international migrant is someone who changes his or her country of usual residence,

irrespective of the reason for migration or legal status. Generally, a distinction is made between short-term or temporary migration, covering movements with a duration between three and 12 months, and long-term or permanent migration, referring to a change of country of residence for a duration of one year or more.[5]

Different definitions of migration are used by different government resources,[6] but they tend to share criteria such as country of residence/birth and length of stay. Facts like these help data collectors to find reliable starting points on which they can base their calculations. However, seeking a clear-cut migrant categorization compromises the data's ability to reflect the real picture, which is flexible and fluid.

Going back to the debate about whether to include students in the number of net migration, among the evidence of socioeconomic benefit international students bring to the UK, and the local public service pressure that comes with it, it is the argument about the *temporariness* of students (i.e. will students remain after their study?) that is central to the debate (The Migration Observatory, 2015). In theory each student-visa holder is open to the option of switching to other visa types such as work visa or family visa, thus making them potential long-term migrants. In reality, however, the level of difficulty for students to switch to full-time employment in the UK has become greater and the number of successful visa-switchers has dropped massively since 2012.[7] Therefore, do we call a foreign-born student a 'migrant' as soon as she/he crosses the border of the UK with a student visa, or *after* that person switches from student status to a more permanent basis? And what counts as a 'more permanent basis'? How is a three-year work contract more permanent than a three-year studentship?

With these questions in mind let us turn to scholarly work for some insights. Having devoted 'a lifetime of his scholarship to tracking and explaining the various cycles of Chinese migration and settlement' (Huang, 2010, p. 1), Wang Gungwu describes the 'delayed' migration among international students as *migranthood*: the condition of a migrant in the space 'between that of a student and that of a migrant' (Wang, 2007, p. 167). Wang distinguishes student-turned-migrants from traditionally defined migrants who leave 'their home without intending to return', thus students are not traditional migrants. But being a student may lead to 'delayed' migration. Wang argues that the post-student migrants are flexible and unpredictable because they respond to the global demand for skills. In the meantime, post-student migrants are also 'the product of economic and technological globalisation' (Wang, 2007, p. 176).

However, time is a concern. Study abroad and migration (assuming they are two different processes) – which happened first? Is overseas education used as a means to long-term migration or is long-term migration inspired by overseas education? Empirical research on the Chinese overseas students or migrants shows the co-existence of both processes. With studying abroad becoming easier and other means to enter a Western country becoming harder, there has been a growing phenomenon of individuals applying to study in an overseas language school with low entry requirements as a way to 'buy a visa' (Fong, 2011, p. 115). This cohort tended to come from less well-off families with a poor academic background, and their objective was to work in the host country under a student visa. Very few made it to a degree course or a professional job and faced the possible risk of failing to extend their visas (Fong, 2011). Since the early 2000s, a small percentage of UK language schools (estimated to be 10% in 2006) have abused the visa system and faced closure (Watson, 2014, BBC, 2006, 2005).

At the other end of the spectrum, well-off Chinese families, particularly from Hong Kong and Taiwan (more recently, from mainland China [Liu-Farrer, 2016]), were found to have joined the citizenship of developed Western countries, typically the US or Canada, so that their children can have better access to locally provided education (Tsong & Liu, 2009, Huang & Yeoh, 2005, Waters, 2005, Ong, 2003). A common pattern found among the trans-Pacific Chinese families was characterized as an 'astronaut family'; the term referred to the process where one parent accompanied the child to the host country while the other parent (usually the father) stayed in the home country to earn money; he would travel regularly between his family and work. Similarly, widely used terms like 'Pacific shuttle', and 'parachute kids' (Ley, 2010, Tsang et al., 2003, Zhou, 1998) also reflected an education-motivated, child-centred trans-Pacific migration arrangement. In this scenario well-informed parents played the dominating role of decision-making, and children were found to leave their country of birth at a relatively young age, typically in their early to mid-teens.

The latter pattern is usually referred to as 'education-motivated migration' (e.g. 'astronaut family'). I would call the earlier 'buying a visa' process 'migration-motivated study abroad'. Compared to the highly calculated feature of these two migration/study abroad processes, a more common process was found among the mainland Chinese post-student migrants in the UK: the tendency of switching to 'migranthood' emerges towards the end of their study abroad where uncertainty and changing perception of self, family and space impact upon the student/migrant's decision-making process.

Although 'migranthood' captures the flexibility and fluidity of migrant-in-transition, it is an underdeveloped term. Wang Gungwu did not indicate when, or whether, 'migranthood' ends, nor did he explain how or whether post-student migrants identify themselves with such a 'state of being'. For example, is Qianqian's status (arrived 3 years previously, renting, single) more like 'migranthood' or is Bolin's (arrived 11 years previously, property owner, married with children)?

The lengthy discussion about the concepts of study abroad and migration serves the purpose of demonstrating the complexity of the real picture. Drawing on his insight in study abroad research, James Coleman criticized the existing attempt to 'achieve significant generalizations' which resulted in a 'sometimes distorted reality by narrowing our definitions and our measures, and by leaving crucial information unconsidered or even unstated' (2013, p. 17). The life-changing experience of study abroad deserves an approach which examines its long-term impact. This research follows a framework that captures an individual's evolving mobility trajectory as it unfolds with changing circumstances at different levels which not only takes place in a relatively more changeable period of a person's life (from education completion to career/family establishment) but is also embedded in a transnational context.

Education and Migration to the UK

Chinese settlement in the UK started relatively later than that in the Asia-Pacific regions. The UK's first Chinese visitor was recorded in 1681 (Benton & Gomez, 2011). However, large-scale migration from China to the UK began after the mid-19th century. The early Chinese diaspora originated mainly from Canton and Hong Kong (Benton & Gomez, 2011). Such migrants generally came from a poor background and did menial work (Liu, 2011). A most common early pattern among this wave of migrants was the objective to make money in the UK, and return home for retirement. A shift from sojourner to settler occurred from after World War II and the following several decades; a period also marked by the unstable political and economic environment in China (Benton & Gomez, 2011).

From the 19th century to the early 20th century the UK Chinese diaspora experienced changes of business openings and opportunities. The various niches have been summarized by scholars as 'salt-soap-soya'. This designation refers essentially to the seafaring groups of the late 19th century, the laundry business in the early 20th century and the catering industry from the mid-20th century (Benton & Gomez, 2011). There are later signs of the

Chinese diaspora's economic activities expanding, which indicates their attempts to break away from the narrow catering niche, and their seeking greater social mobility. The percentage of Chinese workers (regardless of place of birth) working in the catering industry fell from an estimated 90% in 1985 to slightly more than half in 1991 (Chau & Yu, 2001). Recent research shows that a larger number of Chinese can be found working in the business sector and health and education service (Knowles, 2015).

Meanwhile, the early diaspora's second generation, the British-born Chinese, have developed a very different profile; they have enjoyed greater social mobility, and are not prepared to be bound by their ethnic identity. They are better educated, and culturally more assimilated to British society than their parents were. British-born Chinese are more likely to have professional jobs and have become middle class, rather than continuing in their parents' take-away business (Benton & Gomez, 2011, Song, 1999). This group of the Chinese diaspora tends not to identify itself only as Chinese, but as having 'segmented identities', where being neither *Chinese* nor *British* dominate unconditionally (Parker, 1995).

The migration from China to the UK sharply increased between the 2001 Census and the 2011 Census (see Fig. 1). In 2012, 40,000 Chinese migrants arrived in the UK, and China ranked the top of migrant-sending countries to the UK for the first time (ONS, 2013b). The arrival of the new Chinese migrants from mainland China has changed the Hong Kong (Cantonese) dominating profile of the UK Chinese. The percentage of people from mainland China among the ethnic Chinese population in the UK rose from 13% in 1991 (Cheng, 1994) to 40% in 2011 (ONS, 2012).

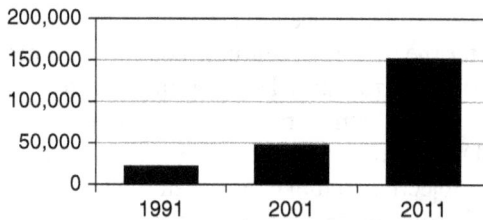

Fig. 1:   China-born residents in the UK (Census).
Source: ONS (2013a).

The demographic profile of the new arrivals has been consistently found to be younger (Biao & Shen, 2009). The large number of recent young arrivals reflected the high proportion of students: students aged 16 and over comprised 45% of the Chinese who arrived between 2001 and 2011 (ONS, 2013a) and the number has been increasing. The student-dominant feature distinguishes the current wave of Chinese migrants from the previous wave (Hong Kong migrants in the fifties to sixties) who tended to be part of a migration network based on relatives and clans (Watson, 1977). Although there is no statistic that shows how many of the 21st century arrivals belong to the one-child generation, it is safe to infer from their age that the majority of the student arrivals does. Most students were funded by their parents; thus, they reflect a largely middle-class family background.

The students who remained after their studies were commonly found in professional jobs. Having limited connection with traditional Chinese communities, the 'elite' Chinese migrants may have benefited from their personal, social and economic networks both at home and in the host countries. What the 'elite' Chinese migrants had in common with the traditional Chinese diaspora was the significant role of the family in generating and sustaining their transnational networks. However, the one-child transnational family represents a unique form of family: it is the combined product of socioeconomic changes in and outside of China.

The Transnational One-Child Family in Time and Space

One-child Chinese migrants are at the centre of several intense relations. As individuals their migration took place during one of the most uncertain stages of their lives: important life events such as completing education, starting a career, getting married and becoming parents, tend to happen to people in their twenties (although starting a family is sometimes deferred). Each life event is intertwined with the on-going decision about return migration or re-migration to another country. Yet the longitudinal feature of the migration decision-making process has not been given much attention. As migrants whose social, economic and cultural lives are divided between the host country and China, they are very sensitive (and vulnerable) towards any policy and social changes in both countries. Therefore, the question remains whether overseas education and migration will lead to transnational advantages or transnational compromises. As the only child in the family, crucial aspects of a migrant's life, such as care, emotion, and expectation are intensified; thus making the one-child transnational family a unique 'transnational social field' (Levitt & Schiller, 2004) to investigate how family and migration impact on each other.

To put this micro-level family dynamic in the bigger picture of time and space (Fig. 2), we see the continuity and discontinuity of intergenerational relations, as well as the family (physical and social) space divided between China and the UK. When viewed from a vertical (time) perspective, family

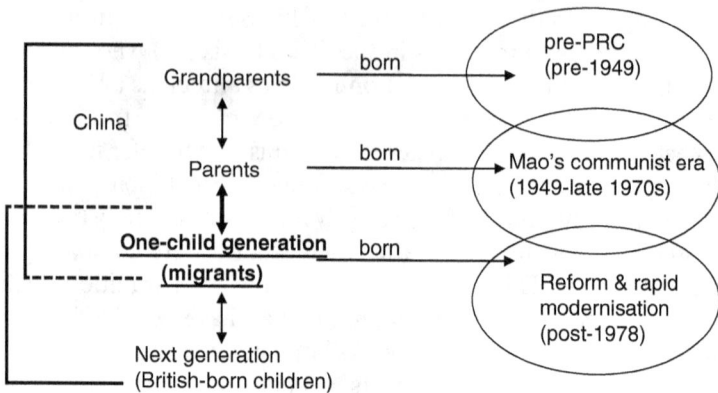

Fig. 2:   Intergenerational relations in the one-child family in space and time.

relations can be influenced by the intergenerational relations of the previous generation; likewise, family relations can also influence the obligations and expectations between the current and the next generation. When viewed from a horizontal (space) perspective, family relations were subject to changes according to the changing physical and social space in which parents and children found themselves. When combined with these two perspectives, the transnational one-child family constitutes the cohort that experienced the most intense space and time changes within two generations; historically, the family members experienced the most radical political upheavals and drastic economic reforms[8] in modern Chinese history. Structurally, these nuclear families were made up of the 'baby boomer' generation[9] and the 'one-child' generation; geographically and socially, only-children and their parents lived separately in the 'West' and the 'East'.

The one-child generation, their parents and their grandparents were born in sharply and distinctively different political and economic periods in Chinese history. For the one-child migrants who had child(ren) (or planned to have children) in the UK, their British-born children would be brought up in yet another, different, environment. Will the 'traditional family contract' based on Confucius' teaching survive such significant changes through the four generations? Which elements will remain and which parts will diminish?

Studying One-Child Migrants As One of Them

This is not the first book that looks at the one-child generation in China or overseas, but it is, as far as I know, one of the very few books written by a one-child researcher about her own cohort. Whether qualitative research is better conducted by an 'outsider' or an 'insider' is open to discussion. This research does not intend to argue that the 'insider' approach was inherently 'superior'. What is important to point out here is that most published qualitative studies on the Chinese one-child generation have been done by 'outsiders'. These 'outsiders' include Western scholars[10] (Kajanus, 2015, Goh, 2011, Fong, 2011, 2004) and Chinese scholars of an older generation[11] (Liu, 2008a, b). For the non-Chinese researchers, apart from the culture shock and the language barrier, their 'foreign' identity was a marked feature throughout their research. Such a feature was particularly pronounced in Anni Kajanus' fieldwork in Beijing. Being 'white and Western', Kajanus believed her 'foreign' identity attracted young Chinese people to participate in her research. Consequently, she was 'often treated as a guest', and noted her informants' clear effort to show 'the 'foreign friend' the 'best part of Chinese society and culture' (2015, p. 41).

The outsider identity is not as immediately pronounced among researchers who are Chinese (or Chinese of a Western nationality). However, there was a methodological setback in their research that was mainly to do with sample recruitment. Most of these researchers entered the lives of their one-child participants as their teacher or through schools or universities. For example, Vanessa Fong (2004) offered free English lessons in exchange for access to her students' family lives. Fengshu Liu (2008a, b) worked in a university in China and her participants were recruited through her former students.

However, being an 'insider' does not make the sample recruitment any easier. The word 'invisible' has been repeatedly used in media and in academic research when describing the Chinese in the UK (Barber, 2015, Luk, 2008, Parker & Song, 2007, The Guardian, 1993). The mainland post-student Chinese migrants were more difficult to reach than the traditional Chinese diaspora in two ways. First, they were professionally dispersed in mainstream industries (instead of concentrating in the catering business). Such a feature was also likely to lead to the further geographical dispersion of the professional cohort. Second, there was a lack of professional new Chinese migrants in Chinese associations, partly because the established associations were catering for traditional Chinese settlers, and partly because the resourceful middle-class migrants did not feel the immediate need to create and participate in diasporic associations (Liu, 2011, Benton & Gomez, 2011). Even so, at the beginning of the sample recruitment, various Chinese associations (such as the British Chinese Society and the Chinese and Oriental Students Society) and university alumni associations were contacted, but there was no response.

To overcome the above challenge, the internet was used, in addition to the researcher's personal contacts, as another resource of recruitment. I observed active participation of new Chinese migrants on the two major mainland Chinese public forums in the UK: LKCN (http://lkcn.net/bbs/index.php?act=idx) and Powerapple (www.powerapple.com). These two online forums were used as fields of recruitment and produced positive responses. In addition to public forums, social network services (SNS) also gave rise to more specified online groups, such as various professional and academic online groups formed by mainland Chinese in the UK, where the target cohort of this research was more likely to be found. It was relatively straightforward for me to gain access to these Mandarin-speaking forums and SNS groups because of my insider identity.

While the internet recruitment attracted a reasonable amount of interest, the person-to-person recruitment was slow. Most participants did not 'snowball' into a greater number of contacts. The majority of participants indicated the limited social contacts they had with fellow Chinese migrants. Since most of the middle-class Chinese migrants arrived in the UK as students, the initial Chinese friends they made were mostly their fellow students. 'Now they've all gone back' was the most frequently expressed explanation for the lack of Chinese contacts in the UK. Working in non-Chinese companies also limited the participants' opportunities for making Chinese friends, compared to their counterparts who worked in the Chinese catering business.

Furthermore, there appeared to be a lack of active involvement with Chinese communities among the professional Chinese migrants. Being highly educated, fluent in English and resourceful, this cohort clearly had the ability to develop its social circle outside of the Chinese community. Although the majority reported a generally limited social circle in the UK, they appeared to be indifferent or casual about the limited number of Chinese friends but showed more anxiety about how difficult it was to 'make friends with the locals'. This attitude is similar to Knowles' (2015, p. 17) discovery in the latest study on affluent Beijing migrants in London. She found that her informants did not 'lead particularly Chinese lives' nor did they 'live in what is referred to as the Chinese community': they were 'integrated in a London cosmopolitan way'.

A breakthrough in the recruitment of more participants in the UK, was, interestingly, made by contacting returnees in China. Similarly to other members in the cohort I maintained contact with my friends who returned to China after study/work abroad. Through the network of the returnees, a substantial number of UK participants with a variety of backgrounds were recruited. This feature of 'transnational recruitment' reflected the emerging transnational social field of the new Chinese migrants. Such an adjustment in the recruitment process was also an example of how the profile of participants and recruitment strategy influenced each other during the research process. As Bryman (2008, p. 185) pointed out, snowball sampling is useful in 'reflecting the relationships between people'. Fig. 3 shows the three channels of sample recruitment (contacts in the UK, contacts in China and the internet) as well as the *limited* 'relationships between people'.

The diagram shows the variety of sources and the process of recruiting participants. The matching of number and individual participants can be found in the Appendix.

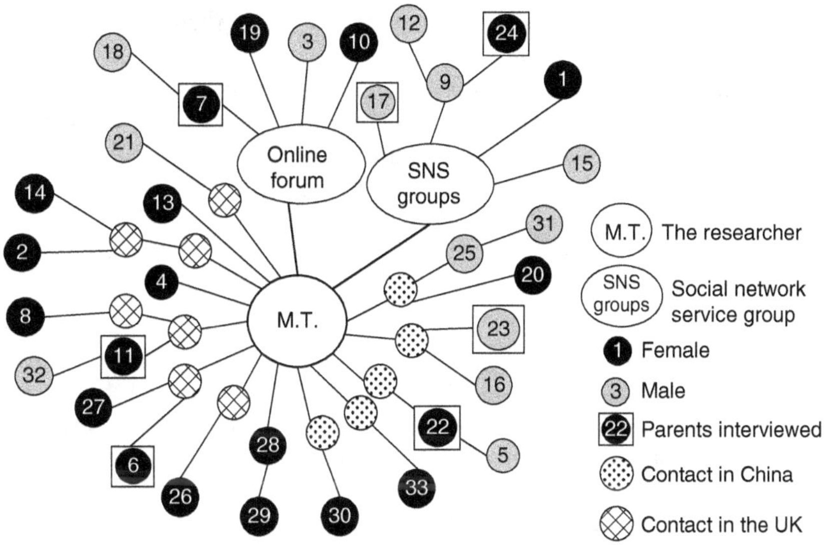

Fig. 3:   Participant recruitment network [inspired by a figure used in Göransson's book (2009, p. 43) and reproduced here with permission from the original author and the University of Hawaii Press].

Interviewing both the child and parents from the same family has been rare in transnational family research largely because of the difficulty in accessing both child and parents in a transnational setting. The recruitment of parents began later than the recruitment of migrant participants. After the completion of each interview, the participants were asked whether they would be willing to connect the researcher to their parents in China. This request was met with three types of response. First, the participant did not want to ask their parents to take part in the research.

Second, the participant asked, but parents declined the interview request. Third, the participant and parents both responded positively to the interview request, and they constitute the seven sets of parents in the sample.

The different types of responses reflect the matter of *trust*. For most parents in this study, taking part in social research was new to them. The parents' generation experienced the Cultural Revolution and were understandably wary of taking part in an 'interview' with a researcher (i.e. a stranger) from a public institution. For example, during an interview with a father from the Inner Mongolia region of China, I was asked several times whether the interview would be 'leaked' to the Chinese Communist Party even after repeated assurances of the confidentiality entailed in the research. Parental suspicion towards 'interviews' was also part of the reason why some participants were reluctant to contact their parents for the researcher. For example, Zhiming (male, 31, sales manager) was recruited through the internet. He was supportive of the research, but when asked about research contact with his parents Zhiming hesitated for a while and politely refused, explaining that his parents might think he had 'got into trouble in the UK' and was subject to 'investigation'.

The Participants

The sample recruited in the UK comprised 20 women and 13 men. There is currently no reliable research that documents the gender ratio among middle-class one-child Chinese migrants in the UK. Consistently, more Chinese women than Chinese men graduated from UK higher education institutions between 2001 and 2011. Women outnumbered men in Master's programmes and undergraduate programmes by a ratio of 1.5 to 1 in 2008/2009 (Iannelli & Huang, 2013). Therefore, it is reasonable to infer that more women remained after education than men. Furthermore, the total number of 40 participants constituted enough variety for the purpose of this research.

In terms of places of origin (see Fig. 4), the participants came from a variety of regions in China. Such diversity reflected what the literature highlighted about the new Chinese migrants: they not only came from transnational coastal migrant regions like Shanghai and Canton (near Hong Kong) but also from inland regions which had not been traditionally migrant-sending places. However, there was no identifiable pattern between participants' places of origin and places of residence in the UK. Participants were distributed in various parts of England. Nevertheless, the concentration of the Chinese population in London is clear.

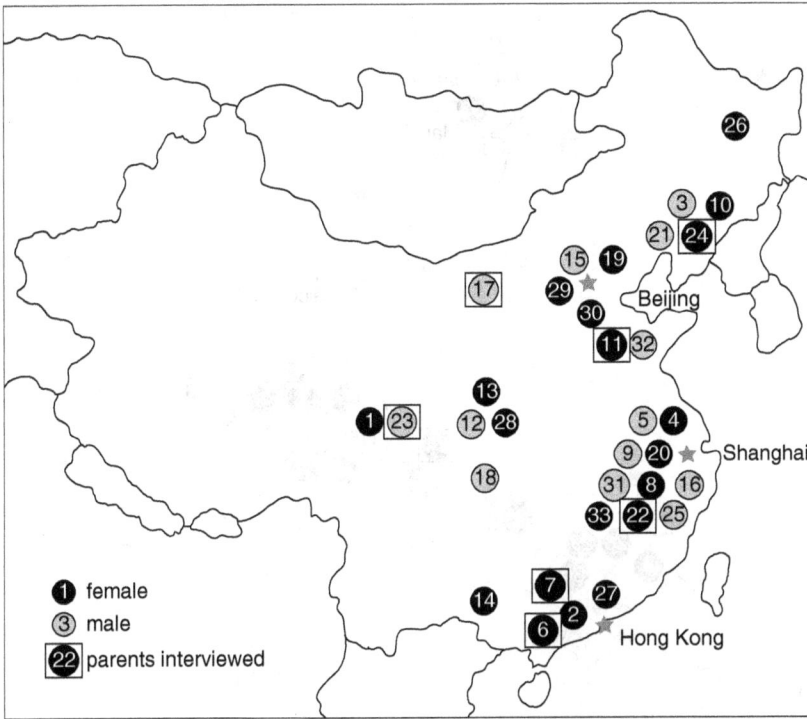

Fig. 4:　Participants' place of origin in China.

Such a London-dominant Chinese population distribution also reflected the latest report of the young Chinese migrants (aged 23–39) in London (Knowles, 2015).

However, Knowles (2015) pointed out that although London had the biggest Chinese population in number, Cambridge had the highest concentration of the Chinese population (the Chinese constituted 3.6% of the population). A relatively high Chinese concentration can also be found in cities with Russell Group universities.[12] Most participants had moved at least once: they arrived in the UK where their university was and later moved to where their job was (if the university was not in London). Job opportunities were greater in London, and nearly half of the participants who lived in London were in finance-related jobs (see the Appendix).

These maps of sample distribution are by no means representative of the one-child migrants' population. The objective of the study was not to recruit a statistically representative sample but to recruit a sample with a diverse background in order to reduce bias. Major qualitative studies

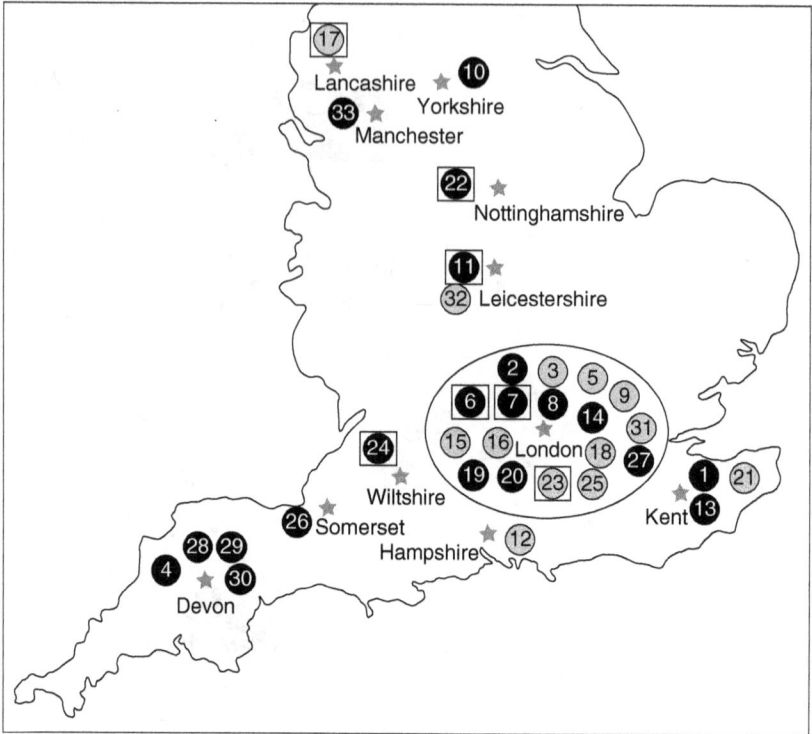

Fig. 5: Participants' place of residence in the UK.

into the one-child generation tended to be limited to one Chinese city (see Kajanus, 2015, Fong, 2011, 2004, Goh, 2011). Although Kajanus (2015) and Fong (2011) followed their participants as they went abroad as students, their research subjects were geographically limited to their place of origin. This study is the first in which qualitative research on the one-child generation contains participants from vastly different regions of China; such regions in China have distinctive cultural and socioeconomic features which were likely to shape its people's perceptions. Based on a very limited observation in this study, participants from north China (including Beijing) were relatively more politically sensitive, while participants from south China were relatively more business oriented. Although such an observation is not generalizable, an inclusive one-child generation sample certainly contributed to more balanced data.

Similarly, this research is also the first qualitative research about the new Chinese migrants with participants recruited from different regions in England. The sample included traditionally Chinese-concentrated places like London as well as the more white-dominated regions like Devon. In a very general sense the participants from London tended to be younger and more career oriented. The non-London participants contained a greater proportion of married women. A common reason for these women to live in locations other than London was because their English husbands were settled in various parts of England.[13] Such a feature between London participants and non-London participants was only indicative and not generalizable. Nevertheless, if participants had been recruited from a single location, like London, this book may have risked the possibility of overrepresenting the Chinese migrants who remained mainly for jobs and underrepresented those who remained mainly for families.

Chapter Structure

Chapter 1 sets the broad historical, social, political and cultural context from which a significant amount became a legacy for only-children and their parents in both subtle and gross manifestations. Chapter 2 offers a re-visit into four themes: 'little emperor', authoritarian Chinese parenting, gender and education. Growing up in a more competitive society, only-children from middle-class families had more resources and choices than did children from less-affluent families. The contrast in the upbringing of the parents' generation and the one-child generation signals the beginning of a challenging and dynamic intergenerational relationship.

With the coming of age of the one-child generation, both parents and children were about to face a journey of uncertainty to the UK. The country that was once deemed the 'the capitalist enemy' in the parents' generation, now became the destination that would ensure a global advantage for their only child. Chapter 3 explores questions including: To what extent is a migration decision rational? Since more than half of the participants initially intended to return to China, what changed their minds? And what role did parents play in these decisions?

Chapter 4 focuses on the migrants' lives in the present. I found a predominately parent-to-child intergenerational flow of money and care regardless of the child's income level and age. It is the first time in Chinese international migration history that a predominately China-to-overseas financial transfer has taken place, especially between family members at home and working adult children in a developed country. The chapter explores the rationale behind this unusual remittance pattern. Chapter 5 shows the simultaneous impact of time and space on filial piety as a guide to the Chinese family contract, as well as the initiatives and compromises made by family members at the centre of the changes. The final chapter draws the main threads of the book's themes to a conclusion while also offering a selective summary of a few of the cohort members' subsequent stories.

Notes

1. Major figures of the 2010 Chinese Census can be found on the website of National Bureau of Statistics of China at http://www.stats.gov.cn/english/ NewsEvents/201104/t20110428_26449.html
2. Even in recent years the 'little emperor' phrase (or 'little emperor syndrome') is still frequently used in mainstream media. For example, see BBC (22 November 2013), 'No Siblings: A Side-Effect of China's One-Child Policy'; *The Independent* (10 January 2013), 'One-child policy: China's army of little emperors.' See Bakken, B. (1993). Prejudice and danger: The only-child in China. *Childhood*, 1(1), pp. 46–61 for the author's critical discourse analysis on the stereotypes of the 'spoiled one-child' generation during the 1980s.
3. The Organisation for Economic Co-operation and Development (OECD) currently has 34 member countries, including the US, UK, Australia and other developed European countries.
4. For the changes of numbers of net migration during 2010–2016 and their political implications see resource from The Migration Observatory at Oxford University: 'The Net Migration Target and the 2017 Election' (4 May 2017). Available at http://www.migrationobservatory.ox.ac.uk/resources/commen- taries/net-migration-target-2017-election/ and 'Net Migration Falls, With Lowest Net Migration from EU8 Since They Joined the EU – But "Tens of Thousands" Target Still A Long Way Off'(25 May 2017). Available at http:// www.migrationobservatory.ox.ac.uk/press/net-migration-falls-lowest-net- migration-eu8-since-joined-eu-tens-thousands-target-still-long-way-off/
5. See United Nations' website https://refugeesmigrants.un.org/definitions
6. See Anderson and Blinder (2017) for a comparison of definitions of migrant as represented in government data sources. Available at http:// www.migrationobservatory.ox.ac.uk/resources/briefings/who-counts-as-a- migrant-definitions-and-their-consequences/#kp1
7. Apart from the increasing competition in the British job market after the 2008 financial crisis, the state policy has made the UK unwelcoming to non- EU job-seekers. Restrictions on work visas were introduced including the requirements of the minimum salary, the lack of freedom in job choices, and the increasing complex application procedure (Home Office, 2015). Furthermore, with the cancellation of the PSW visa in 2012, the number of students who obtained a work visa after study immediately dropped by 87% (Universities UK, 2014).

8. The parents' generation grew up during the Great Leap Forward followed by the Great Famine (1959–1961) and the Cultural Revolution (1966–1976); immediately after came the Economic Reform (1978) which transformed the planned economy to a market economy.
9. China's baby boom took place during the early to mid-1960s when the fertility rate increased from 3.3 (1961) to 7.3 (1963) (Poston & Duan, 2000). The majority of cohort members' parents were born between the mid-1950s and the mid-1960s.
10. Kajanus is Finnish, Goh was born and raised in Singapore and Fong was born in Taiwan, and raised in California.
11. Liu was born and raised in China.
12. The Russell Group represents 24 leading UK universities. See http://russell-group.ac.uk Accessed 12 February 2016.
13. All the participants are heterosexual.

Chapter 1

China's Modernization: A Generational Leap

> Never in history have so many people made so much economic progress in one or two generations.
> (Li, 2010, p. 3)

My summer holidays usually involved time with my grandparents. My parents were both working full time, and so I was sent to spend the two months in summer with my paternal grandparents who lived in a nearby city. My grandmother was born in 1940, she went to a teacher-training college and became a primary school teacher in 1959. She taught Chinese literature, but in my young 10-year-old mind I thought she should have taught mathematics because she was very good at numbers, especially to do with saving money. Having retired from a state school with a good pension and enough savings, she was, however, against spending, and she was a passionate supporter of frugality.

My grandparents lived in a pleasant flat, but their bathtub was always half-full of water. The water dripped constantly from the water tap above. It was turned on only slightly to the precisely-measured degree which was loose enough to have 24-hour dripping water, but could not be sensed by the old-style water meter. In this way, we could use the water for most of our daily activities for free. However, compromises had to be made in exchange for 'free' water: there was no separate shower facility so we had to clean ourselves from a bucket. For a child frugality meant inconvenience, discipline and no treats. Although in the 1990s, my generation was called 'little emperors' and 'little empress' and the older generation was supposed to pamper or spoil us, I did not identify with such images nor did the many one-child participants I interviewed for this research.

Education, Migration and Family Relations between China and the UK:
The Transnational One-Child Generation, 23–45
Copyright © 2018 by Emerald Publishing Limited
All rights of reproduction in any form reserved
doi:10.1108/978-1-78714-672-320181003

It occurred to me only much later that my grandparents' frugality may have been rooted in the resource shortage they experienced in the planned economy from the 1950s to the 1980s, including the period of the Great Famine (1959–1961). In 1959 the monthly ration of grain allocated to my grandmother was 30 kg, and it was reduced to 29 kg in 1960. My parents were born in the mid-1960s. They grew up in a planned economy when, in their words, 'everybody was poor'. However, the state of being 'poor' is relative. In most cases my parents were referring to the lack of diversity in income resources and consumer goods 'back then', in comparison to the market economy we have today. Nevertheless there were variations in the income level within the planned economy. For example, my father's childhood had more financial security because both his parents were professionals while my mother's parents were not. Nevertheless, growing up in cities, access to food security, education resource, and medical care was much easier for my parents compared to the people who grew up in the countryside.

By the time my parent's generation started working and establishing families in the 1980s, the modernization policies that were taking shape in the 1970s started to impact on their lives. The 1978 economic reform and the 1979 one-child policy transformed the profile and outlook of Chinese families during the final three decades of the 20th century. At the same time the social, economic and political changes posed challenges for families. Although most of the significant policies we focus in this book were national-level policies, their impact on Chinese families was not clear-cut. To understand the generational leap between the one-child generation and their parents' generation, we need to go back in time to the social changes before and after the economic reform and the one-child policy.

Pre-1978 Social Stratification

During Mao's communist era (1950s–1970s), households were classified into 'red' and 'black' categories. The former referred to the revolutionary class including landless peasants, factory workers and cadres. The latter referred to the so-called 'anti-revolutionary classes' including landowners, 'right-wingers' (mostly intellectuals) and urban property owners. The classification was largely based on the occupation of the individual's father as well as the individual's 'political performance' in party-led campaigns (Bian, 2002). Classes in the 'red' category, which were regarded as the 'former exploited classes', were favoured in school admissions and job assignments, while the 'former exploiting class' suffered systematic discrimination (Walder, 1989). Once labelled a certain 'class', it was extremely difficult for an individual to switch from one class to another.

In the late 1950s, the state introduced a strict household registration system (*Hukou* 户口) which limited the physical and social mobility between urban and rural residents (Whyte, 2012, Wu & Treiman, 2004). Households registered with their local office were categorized as 'urban' or 'rural'. Based on the household registration system, urban residents participated in work units[1] (*Danwei* 单位), and rural residents belonged to communes where they took part in agricultural production. The rationing system, which lasted until the late 1980s, was carried out through work units and communes. Unlike the communes system, which was replaced by the Household Responsibility System[2] (家庭承包责任制), work units still exist today.[3] In cities, the work units allocated jobs largely based on the individual's political 'class'. A job in a work unit was commonly referred to as an 'iron rice bowl', unlike a bowl made of clay or china which is easy to break, indicating the sense of security that came with it (Whyte, 2012). Work units provided for a wide range of welfare including housing, medical care, childcare and children's schooling (Li, 2005).

Mao's regime placed the emphasis on an egalitarian income distribution and stressed 'moral instead of monetary incentives' (Walder, 1989, p. 407). The salary and welfare provided by work units were (supposed to be) guaranteed for a lifetime. This politically rigid, economically unsustainable system soon faced the pressure of staff redundancy in the 1960s. Two years following the start of the Cultural Revolution in 1966, 16 million urban youths were allocated to rural areas to be 'educated through hard manual work' (Guan, 1995). The number of adolescents involved in the 'sent-down movement' accounted for 10.5% of the urban population in 1979 (Pan, 2002). The movement was arguably a measure to suspend the outbreak of the urban employment crisis; it consequently slowed down the rate of urbanization (Li, 2005, Walder, 1989).

Urban children from all 'classes' (red and black) were forcibly 'sent down', and even parents from a privileged background could not prevent it (Unger, 1980, Bernstein, 1977). The 'sent-down movement', which lasted for a decade (1968–1978), disrupted a generation of young people's education and career paths (Zhou, 2013, Guan, 1995). In my research, parents who were born between the 1940s and early 1950s were affected by the movement, like Bolin's father, whose education was stopped two days before the start of the Cultural Revolution. Another father, from

Guangdong Province, who was also part of the 'sent-down movement', described his generation as the 'lost generation', a generation which had been *dan* 耽 (delay) *wu* 误 (mistake) – delayed by mistake.

When the great waves of the 'sent-down youth' returned to the city at the end of the Cultural Revolution, the state attempted to solve the massive job demand by allocating more jobs to the already oversubscribed state-owned companies, meanwhile encouraging individuals to turn to self-employment. The former method eventually led to a large number of staff redundancies during the economic reform of the 1980s and 1990s; the latter attempt witnessed the emergence of various non-state businesses (Whyte, 2012, Wu, 2006, Li, 2005). In addition, some of the 'sent-down' members resumed their education after 1976, while the rest were not able to do so for physical, psychological and administrative reasons (Zhou, 2013). Such a difference in education levels further divided the socioeconomic profile of that generation when skills and qualifications became essential in the reformed labour market.

Post-1978: Emerging Middle Class of China

The post-1978 economic reform witnessed the widening of the gap between the rich and the poor as well as the rise of the group in-between. The middle-range income group was commonly referred to as the 'middle class'. A significant number of laid-off workers in the 1980s and 1990s (mainly in cities) became private business owners (Wu, 2006) while the rest of the laid-off workers struggled in poverty (Li, 2005). The former 'red' and 'black' divide rapidly blurred. However, the legacy of the communist institutions from the pre-1978 period still had an influence in shaping the new middle class: the emergence of a private sector in China was mainly the product of the transformation of state-owned enterprises. Such companies had, to a large extent, inherited personnel, a managerial system, and a political culture from their former context (Goodman, 2008).

China's middle class has unique attributes defined by the pace of its emergence, its scale, and the political environment. China's dramatic economic development and social change started with fiscal reform in the 1980s: 'wealth creation' and 'wealth concentration' redistributed all forms of resources. The rapid privatization of state-controlled enterprises opened up the market and made available goods, jobs and services, as well as intensifying competition for economic, cultural and political resources. Within two decades social stratification became the salient feature based on the individual's performance in a market-orientated economy (Bian, 2002). So rapid was the economic change that Biao and Shen were able to claim that, 'class formation and class closure are underway' (2009, p. 513).

'Middle class' is an overused term. It has become more difficult to define with the formerly deprived population becoming 'richer than before' (Donald & Yi, 2008, p. 71). However, 'middle class' is also a useful term that reflects, to some extent, a group's economic, social and cultural characteristics all at once. Overused as it is, I struggle to find a better term which helps more sharply to convey the essential features of this group to a diverse readership. Therefore, we will have to settle for a broad stipulative definition regarding the general demographic that the term 'middle class' refers to, but keep in mind that in China there are different 'middle classes'. In China, the projection of the middle class derived initially from advertisements that were associated with 'real estates, automobiles and other expensive commodities' (Li, Chunling, 2010, p. 140). In general, the most direct middle-class aspirations were a 'relatively high and stable' income, a 'professional or managerial' occupation, a 'higher' education and the enjoyment of a 'comfortable' lifestyle (Li, Chunling, 2010, pp. 139–140).

Little did the major middle-class aspirations resemble the traditional Chinese culture; rather, the aspirations originated from the image of the affluent West. According to her in-depth study of average income Chinese families in Dalian, China, in the 1990s, Vanessa Fong reported an overwhelming admiration by Chinese parents and children for the 'First World' (2004). Drawing on Immanuel Wallerstein's analysis of a 'capital world system' (1974) which divided the world into 'core' (First World), 'peripheral' (Third World) and 'semi-peripheral', Fong employed the 'culture model of modernization' promoted by the 'capital world system' as a way to explain Chinese people's admiration for the 'West': it 'motivates people to desire First World affluence and believe that participation in a modern economy will enable them to attain that affluence'[*sic.*] (2004, p. 14).

Unlike the emergence of the middle class in Europe, China's middle class is believed to have emerged as a state-planned phenomenon rather than 'a real historical force' out of 'a history of political struggle and mobilization' (Crossley, 2012, p. 96). The Chinese middle class grew in a society that had a state-imposed and state-maintained economic policy which incorporated both agrarian and urban-industrial bases (Li, Chunling, 2010, Li, Cheng, 2010, Goodman, 2008). The context of the emergence of the middle class was 'a very particular post-socialist Chinese

'situation' where social, cultural, political and economic forces, including the party, the state and multinational capital, intersect and jostle for
legitimacy and success' (Donald & Yi, 2008, p. 76). The Chinese leader-
ship 'called for "enlarging the size of the middle-income group" to give
hope to the country's still massive underclass' (Li, Cheng, 2010, p. 11).
Developing a middle class was said to be a way of expanding individual
initiatives and self-driven economic growth (Goodman, 2008).

The membership of the middle class expanded rapidly. The scale of
the middle class in China varies depending on the source of information
as well as the criteria of definition. *The Times* estimated that the membership of the Chinese middle class was 250 million (Lewis, 2013b), the
McKinsey model suggested that the number of middle-class people was
290 million in 2011, and will be 520 million by 2025 (Farrell et al., 2006).
Because residents in the cities have more opportunities to enter middle-
class professions and education, the urbanized feature of the distribution of middle-class membership is significant. The Chinese government
announced that 78% of city residents will be members of the middle class
by 2020 (Li, Cheng, 2010). Meanwhile, because sociologists are adopting
different measuring criteria (Li, Chunling, 2010), the estimated size of the
current urban middle-class ranges from 8% to 50%.

Numbers aside, the middle class in China is heterogeneous; individuals
from variously labelled political 'classes' could acquire middle-class status
from different channels: being an educated professional, involved in a private entrepreneurship, and being a part of the political personnel (cadres).
Within only a decade intellectuals from the former discriminated 'black'
classes became respected because of their qualifications and expertise; the
'capitalists' changed from being at the bottom of the pre-1978 political ladder to being the elites in the market economy. Moreover, the former cadres
were also able to convert their 'political capital' (Wu, 2006) and transform
themselves into entrepreneurs in the 1980s. As a result, instead of sharing
a 'homogeneous middle-class identity and culture' (Li, Chunling, 2010,
p. 155), the current Chinese middle class has different levels of education,
financial affluence and socio-political attitudes.

Parents' Generation: Opportunities, Competition and Wealth

The first decade of the economic reform saw the gradual change from
equal to competitive salaries in state-owned enterprises. Job security
in work units was further challenged in the 1990s when a large number of state-owned enterprises went through privatization, and a great

proportion of their employees became a redundant workforce. The number of people employed in work units plummeted from 113 million in 1995 to 41 million in 2002 (Whyte, 2012). Furthermore, the rise of private business and the entrance of foreign investment accelerated competition for jobs and promotion within the work units as well as in the wider labour market.

Individuals in the middle of the rapid institutional transitions were faced with the urgent need to adjust themselves from the former work unit system to the market economy competition. As mentioned earlier, the rise of private business in post-reform China was, to some extent, the result of the failure of the state to reduce the rate of unemployment in state-owned enterprises. However, a significant proportion of the working population in the 1990s was not so passive; they became aware of the diversity of business opportunities and the risk of the household's dependency on the inefficient work units. During the massive cut of state-owned enterprise employees in the mid-1990s, 20% of the staff were not forced to leave, but they chose to resign for better-paid opportunities (Li, 2005).

In my interviews with one-child generation participants and their parents it was common to hear about the changes in the career paths of the parents as they experienced institutional changes during the latter three decades of the 20th century. Some parents switched from the public to private sector (from work units to self-employment, or starting their own business). Ran's (male, 27, software engineer) parents were trained in chemistry in a college in western China. They began their job at a state-owned chemistry factory as technicians. Ran's father was later transferred to a sales position and progressed to the higher management of the factory. During privatization of the factory, Ran's mother was given a chance of early retirement. She took the compensation and became a businesswoman who traded in the catering industry. Ran's father remained in the factory as manager after the factory was bought by an investor. However, not being satisfied with the new system, Ran's father left the factory and became a freelance consultant who took temporary contracts with different companies.

Some parents changed the field of their expertise in response to the labour market's demand. Jinhai's (female, 27, auditor) father came from a southeastern coastal city. He had a degree in aquaculture and worked in a fish farming research centre – a work unit. As the finance sector rapidly grew in the area, Jinhai's father taught himself accountancy and obtained relevant certificates which enabled him to work in an accounting firm. However, not all the parents left the security of work units in pursuit of a more profitable private sector career. Liang (male, 31, sales manager) was from northeast China, and his parents did not have a professional background because their education was cut short by the 'sent-down movement'. They worked as ordinary clerks in a state-owned enterprise. The job was not demanding, so they developed a side-line private business and traded spare parts for computers. Whether a work unit employee was allowed to develop a side-line business was unclear; from Liang's memory his parent's strategy, which took advantage of both the work unit system and the market economy, was not uncommon.

Nevertheless, the majority of parents in this research had sustained their jobs in state-owned enterprises, partly because the parents who survived the massive staff cuts in the 1990s were already established employees (in middle or higher management positions) in their institutions. What we see from the various career routes of these parents is that the individuals actively generated resources during a period of transformation and became successful survivors of the social stratification. This initiative made these parents more likely to be open minded about new opportunities and challenges, for example, sending their only child to study overseas.

Accompanying the opportunities in China's marketization is the middle-class families' growing disposable income. The household saving rate among the Chinese families is famously higher than most other countries in the world. The gross saving rate from late 1980 to 2015 (Fig. 6) shows

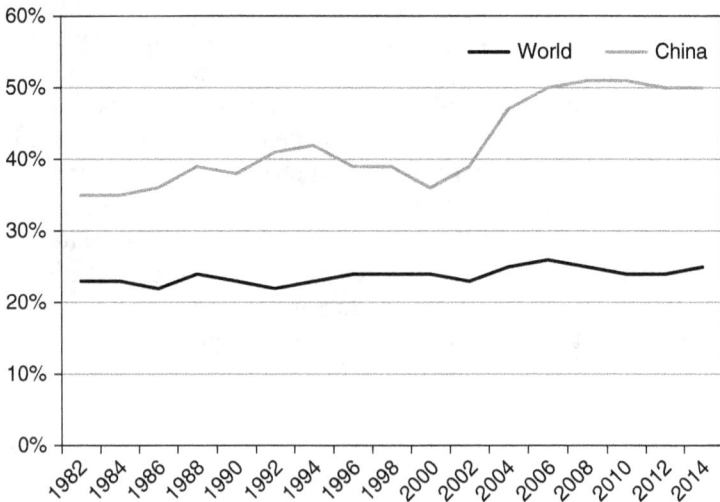

Fig. 6:   Gross savings rate as a percentage of the GDP. *Source*: World Bank National Accounts data and OECD National Accounts data files (2017). Available at http://data.worldbank.org.

that the Chinese gross saving rate as a percentage of the GDP is much higher than the world's average, with a sharp surge from 2000.

The population that became middle class in the post-1978 economic reform was largely the generation that was born in the 1950s and 1960s. In spite of the diversity of their educational and political background, what these middle-class Chinese had in common was an increase in household assets and a shared experience of the social and economic upheavals during the second half of the 20th century. The high post-1978 household savings rate was the result of household income growth, a destabilized former communist-style welfare system and the reduction in the number of children after the one-child policy (Ma & Yi, 2010, Kuijs, 2006, Modigliani & Cao, 2004).

Wealth was new to most of the cohort's parents' generation. Based on some parents' memories of their childhood and early working years, most parents in this research had a financially deprived upbringing and a low household income period from the 1960s to the 1980s. Although some younger parents who were born in the 1960s were not directly affected by the 3-year Great Famine (1959–1961) and the Cultural Revolution (1966–1976), the memory and lifestyle of the grandparents' generation still retain their impact upon both the parents and their child. This kind of background and traumatic historical experience resulted in most parents' desire for financial security and the tendency to save their newly-acquired wealth for the next generation.

The One-Child Policy: The Implementation

In the West people born in the immediate post-World War II period are usually referred to as the baby-boomer generation. It was rarely mentioned that the parents of the one-child generation were also baby-boomers born after the founding of the People's Republic of China. Except for the Great Famine period during 1959–1961, the birth rate in China remained high, especially during the 1960s (Fig. 7). The high birth rate was, to a large extent, due to Mao's pro-natalist policies in the 1950s and 1960s when he believed that a large population was the key to the development of the country (Howden & Zhou, 2015). The encouragement to have children was also in accordance with the Confucian basis for family reproduction, where a large family was held to be an insurance for the parents' old age care, and to carry on the family line (Milwertz, 1997). In addition to the political and cultural factors, the pro-natalist policies meant that the state was to be responsible for the basic needs of raising the children, which

Birth/death rate :1949–2015

(number of birth/death ÷ average population × 1000‰)

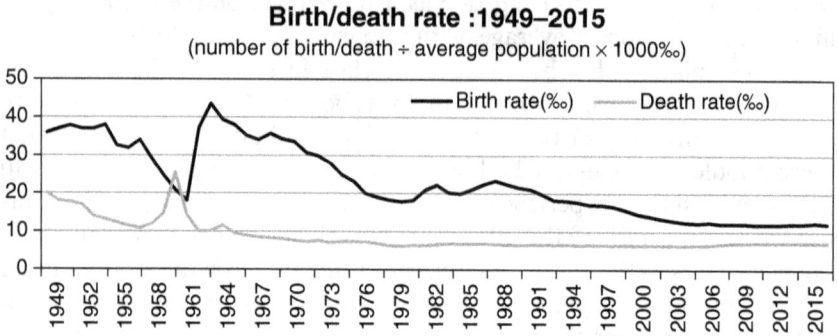

Fig. 7:   Birth/death rate (1949–2015). *Source*: National Bureau of
Statistics of the PRC.

encouraged families at various economic levels to have multiple children
(Howden & Zhou, 2015). Therefore, it was common for parents of the
one-child generation to grow up in a big family with several siblings. By
the time the baby-boomers started to establish their own families, they
were restricted by the 1979 one-child policy.

How was it possible to strictly control the biologically reproductive
behaviour of such a vast population and suppress the basic desire in
people to want more children? The one-child policy was not a one-off
decision. The build-up towards the policy as we know it today found its
earliest form in the mid-1950s when the state began to encourage individual population control (Greenhalgh, 2008). However, these attempts
were 'on-again, off-again' in Mao's regime until his death in 1976 when
birth planning officially moved to the central political agenda (Greenhalgh, 2008, p. 53).

A few years before 1976, the 'later-longer-fewer' (later marriage and
child-bearing, longer time between the birth of children, fewer children in
total) policy was developed tentatively by Premier Zhou and other leaders
who were concerned about the rapidly increasing population. Although
carried out cautiously among the local (in cities and towns) governments,
the rapid decline in the birth rate from the late 1960s reflects the effective-
ness of the 'later-longer-fewer' policy (Greenhalgh, 2008). The drafting
of the tough one-child policy from 1976 was a process of entanglement
between political ideology and statistical models, which have been well
documented in Susan Greenhalgh's book *Just One Child: Science and
Policy in Deng's China* (2008). In the mid-1980s the strict nation-wide[4]
'one for all' rule was relaxed in rural areas; families whose first-born was

a girl were allowed to have a second child. This modification was partly a response to the strongly pervasive son preference in rural families, partly a compromise to the labour shortage and the lack of old-age security in rural China (Milwertz, 1997). The Chinese Census in 1980 and 1990 showed that the percentage of the urban population was 20.9% and 26.4%, respectively, which means that after the rural one-child policy relaxation in the 1980s, the one-child-only rule actually applied to only a minority of the Chinese population.

In cities the policy was carried out and monitored through both the residential committee system and the work unit system. Cecilia Milwertz gave an in-depth study in her book *Accepting Population Control* (1997), which was based on her empirical research in China during the 1980s and 1990s. These valuable first-hand data showed a rigorous birth control process: work units had limited quotas each year to allow only a small number of births in the unit. A married woman had to apply for a birth plan certificate before the birth of the child. The certificate then needed to be endorsed by the residents' committee where the woman was registered to complete the application of the birth planning quota. The punishment for birth outside the plan came in the form of expensive fines and/or job loss – the 'iron rice bowl' (of the mother and father) – in the work unit.

The policy was particularly strongly implemented among urban couples for whom job security was closely tied to the number of their children. As Milwertz observed in the 1990s, urban mothers accepted the policy 'as a matter of course' in so far as 'the policy applies unequivocally to all city district citizens' (Milwertz, 1997, p. 121). Any one-child policy breach tended to happen among the small number of urban (semi-urban) residents who were working in the private sector, or had their own business in the 1980s, like the parents of Qianqian (female, 27, purchasing assistant), who had two children while running their own company in Beijing. Another non-one-child migrant, Feng (female, 34, IT manager), grew up in a semi-rural town at the fringe of the city in southeast China. Her father had 'had his own business' since Feng was little a child. She also reported that entrepreneurship was common in her hometown and that 'it was the norm to have more than one child'. A father from a semi-rural town in south China, who had only one daughter, said that he knew many friends who 'tried everything' to have more children. It is perhaps not surprising that policy breaches tended to happen in the less urbanized areas, and where the average educational level was also lower. At that time, highly educated professionals were more likely to be employed in work unit. Therefore, to what extent education level, or fear (of losing a job), played in urban middle-class professionals' adherence to the policy, is not immediately clear.

The One-Child Policy in the Landscape of Socioeconomic Development

Based on the reduced family size, the one-child policy was a success. However, to what extent China's reduced birth rate is a *result* of the one-child policy, is questionable. The birth rate was already in sharp decline before 1979, but we cannot learn what the population size would be had the one-child policy not been implemented. Nevertheless, an experiment carried out since 1985 can give us some indication. Liang Zhongtang was a party school researcher and teacher in Shanxi Province. He is well known for challenging the strict one-child-only policy and proposing a less severe 'two-children'[5] policy which he believed would equally reduce the population increase to a similar level. In 1985, he was allowed to carry out his experiment in Yichen, a rural town in Shanxi Province (central China). The 1990 Chinese Census showed a lower birth rate in Yichen (15.85‰) than the national level (20.98‰, including urban and rural areas). In the latest Census in 2010, Yichen's birth rate (11.18‰) decreased from its 1990 level, but it was slightly higher than the national level (10.38‰) (Wu, 2014). In addition, Yichen reached this result with less human cost: it has a healthier gender ratio and a lower abortion rate compared to the national level.

We cannot assume that Yichen's experiment is replicable to the rest of China, but it points to the suggestion that the child-bearing pattern among couples in post-1978 China may have had more to do with the socioeconomic factors and less to do with the one-child regulation. However, Milwertz (1997) also revealed a complex relationship between the number of children desired by Chinese mothers and the number of children these women were prepared to have. In the survey she conducted in Beijing and Shengyang, two major north Chinese cities, she asked 857 women questions regarding their ideal number of children, and whether they would have only one child regardless of the one-child policy. While around half of the women said two children would be ideal, still 38% of women in Shengyang and 21.4% of women in Beijing regarded only one child as ideal. In comparison, 62.9% of women agreed that they would have only one child even if there were no one-child policy, while 25.5% of women did not agree (Milwertz, 1997, pp. 69–70).

The ages of the women in the survey ranged between the early twenties to late thirties: they were involved in intensive child-rearing. But a person's preferences are subject to change at different stages of life. Bolin's mother (see Prologue and Introduction), for example, in her late sixties regretted having just one child, though when she was young she decided to abort the second child because of the busy working hours. When females made conception choices, the limitation of the policy was only one of the factors. Because the rationale of the one-child policy was rooted in China's quest for modernization, there is a sense of taken-for-grantedness among parents in accepting the policy as if it was part of the package that came with the post-1978 development. I use the following lengthy quote of Ran's father, who was 56, born in a rural family and now a well-off consultant, to demonstrate the parents' generation's acceptance of the policy in the context of a pre-1978 deprived upbringing, and the rapid post-1978 socioeconomic changes.

> Many people can't understand, for example, I had six siblings, yet I have only one child, do I feel sorry about it? No, I don't feel sorry at all. Why? One reason is the policy's restriction. The other reason is that my wife and I didn't have much money. We were struggling with only one child because of the long working hours and low income. We felt a great pressure with just one child, so we didn't want a second child. Later on with better economic conditions, we did think about the idea of having another child, but the desire was not strong. If you ask me how do I feel about the loss of sibling companionship, I tell you it was painful for me to have so many siblings. Our family was poor. My sister and I were the oldest girl and boy, so we were the only two children who had new clothes. Actually most of the new clothes were just for me because I was a boy. When I outgrew the clothes, they were left for my younger brothers and sisters, who hardly had any new clothes. How could you feel happy with the siblings in this situation? The big happy four-generation-under-the-same-roof kind of family in old China refers to the rich landowners' family, not poor peasants' family like mine. Our family was actually not too bad because my father was a peasant leader in the village. There were some children who died of illness or hunger in other families, because of poverty. When those families' children grow up, would they give birth to a second child if

> they can't even afford to take good care of their first child?
> No, because they wouldn't want their second child to suffer
> like their dead siblings did. So we didn't have a strong desire
> to have a second child. We are educated. My parents were
> uneducated and illiterate. What could they teach us? All my
> Mum ever told me was to save money and to study hard.

We cannot truly learn whether given the freedom Ran's father would have had more than one child; his justification for accepting the notion of a one-child family demonstrates that in the context of the family's social upward mobility the number of children became a relatively minor concern. In contrast, the need to invest in the next generation's education became the priority: quality mattered more than quantity. This father's reflection of the family's economic changes was very similar to his counterparts in Singapore. Middle class Chinese Singaporeans born in the 1960s and 1970s experienced rapid economic growth in the late 20th century, which Kristina Göransson (2009) described as the 'sandwich generation'. This term does not mean the mid-age couple struggling between the needs of the elderly and the young; it refers to the generation between the 'old traditions' and the 'modern world'.

Like Ran's father, and many other parents in this study, the Singaporean 'sandwich generation' in the 21st century enjoyed a comfortable lifestyle and were able to provide high-quality material and educational resources for their next generation. Such a lifestyle stood in sharp contrast to that of their childhoods (Göransson, 2009, p. 35). As Göransson pointed out, the so-called sandwich generation was a class-related phenomenon and did not apply to all members of that age group. Similarly, in the post-1978 social stratification, some families remained poor. The widening income gap pushed most households at all income levels to work harder to climb up the social ladder and avoid falling behind. This implies that both men, and women, had to quickly adjust their roles in the society and in the family.

Emancipation of Women or Work–Family Double Pressure?

'Women hold up half the sky'. This famous slogan which was repeatedly used in gender-equality propaganda, is believed to be a proverb that originated in Hunan Province. Its first appearance as a political slogan was in the Communist Party's newspaper, *People's Daily*, in 1958, when an article titled 'A labour force not to be ignored' (不可忽视的生力军)

reported that Hunan Province witnessed women's active agency in production activities from the beginning of the Great Leap Forward in 1956 (Gen & Zhang, 2015, p. 73). During Mao's planned economy in the 1950s, the proportion of women who participated in paid employment rose from 10% to 90% (Li, 2005). Such an unusually high female employment rate is, to a large extent, politically inflated. The idea of being a housewife was stigmatized in the women-initiated labour participation movement; housewives were 'viewed as lesser beings with no desire or conscience to make contributions to national construction' (Fang & Walker, 2015, p. 7). Arguably the sudden increase in women's paid labour participation was largely in response to the communist ideology. The high employment rate of women was also made possible by the public service provisions (such as nursery and canteen) in work unit which eased women from the conflict between work and family.

In 1987 the US Sociologist Lawrence Hong claimed that 'the one-child policy may have benefits for Chinese women that ultimately outweigh its adverse effects' (Hong, 1987, p. 318). One of the reasons he gave for such a belief was that the low fertility rate following the policy was likely to minimize women's time spent on pregnancy and child-rearing; thus women

> could find it worthwhile to invest their time and energy in activities traditionally dominated by men. With ideology on their side and time at their disposal, it would be difficult to deter women from having a greater and more equal role in society. (p. 324)

However, what Hong failed to see was the massively increased time and energy needed for the 'cultivation of the perfect only child' (Milwertz, 1997, p. 121). In Milwertz's research in two north cities in the 1990s, most urban mothers with one child reported the exhaustion of time and money when raising their child: the costs ranged from paying for piano classes to buying good clothes; the time spent on the child included sending the child to various extra-curricular activities, and helping with their homework every evening.

Women who grew up in Mao's era took it for granted that employment was an important component of an individual's life (Wang, 2003). However, since the post-1978 reform put efficiency and economic development as the priority of companies, the family-friendly welfare in the planned economy period was quickly reduced. The late 20th century also saw a wider gender gap in income: the average annual income of urban women was 77.4% of men in 1990, it dropped to 70.01% in 2000 (Fang & Walker, 2015). This factor also contributed to the economic justification that if one of the dual-earners was to resign to look after the family, it should be the wife. Increasingly women had to withdraw from paid employment to take up their traditional domestic role. Urban women's employment rate dropped consistently according to three Census: 79.75% in 1982, 75.45% in 1990 and 62.81% in 2000. Although the ageing population made up part of the reason for the urban employment rate's decline (in both genders) (World Bank, 2006), women in the marketized economy found it increasingly difficult to balance the demands of work and family.

Fang and Walker conducted an in-depth investigation in 2006 and 2007 into women in Chinese cities aged between 22 and 55 who resigned from their full-time job to fulfil their domestic roles as a good wife and mother. They found that women's reversion to a domestic role was largely to do with 'the push coming from the labour market in which women face occupational segregation, while at the same time, the traditional gender order pulls them toward the family' (Fang & Walker, 2015, p. 14). What was alarming was the moral dilemma expressed by women from various income and educational backgrounds, including some women who had a better job (higher paid and higher status) than their husbands. For example, a woman in Fang and Walker's research had a successful career as well as her husband's support in childcare. Being 'upset by her lack of ability to care for her child', she decided to resign from her high-salary position because of 'the inner pressure produced by the traditional gender order' (2015, p. 13). Nevertheless, we should not jump to the conclusion that women experienced a reverse in upward mobility. The fact that a woman could *choose* to stay in her job or to resign indicated a degree of freedom, backed by household economic availability. Interestingly, women in Fang and Walker's research refused to identify themselves with the stigmatized term 'housewives' (家庭主妇), but used a new term; 'full-time wives' (全职太太) to indicate their flexibility and mobility in switching between the job market and the family.

In spite of having decreased in the post-reform period, China's female employment rate remained much higher than most countries in the world.[6] Compared with families with more than one child, the childcare pressure in one-child families was less demanding. Among the six two-children families in this research, two mothers stayed at home to look after the children, while only one out of 27 one-child respondents' mother did so.[7] Although most participants reported a traditionally gendered arrangement, where the father was the main breadwinner and the mother was more involved in domestic tasks like housework and childcare, a small number of only-children reported the opposite: that the mother took a dominating role in bringing in family income and making family decisions, while the father had a stronger domestic role. However, these cases were rare. More often found are the cases where mothers in professional jobs had to balance the traditional expectation of a wife and daughter-in-law, self-aspiration to career success and their expectations for their only child.

Beiyao's mother had been frustrated by the clash between not only full-time employment and motherhood, but also between the more conservative son-preference in the older generation, and the widely-spread notion of 'sons and daughters are equally good' promoted by the one-child policy propaganda.

Beiyao's family is from Liaoning Province in north China. I met Beiyao at her home near London when she just had her son (a month previously) and her mother was in England looking after both Beiyao and the baby. Beiyao was a PhD graduate and was working as a process engineer in Chemistry; her mother had just retired as a high-school English teacher. Born in 1959, Beiyao's mother was part of the 'sent-down movement'. Fortunately she resumed her education afterwards and graduated from a teacher-training college. She continued to pursue higher degrees part-time while working full-time as a teacher. Her husband was a fellow teacher and was later promoted to work in the local government. Beiyao's mother revealed that the promotion was first offered to her, but she declined the offer and recommended her husband instead:

> I had many promotion opportunities, but I gave them up for my daughter. As long as I am a teacher, my working time would coincide with my daughter's schooling time, so I can concentrate more time on her.

The mother's determination to ensure her daughter's success was influenced by the gender discrimination from her husband's family since the birth of Beiyao. The in-laws preferred a grandson and refused to help out in childcare. The name the mother gave to Beiyao literally means 'better than men'. She became pregnant again when Beiyao was a child, but she had to have an abortion so that both her and her husband would not risk losing their jobs. Without any help from the grandparents' generation, and with both her and her husband working full time, Beiyao's mother struggled very hard with career advancement and childcare.

She described the desperate measure she took when she had to go to work and the four-year-old Beiyao refused to go to nursery. The mother had no choice but to leave her daughter alone at home: 'My work place was not far from home. I left food on the table and a bucket on the floor so she could go to toilet herself. I said "you stay here and read your picture books, Mum will come back to check on you every other hour". She said "OK". Beiyao had been a top student since childhood and she had a Master's degree from a top university in China, another Master's degree and a PhD degree from a high-ranking British university. Yet when reflecting on the past, Beiyao's mother viewed her compromise in a tone suggesting that she had suffered an injustice:

> To be honest, my generation didn't live for ourselves, we were always thinking about others' needs. Look, we did things for our parents and parents-in-law. As for our husbands, we have to support our husbands, let him advance in his career without worrying about the family. We live on an ordinary salary, so we women have our own jobs, too, and we must do equally well in our career, that's a lot of hard work. Also, we need to look after our child, and hope our child will achieve high. We are brought up to have the traditional female virtue, and we are expected to serve the elderly, the country and our families. As for raising our own child, it is either 100% hope or 100% failure. We women's life is really really hard.

Women were, ideologically, emancipated from the gendered role in the patrilineal family culture and were free to pursue a career equally as men. But men, as a whole, were not culturally ready to fill the domestic gap that was left by fully employed women. Why was there such an uneven gender change in Chinese society in the post-reform period? Fang and Walker (2015, p. 4) provided a well-summarized explanation below:

> In the context of state socialism, the liberation of women embodied the legality of the state. Women were granted equal political, economic, educational, employment, and marriage rights within a short period of time, whereas Western women had to undertake a long battle for such rights. The main problem with this social progress was that women had no choice but to adapt to it and no time to consider its consequences. Thus women's subjectivity and identity did not develop along with their labour market liberation. This is not to suggest that gender equality was achieved in the pre-reform era; it remained unfulfilled and problematic.

Modernization and Caring for the Older Generation

As mentioned before, the parents' generation stands between the 'old traditions' and the 'modern world'. One of the most important 'old traditions' in Chinese families is the requirement of filial piety[8] (Xiao 孝) from the younger to the older generation. In Chinese families the notion of filial piety has been the dominant 'cultural logic' for more than 2,000 years (Zhan & Montgomery, 2003). It is arguably one of the oldest forms of family contract that bind parents and children through practical duties and the provision of emotional support. The tradition of filial piety, which was embellished by Confucius (551–478 BC) and reinforced by Mencius (372–289 BC), has been the governing principle with regard to the family obligations of the younger generation for centuries.

Children were expected to fulfil a parent's practical and financial/material needs; look after a parent's emotional wellbeing. More specifically, the eldest son and his wife have historically had the main responsibility of taking care of the son's elderly parents (Song et al., 2012, Zhan & Montgomery, 2003). Filial piety also traditionally prescribes obedience and respect from the younger to the older generation regardless of an individual's age (Keller et al., 2005). Such a pattern was also found in other East Asian societies, such as in traditional Japanese and Korean family culture, which was also characterized by Confucian filial obligation (Lee, 2010; Park et al., 2005). Outside the family, filial piety requires 'conducting oneself so as to bring honour, and avoid disgrace to the family name' (Chow & Chu, 2007, p. 93). Likewise, an individual's 'filial demonstration' towards his/her parents establishes him/her as 'a reliable, trustworthy and honourable person' in the eyes of others (Ikels, 2004, p. 5, Whyte, 2004).

In practice, the son (or the eldest son) provided the financial contribution while the daughter-in-law carried out everyday care. Therefore, sons were regarded as long-term members of the family while daughters were temporary members who eventually devoted themselves to the husband's family (Greenhalgh, 1985). Apart from caring for elderly parents, filial piety also emphasized a superior–inferior relationship within the family: children were expected to show respect, obedience and loyalty to parents (Fong, 2004, Baker, 1979). In fact, the traditional norms of filial piety were highly patriarchal and gendered. Such a pattern of elderly care in Chinese families has not changed fundamentally for 2000 years (Zhan & Montgomery, 2003).

However, the varying definitions of this ancient term are vague; it is easy to make the mistake of assuming 'filial piety' to be the preeminent cultural explanation of (almost) all phenomena in Chinese families. Part of the confusion is caused by the fact that the concept of filial piety has not remained static; its meanings and forms have been subjected to modification through ancient dynasties and modern states. The definition of filial piety in the 21st century varies slightly according to different scholars in different contexts (Schans & de Valk, 2011, Chow & Chu, 2007, Croll, 2006, Ikels, 2004).

Although filial piety is still the most important value underlying the practice of the support of the elderly in communist China (Fong, 2011, 2004, Bodycott, 2009, Deutsch, 2006, Chow, 1991), recent research has indicated evidence of changes with regard to the norm and practice of filial piety in the 21st century. Two survey analyses were conducted, respectively, on two north Chinese cities (Zhan & Montgomery, 2003) and one rural province (Song et al., 2012). The findings showed that in both cities and the rural region, parents were increasingly cared for by daughters instead of daughters-in-law. Furthermore, daughters in cities tended to provide equal financial support as sons. Most care-givers in the two surveys were between 30 and 50 and were likely to be the parents of only-children.

I interviewed six sets of parents (eight participants, including two couples and four interviews with either the father or the mother). It is a small sample, but when asked about how their own elderly parents (or parents-in-law) were being looked after (or had been looked after when they were alive), participants reported various caring arrangements. The eight parents all had siblings, but it was difficult to observe any dominating factor, including the order of the adult child, gender and income level, which determined the caring arrangement.

Yizi's (female, 31, advertising manager) mother (55, school teacher) described her husband as a 'very very filial person...You can't imagine how filial he is towards his father'. Yizi's paternal grandpa was in his late eighties, he relied on his wife for old age care until his wife passed away in 2008. According to Yizi's mother, Yizi's father had an older brother and an older sister, but the brother travelled frequently for his work and the sister often visited her son in a different city, so Yizi's father took himself to be the main carer of their father. I did not have the chance to talk to Yizi's father, but I learned the details of his filial conduct from the accounts of both Yizi and her mother. From Yizi's words we can see the underlying emotional dynamic among the parent's generation with regard to looking after aged grandparents:

> My Mum sometimes complains that my Dad is being too filial.... Although my aunt lives in the same neighbourhood

with my grandpa, they don't get on with each other. So my Dad carries the main responsibility of looking after grandpa. He usually drives to see my grandpa, it's a 6-hour drive. Each time he stays with my grandpa for a month, does grocery shopping and the laundry. Also, he cooks for grandpa 3 meals a day, plus 2 snacks. My grandpa doesn't like hiring helpers because he doesn't like strangers in the house. So my Dad does everything.

In Yizi's family the aged grandfather was being looked after by the younger son (not the older son, or daughter, or daughter-in-law) who lived further away (not the one who lived the closest). From Yizi and her mother's description Yizi's father seemed emotionally committed to his caring role in spite of the uneven share of the caring responsibility between the siblings. In comparison, Zhaohui's (female, 23, postgraduate student) family showed a more balanced pattern in terms of sibling share of parental care. Zhaohui's paternal grandmother had lived with Zhaohui's family since Zhaohui was a child. Zhaohui's mother became paralysed a few years before my interview in 2014, so Zhaohui's father became the carer for both his wife and his mother. Zhaohui's aunt (the father's sister) lived in the same block of flats, so she visited every day and helped out with the caring for their mother. However, the emotional commitment of Zhaohui's father was very different from Yizi's father.

Zhaohui's father was a semi-retired accountant; he was a man of few words. I made a positive comment on his filial behaviour of providing daily care to his mother. He responded: 'I wouldn't say I'm being filial, we are just keeping each other company.' Zhaohui's father said that he had the chance to leave his hometown and work in a big city, but his father was ill at that time, so he remained to be near his parent. Zhaohui's paternal grandfather passed away before she was born, and Zhaohui's father never left the hometown.

'I now regret it. The moment had passed, the opportunity was gone, I couldn't leave even if I wanted to.' As a local civil servant, the long-term job security also pulled him towards remaining in the hometown. He employed a carer to fill in the caring gap, 'but the carer became ill, and it has been difficult to find another one, so I'm doing it by myself'.

The feeling of regret with regard to parental care was shared by Bolin's (female, 38, export manager) parent, but for a different reason. The regret came from the absence of practical care towards their parents. At the time of interview, Bolin's parents were both in their late sixties and Bolin's grandparents had passed away. Both Bolin's mother and father were factory workers. Their jobs were demanding and they struggled with just looking after Bolin, so parental care had to be compromised:

> Now that I am old, I sometimes think 'Ai, why didn't I look after my parents properly?' My parent passed away very early. Look at my husband, he also regrets. His mother had five children, they all lived in the same city. But the old lady spent her final five years with a paid carer. The carer said each Sunday my mother-in-law would sit by the window and expect her children to turn up.

In spite of having siblings, the parents' generation has already revealed the dilemma between work, childcare and parental care in the context of a modernizing and increasingly demanding Chinese society. Co-residence has been essential for adult children to carry out everyday parental practical support. While multigeneration families living in the same household were widespread in agrarian society, it is relatively uncommon in today's Chinese cities. Since 2011, the population in Chinese cities has surpassed that in rural areas (compared to the urban population rate at 20% in 1981) (World Bank, 2015). Apart from the compressed living space in urban areas, longer life expectancy of older people, the smaller number of adult children and demanding jobs, have all contributed to the shift to separate, nuclear family living arrangements. Furthermore, women's participation in full-time employment has reduced their availability for traditional domestic roles, including looking after elderly parents (usually parents-in-law) at home.

The evidence indicated three trends in modern Chinese families: the practice of filial piety had become more flexible because of the increasing mobility and unavailability of adult children; the elderly population had less authority as the traditional extended family shifted to a small nuclear family; lastly, gendered filial piety expectation had become blurred as sons and daughters were equally expected to support their parents.

Nevertheless, it is the emotional side of parental care that is more difficult to settle. The sense of regret following compromises is likely to linger among the living; and how individuals interpret their 'filial' or 'unfilial' behaviour continues to change with time and ageing. As we saw in the Prologue, Bolin's parents were psychologically prepared to rely on paid care/nursing home for their old age care and leave Bolin out of the difficult situation between family responsibilities in China and in the UK. But would Bolin accept such an arrangement? Would she not have regrets in the future, like her parents did about their 'abandoning' Bolin's grandparents? Such matters faced by the one-child generation will be discussed in Chapter 5. Before we reach the later stage of their lives, we will start with the beginning of the parent–child relationship. The next chapter focuses on the upbringing of the one-child generation.

Notes

1. The work unit is the communist equivalent to the word 'company'.
2. From the 1950s, the Chinese rural production systems were organized in a collective manner, yet they were ineffective. The Household Responsibility System developed since 1979. This system contracts land, resources and output to individual households, which remarkably increased the level of efficiency in agricultural production (Lin, 1988).
3. The work unit System underwent a complex reform and reconstruction after 1978. In the 2000s the urban population was largely to be found working in the private sector, public sector and the public-private-mixed companies. The legacy of the work unit system is largely in state-supported organizations such as state-owned enterprises and public service-related institutions.
4. The one-child policy was applied only to the Han ethnic majority; ethnic minorities were excluded from the regulations. According to the Chinese Census in 1982, the ethnic minority population made up 6.7% of the whole population.
5. Liang Zhongtang's 'two-children' policy allowed all couples to have two children, but the child-bearing was to be delayed: the first birth should take place when the wife was around 24, and the second birth was to be when she was about 30 (Liang & Tan, 1997).
6. According to the World Bank, the female labour force participation rate for China in 1990 and 2000 kept over 70%; for the UK it was 52% and 54%, respectively, while the rate for the world average was around 50%. Details for the data can be found on the World Bank website http://data.worldbank.org/indicator/SL.TLF.CACT.FE.ZS?locations=CN-1W-GB.
7. It is important to note that two-children families tended to be from rural areas and that the number of children may not be the dominating factor of the mothers' employment (or unemployment).
8. See more discussions on filial piety in Chapter 5.

Chapter 2

Growing Up, Gender and Education in China

> Children of China's one-child policy became First World people too quickly for their families and societies to keep up. They faced intense parental pressure and competition for elite status in the educational system and the job market, as well as the accusation that they were spoiled because they had unrealistically high expectations. (Fong, 2004, p. 3)

Almost all the scholars who studied the one-child family found that in each family the only-child was seen as the 'only hope' and that the one-child generation faced great pressure from their families to become high achievers (Lin & Sun, 2010, Liu, 2008a, b, Deutsch, 2006, Fong, 2004). Almost all parents around the world hope their children achieve some kind of success, but the definition of 'success' is context-specific, and how parents (are prepared to) help children towards that goal varies even more greatly in different cultures and social classes. Chinese families (in China or in Western countries) were consistently reported to have very high expectations of their children, particularly in terms of academic performance and career success.

For example, in her study of Chinese families in Singapore, Kristina Göransson found that the Chinese were, in general, more successful than the Malay demographic in Singapore and that young Chinese parents invested more time and money on each child than the Malay parents in order for them to be 'the best of the best' (Göransson, 2009, p. 181). Average Asian Americans (Chinese, Japanese, Korean and Indian) were found to have higher education expectations and education attainments than average white Americans (Goyette & Xie, 1999).

Education, Migration and Family Relations between China and the UK:
The Transnational One-Child Generation, 47–72
Copyright © 2018 by Emerald Publishing Limited
All rights of reproduction in any form reserved
doi:10.1108/978-1-78714-672-320181004

Among Chinese families high expectations and intensive parental investment or sacrifice were found across all social classes. In poorer families parents 'sacrifice' their basic needs for the education of their children. For example, in Leung and Shek's research (2011), a Hong Kong father kept wearing mended clothes but bought expensive electronic devices for his children's study. At the other end of the spectrum Johanna Waters (2005, 2002) revealed the long-term separation endured by affluent middle-class parents when the wife accompanied the children to study in Canada while the husband spent most of his time in Hong Kong earning an income to support the children's overseas education and living costs.

What about one-child families in China? What kind of expectations and competition did the future transnational Chinese migrants grow up with? Throughout the 1990s and the 2000s, ethnographers spent lengthy time on fieldwork in selected cities of China and collected first-hand data regarding parent–child interaction when the one-child generation young children, teenagers or university students (Kajanus, 2015, Goh, 2011, Fong, 2004). The families they observed ranged from poor to rich. While individual families strived to push their only child one step further up the education ladder, social stratification and class solidification quietly pulled these families apart from each other. Vanessa Fong was one of the first scholars to make in-depth observations of one-child families. The (lower) middle-income families in Dalian gave her the impression that the Chinese only-children were brought up with 'First World living standards and educational opportunities', but their ambition clashed with 'Third World parents and society' (Fong, 2004, p. 3).

When discovering that the many only-children she studied in the 1990s went to the 'First World' as students, she did not hesitate to express her surprise:

> Few of them seemed wealthy enough to pay for study abroad or were high-achieving enough to qualify for scholarship abroad … In retrospect, I realize that I had underestimated the extent to which obstacles to study abroad could be overcome by the confluence of four factors. (Fong, 2011, pp. 2–4)

The four factors Fong stated were the financial support from extended families, the rapid increase of urban families' incomes, the expansion of the international education infrastructure and the growing desire to study abroad among the one-child generation.

Chinese families were like boats on the surface of social changes from the late 1970s; they float with what may be a steady support or an unexpected turbulence. Parents of only-children are naturally first-time parents. For those parents who gained upward social mobility, they were first-time middle-class members too. There is little to learn from their own upbringing given the sharp contrast of the two periods of Chinese society. Therefore, child rearing in post-1978 China was a challenge to most parents when they were navigating their own social mobility and simultaneously designing a future for their child. From the child's perspective, growing up in middle-class one-child families was also a challenge as they were the centre of an experiment (both for the family and for the state).

Hindsight is a wonderful thing, especially when it comes to the parent–child relationship in a changing environment. Time washes away the details of intergenerational conflict and short-term reaction. It then reveals a long-term impact and evaluation, when both parties are older (and possibly wiser). The rest of the chapter offers a re-visit to four themes: 'little emperor', authoritarian Chinese parenting, gender, and education. These four themes were repeatedly brought up in previous research and media coverage about the post-1978 Chinese family. Unlike earlier ethnographic accounts, which directly observed the one-child Chinese family, this research focuses on the one-child generation as adults in the UK as they were at the time of interview. The way parents and adult children select the 'memorable details' from the past made the retrospective accounts more valuable in learning about attitudes towards that past and its long-term impact upon them and their families.

The Myth of the 'Little Emperor'

> Soon after China implemented its one-child policy in 1979, reports reached the West of a new breed of plump, pampered creatures who had never learned to share. They were called Little Emperors, and nobody said 'No' to them. It was as if Britain had decided to spawn millions of Prince Andrews. As these children have grown older, they have not, according to many bulletins, grown nicer. They are said to be in love with consumer durables and so obese, due to routine parental overfeeding, that they require regular sessions in fat farms. (Bennett, 2011)

This excerpt was the beginning paragraph of an article titled 'China's little emperors' published in *The Guardian*'s website in 2011. Search the phrase 'China's little emperor' on any internet search engine where the list of results can easily lead one to similar remarks, like the one shown above, about China's one-child generation. It is true that China has a large number of 'little emperors' (and 'little empresses') as those described above. So do most countries in the world. But children in other countries may be referred to simply as 'spoiled children' instead of being given an exotic designation which associates them to the cliché mysterious oriental figure in the Forbidden City.

I do not believe in this media invention. I often felt nervous when reading such descriptions about my generation. After having a quick scan in my mind of the names of children, teenagers and adults I know from China, I struggled to find such 'plump, pampered creatures'. I know several only-child friends who are selfish and demanding, but I can also name a small number of non-Chinese friends, or their children, who *almost* fit the so-called 'little emperor' stereotype. In contrast to the popular stereotype, the one-child participants I came across in the research seemed to be ordinary, well-adjusted people; they had, like most human beings do, multiple sides and therefore they should not be judged by one particular feature of their personality shown at a certain stage of their lives.

It is not just the Western media that is to blame for the crude distinction of a generation profile; the belief that the only-children are necessarily more spoiled, more selfish and less capable of handling pressure is widespread in Chinese societies too, including among my one-child participants and their parents. When talking about the number of children they hope to have, the majority of one-child participants expressed their wish to have more than one child. When asked why, a common reason given was that only-children tend to be selfish, while siblingship helps a child to develop a willingness to share and care. 'It [being an only child] is not healthy for a child's mental development. It has a negative impact on me, and everybody [only children] around me' said Liwen, a 30-year-old only-child working as a tele-communications engineer in London; 'we tend not to think in other people's shoes, we become mentally mature too late.' Liwen made these remarks at the end of our interview. Having talked about his parent's financial and emotional support towards his study for a Master's course and a PhD in the UK, he repeatedly mentioned his sense of indebtedness, and accused himself of being selfish.

Similarly, Beiyao, whose mother's story we became familiar with in the previous chapter, was a 30-year-old only-child who had just had a baby and was planning to have another one. She emphasized the important role siblingship was likely to play in her offsprings' moral education:

> Beiyao: My husband and I are both only-children, we know how lonely it was to be an only child. So one reason [to have another child] is for companionship. Another reason is because only-children have many flaws like selfishness. If you have a sibling you would naturally learn how to be modest and take care of others. There must be some advantage [of having more than one child].
>
> M.T.: The *flaws* you mentioned about only-children, is it your own observation?
>
> Beiyao: I observed some, and the older generation kept saying so, too. My parents have many siblings, they often criticised the one-child generation for being self-centred and so on. In addition, media also reported similar kinds of things about only-children.
>
> M.T.: Do you think you have the qualities which they were critical about?
>
> Beiyao: [Laugh] More or less, yes. I will try to change.

Both Liwen and Beiyao self-identified as 'selfish only-children' and clearly felt ashamed of it. They also showed an imagined notion of sib-lingship and assumed the benefit of having a brother or sister. However, life experience tells us that a truly spoiled selfish person is very unlikely to openly admit to such qualities in him or herself and that siblingship does not *always* bring out the better part of human nature. The interview with non-one-child participants revealed the siblings' willingness to look after each other as well as the stimulation of jealousy and competition between siblings. The two female participants who had a brother, Feng (34, IT manager) and Gaomei (27, purchasing officer), both described mixed feel-ings towards their brother.

Feng was an only child until she was six. The arrival of the brother had a negative emotional impact on Feng as a child:

> I was jealous, everybody liked boys…Maybe I thought too much, I always prepared for the worst, I kept everything to myself … but after a while, I got to like my brother … I felt happy that I could care for him.

Gaomei was the younger child, her positive relationship with her brother declined when her wish to study abroad was opposed by her brother: 'because he thought he didn't study abroad, why should I?' Therefore only-children tended to have a simplified (and romanticized) notion of siblingship and internalized the discourse that only-children were being emotionally disadvantaged as a result of lacking a sibling.

In contrast to the adult only-children's self-accusation of being 'spoiled and selfish', parents' accounts produced two levels of response to the 'little emperor' stereotype. Beiyao's mother, the high school English teacher, was confident that her daughter was not selfish: '…because she has cousins, some were younger than her. I've always educated her to share with her cousins since she was little'. Meanwhile, Beiyao's mother supported the notion that only-children are spoiled. She became a little upset when talking about the clash between the demanding parents who wanted the teachers to focus on their child, and the limited energy a teacher had when facing a big class of students. Furthermore, she believed that the one-child generation was becoming significantly more selfish:

> I've been teaching for many years. It is easy to tell among my students. It has become more difficult to teach these days. Once we had an open day and invited parents to sit in our classes. My colleague received a phone call from a parent afterwards and was accused of being biased because she did not ask that particular child as many questions as she did to some other students in the class. My colleague was reduced to tears. Each child is the emperor in their own home, and they expect full attention when they are at school, too. It is the parents who are to blame. Parents believe their child is the cleverest therefore deserves the best.

It is curious to see the gap between Beiyao's mother's perception of her own parenting and the parenting of one-child families as a whole. There is also a mismatch between Beiyao's understanding and her mother's impression with regard to the selfishness in Beiyao's personality.

Like many 'spoiled emperor' narratives, the parents are placed in the dominating role of giving attention, money and love; while the child is usually posed as a passive receiver who gradually acquired the negative qualities such as selfishness and laziness by being pampered. Nevertheless, numerous research has shown that 'such speculations have not been supported by any substantial evidence in research' (Chen, 2003). Other observers also argued that such a 'theory' was biased and lacked evidence, and merely maintained a 'stereotype' (Bao, 2012, Goh, 2011, Liu, 2008b, Falbo & Poston, 1993).

To give a few examples of such investigations, the Chinese sociologist Feng Xiaotian conducted a survey in 1988 to find out whether parents of only-children were more likely to 'spoil' their child than parents with several children (Feng, 1993). Among 1,293 students (including only-children and non-only children) in five cities aged between 7 and 13, Feng discovered no significant difference in parenting between his two cohorts which could convincingly support the 'more spoiling one-child family' stereotype. Furthermore, Feng pointed out the overall higher income among the one-child families, compared to non-one-child families, directly led to more frequent gift-buying among one-child families. Therefore, it was mainly the different level of affluence that resulted in what appears to be a more spoiling parenting behaviour in one-child families.

Research conducted after the one-child policy was carried out also showed that only-children in China, compared with non-only-children, gained in physical and mental health (Wu & Li, 2012, Jiao et al., 1996); this finding led to the perception that the one-child policy improved the 'quality' of children. However, more recently an investigation carried out between 2009 and 2013 in four rural regions of China challenged this claim. The research was based on 25,871 observations which provided data for comparing health, cognition and non-cognitive outcomes between only children and non-only-children. These school-level students were given formal cognitive tests, mental health tests (anxiety-level measurement) and additional mathematics tests. The result showed no significant distinction between only-children and non-only-children in terms of their health, cognitive and non-cognitive outcomes (Zhou et al., 2016).

Compared with the earlier findings (see Wu & Li, 2012, Jiao et al., 1996), Zhou et al. (2016) stated that 'the gaps among school-aged children with and without siblings appear to have almost disappeared' (p. 14). They attributed the improvement of rural non-only children's conditions to 'some combination of rising incomes and better off-farm employment opportunities' (*Ibid.*). Nevertheless, they also highlighted that rural children, with or without siblings, are overall more vulnerable than urban children and in need of more care, attention and resources.

Children with siblings are generally more in evidence in poorer areas of China, while only-children tend to be concentrated in cities, where consumer culture and rising family purchasing power provided greater possibilities and, to some extent, pushed middle-class urban families to give the 'best of the best', like their counterparts in Singapore do to their off-spring (Göransson, 2009, p. 117). Somehow the identity of 'only children' has overshadowed other factors in the society, such as income gap and the rural–urban divide in the public perception of children born in post-1978 China. The identification of only-children being spoiled selfish individuals is too simplistic. In talking to non-one-child participants regarding their perception of only-children, I found that a more sharply felt difference in material resources rather than in personality.

Demin was born in 1983 in a rural town in Shandong Province. He had a younger sister. From the age of 10, he attended a boarding school in a nearby city where around half of his classmates were only-children. I asked him for his view about the difference between only-children and non-only children.

> Demin: I never divided the students I knew as an only-child and non-only-child, it seems to me the difference is more noticeable between rural children and urban children. I remember when the teacher encouraged us to buy a booklet to practise calligraphy, she said, 'all you need to do is to eat one less pack of chocolate, then you'll have the money to buy the booklet'. She talked as if chocolate was a common feature in our lives, but chocolate for me was a rarity. It was then that I started to realise the difference between me and my urban classmates.
>
> M.T.: What else have you noticed between rural and urban children?
>
> Demin: They [urban classmates] were faster in accepting and mastering new things. It made them *appear* [emphasis mine] to be smarter, but actually it was because they were exposed to these things at an earlier age. For example, they were familiar with piano and learning English since they were little. While for me, I felt anxious and lacked confidence.

It is easy to attribute both positive and negative outcomes of the one-child generation to the one-child identity while the socioeconomic factors at work form a more complex web of geography and class divide. The anxious young Demin from a rural town formed a contrast to his confident urban classmates who took chocolate, piano practise and English classes for granted. This emotional contrast is congruent with Polit and Falbo's finding in the 1980s. After having reviewed 141 studies about only-children and personality development, their findings suggested that 'only-children and others from small families might be more highly motivated because their families would be more likely to have the resources needed to channel motivation into actual achievement' (1987, p. 319). In non-Chinese societies the perceived differences between only-children and non-only-children have also been subject to various tests and analysis, and the evidence has consistently led to the conclusion that a child's personality, mental development or achievement does not have any significant association with being an only-child or not (e.g. Kitzman et al., 2002, Gee, 1992, Polit & Falbo, 1987).

Then why in China have the only-children, the parents and the wider society all breathed air into the 'little emperor' myth? The economist Gary Becker described how parents could help determine the value of the children by making their children feel a sense of indebtedness and/or create a 'warm' atmosphere in their families to increase their children's willingness to reciprocate (Becker, 1993a). I argue that the 'little emperor' myth helps develop a sense of indebtedness among the younger generation by emphasizing the 'unlimited giving and sacrificing' of parents. Furthermore, the 'selfish' feature of 'little emperors' places children on the moral low ground, thus giving room for them to 'redeem' their pejorative status by becoming 'selfless', and provide for parents in the future. The pervasiveness of the 'little emperor' myth showed the underlying anxiety of both generations when faced with a changing intergenerational contract, as well as the older generation's effort (in a broader sense) to 'cultivate reciprocity' (Milwertz, 1997, p. 132). Having cleared the misperception of the 'little emperors', we move on to more in-depth accounts of the one-child generation's upbringing (another aspect of Chinese family life which is frequently subject to stereotypes), and explore the changing parent–child relations in middle-class Chinese families during their children's upbringing.

The Many Faces of a Chinese Upbringing

> Chinese parents tend to monitor their children more closely, moralize more often, emphasize greater sense (sic) of family obligation, value grades more than general cognitive achievement, evaluate more realistically a child's academic and personality characteristics, be less satisfied with a child's accomplishments, and believe more in effort and less in innate ability as a factor in school success. (Hidalgo et al., 2004, p. 640)

European American mothers were concerned with making their children 'feel loved', 'building their self-esteem', 'providing a stimulating and learning environment', and encouraging their children to be self-expressive. (Chao, 2000, p. 236)

The parenting description from Hidalgo et al. and Chao was written more than a decade ago. Comparative research between families in China and families in Western countries was largely congruent with the above summary (Porter et al., 2005, Tsui, 2005, Quoss & Zhao, 1995). The dominant perception of Chinese parenting has been associated with children's high academic achievement and the strict, demanding and authoritarian style of parents; the former is usually regarded as the result of the latter. In the Western media, Yale professor Amy Chua's autobiographical book *The Battle Hymn of the Tiger Mother* generated a sharp critical reaction with regard to extremely strict parenting and children's achievement among Asian American parents (BBC, 2011). The following year a middle-class father in China emerged as an 'eagle Dad' (The Times, 2012) and once again reinforced the perception of the 'authoritarian' parenting stereotype in contemporary China.

The concept of 'authoritarian' parenting, as widely used in family and adolescent studies, is believed to originate from Diana Baumrind's model (1991, 1971) of three parenting styles, namely, authoritative parents (demanding and accepting), authoritarian parents (demanding and rejecting), and permissive parents (permissive and rejecting). The common association of Chinese-style with 'authoritarian' parenting has been criticized for misrepresenting Chinese families using methods based on Western culture (Goh, 2011, Huang & Prochner, 2003, Chao, 1994). Different from a Western perspective, the concept of *guan* (管) is crucial in understanding parental control in Chinese families (Chao, 1994, p. 1112). *Guan* literally means 'to govern' with positive connotations of 'to care for' and 'to love' (Tobin et al., 1989, p. 93), which equates to parental concern and involvement (Chao, 1994). A lack of *guan* is likely to indicate irresponsible parenting. Therefore, Chinese parents and children may stress the feature of discipline and control in the family because *guan* is considered to be the accepted norm of Chinese parenting.

This research does not attempt to ascertain which parenting method had a more successful impact on children; such an abstract framework of parenting and upbringing assumes a static state of family members and distorts the reality of the family dynamic. The very value-laden contrast of 'Chinese style'/authoritarian and 'Western style'/egalitarian child-rearing processes puts families in an over-simplified binary opposition. The children and parents I interviewed all acknowledged high academic expectations from the family, but *how* parents were involved in the child's education (and other aspects in life beyond education) showed variations in parental approaches. Let us learn more about it through three accounts of one-child participants' upbringing: they are Ran, Yizi and Tian.

Ran was born in a big city in Western China. In Chapter 1 we learned about his father's (the former chemistry factory manager) appreciation of the 'generational leap' he experienced; he certainly wasted no time in consolidating the advantage in his son. Ran has been a top student since he started schooling. He attributed his academic success to his parent's severe discipline, including physical punishment. He was hit with a bamboo stick if he did not achieve a full score in tests. Ran said that his motivation to do well in school was mainly to avoid punishment from his parents. However, the 27-year-old software engineer in London did not express any resentment about being physically punished, nor did he feel his experience to be unusual among his peers; on the contrary, he regarded a parental 'push' as crucial for a child's academic performance: 'for a child, studying is a boring process, a child won't naturally enjoy studying, so it is mainly the push from family [that motivates the child to study]'. Ran described himself as being 'typical' in the parental push model.

In comparison, an equally successful migrant in London, Yizi (female, 31, advertising manager) reported a parenting style which was different from the 'usual Chinese family'. Yizi was among the top range of students throughout her primary school to go to university. She regarded her mother's views as being 'very open', and her father was 'even more relaxed'; he would ask Yizi to 'come and watch TV, don't make yourself too tired [studying]'. Similar yet different to Ran, Yizi attributed her achievement today to her parents *not* pushing her too hard:

> They[Parents] gave me a certain amount of freedom and independence. They were not very strict with me, honestly, they let me do what I wanted to do…They never pushed me to study or forbad me doing this or that. They'd support my decisions once I thought things through.

However, the frequently reported 'relaxed attitude' from parents did not mean these parents cared about their child's schooling any less than the 'strict parents'; rather, their influence on the child tended to be more indirect. For example, Yizi had been a 'model child' without much direct parental involvement in her school work. In the interview with Yizi's mother (55, high school teacher), she described her covert approach to *influence*, rather than to *intervene* in her daughter's school work:

> Parental influence had better be at a subconscious level, not by force. Parents shouldn't say 'you must do this and that'. Once you helped the child to develop a healthy value system in her heart, you won't need to worry much about the rest, she won't walk into a wrong path.

Slightly different from Yizi's emphasis on a 'relaxed' parenting style, Tian (female, 31, lecturer) believed that her education and career had benefited from her upbringing with parent-guided *self-discipline*:

> My parents never checked if I did my homework. My Dad always said homework is only a means to an end. Understanding the knowledge is more important than completing homework...I followed this principle. They mostly educated me about basic things like a sense of morality and responsibility. They have planted the tree in good soil, so they just left the tree to do the rest of the growing.

Tian's father was a university-educated manager in a state-owned enterprise. He described his parenting as an evolving process. He admitted that he was 'strict' when Tian was little, but his relationship with his daughter gradually changed to a (in his words) 'Westernized' style during Tian's teenage years. He believed that the ageing process of Tian and himself was an important factor for the change: 'She was older, there was a process for parents to start respecting their child. As I was also ageing, I became less assertive and sharp in communicating with her.' In addition to the ageing process, he attributed his more interactive parenting style to the change in society:

> We are in a different time, although traditional culture is still deeply rooted in China, we are now more advanced...I like reading lots of books, maybe that helped me to accept new concepts...Chinese parents always say children should listen to parents, but I don't agree with it. Why should children always obey you? Are you always correct? Two generations surely will have different ways of thinking...I don't think the young should always listen to the old.

Ran, Yizi and Tian's cases are not atypical; elements of their upbringing can be found in families in this research regardless of region, parental income or education level. It is clear that the notion of *guan* (discipline) still existed in post-1978 middle-class families, but the way to approach it became more subtle. In other words, some parents (and children) had started to re-examine and re-define *guan* in Chinese parenting. Instead of prioritizing 'academic performance' for its extrinsic value, children's education advancement had been incorporated into the process of developing a well-rounded personality. Thus, education's role had a lot to do with its intrinsic values. Compared to the earlier more traditional parental approach to disciplining a child's study, this covert strategy was referred to by respondents (both children and parents) as 'Westernized', 'equal', 'modern' and 'democratic'. These terms were used as if they were interchangeable. It can be inferred from these normative judgements that the so-called 'Westernized parenting' was regarded as better (more acceptable) than the 'traditional Chinese parenting'.

Although a significant proportion of the sample (nearly half) reported that they had experienced a 'relaxed parental attitude', and praised this 'Westernized' style, it has to be noted that the sample of the research was recruited in the UK; most only-children came to the UK funded by their parents. This feature suggests an initial bias towards 'Western culture' among the families in the research, thus enhancing the acceptability by parents and children of a pro-Western-style parenting.

The Chinese upbringing among the middle class one-child generation has many aspects across different families as well as across different time periods within a family. No family was absolutely either 'traditionally authoritarian' or 'unconventionally egalitarian'; instead, the participants' upbringing was usually a hybrid of 'authoritarian elements' and 'non-authoritarian elements'; thus nuances of the different range and intensities of interactions between parents and their children have been established. Such a mixture brings out two questions: how did the seemingly inconsistent elements co-exist among middle-class families in the same society? And how did they co-exist in the same family?

As discussed earlier, within two decades (1970s–1990s), the parents' generation (born between the 1950s and 1960s) experienced a fundamental ideological and institutional shift in the employment system during the early and middle stages of their careers. The assumed lifetime continuity of their careers, in most cases, was interrupted and redirected. This kind of change was likely to impact on parents' expectations for their child's academic/career prospects and the way they brought up their child.

In the case of Ran (male, 27, software engineer), however, while his parents claimed they were 'democratic' and 'encouraging', he referred to their 'authoritarian parenting' style, including physical and psychological punishment; he felt great pressure, and it was difficult to communicate with his parents. Ran's parents were college-educated and worked in higher-management positions in a state-owned enterprise. Ran's father became self-employed after the business was privatized. Ran's mother also left the enterprise and became a successful business owner. Their experience of pre-reform collectivism and the climate and culture of post-reform competition may have shaped their parenting style into being part traditional and part modern.

Ran's mother elaborated on their 'democratic' parenting by saying that 'ever since he was 10 years old, we included his opinion in all the family decisions, we will count him in *as long as he is right* [emphasis mine]'. Clearly, Ran's parents *performed* a 'democratic' practice, but did not completely *believe in* an equal parent–child relationship. In fact, they revealed later in the interview that they valued the traditional patriarchal hierarchy:

> We have been strict about his manners, we demanded that he always respect the elders. In other families children may joke and call their parent 'buddies', this is not allowed in our family.

The contradiction of the 'democratic' element found in Ran's parents represented a dilemma among post-reform parents with regard to how to bring up their only child in a modernizing China. On the one hand the pragmatic, results-driven authoritarian parenting style was more effective in improving a child's examination results, and thus likely to secure a better position for the child in the job market; on the other hand middle class parents became increasingly concerned to 'raise well-rounded children apart from emphasis on academic achievement' (Wang, 2014, p. 765). Parents sometimes expressed their sympathy towards their own child for their lack of play time; yet they also felt that compromises/sacrifices had to be made.

Another dilemma concerns the hierarchy within the family. Since the 1980s the state launched a campaign, 'Raising the quality of the population' to improve 'each person's ideals, morals, education, and discipline'. One of the central messages of this campaign was that 'children are autonomous human beings who should be treated as their parents' equals' (Binah-Pollak, 2014, p. 29). Such a public discourse sharply contradicted the traditional parent–child hierarchy. Combined with the growing job market demand for individuals who were independent, innovative and self-motivated, Chinese parenting was faced with the challenges of both ideological and practice-based transformations.

The response of middle class parents towards these changing norms and policies in the 1980s and 1990s was divided. Although we saw in the examples of Yizi and Tian, where their memory of childhood interaction with parents challenges the traditional Chinese parenting style, only a minority of parents brought up their child in what seemed at the time to be an unconventional way. They were first-time parents whose own upbringing in pre-reform China had very limited practical relevance in post-reform child rearing. These parents were reported to be getting help from reading parenting books. For the majority of parents of the one-child generation, raising their child in a changing China was a process full of experiment, and risk.

At the point of interview the parent participants were in their fifties or sixties. When looking back at their earlier parenting behaviour these parents articulated a change of attitude in favour of a non-authoritarian parenting style. Some parents criticized themselves for being too demanding. For example, Yizi's mother sent Yizi to study violin at the age of four. The violin lessons stopped after two years because Yizi did not enjoy them. Yizi's mother blamed herself for following the trend blindly: 'Like many other parents who sent young children to study a music instrument, I also did the same.' Therefore, bringing up a child in a fast-changing China was for the parents also a process of trial and error.

The parents' child rearing style changes were not only brought out in interviews with parents; this kind of change was also revealed in interviews with the children. Jin (female, 23, student), reported a change in her mother's attitude from being 'strict', and taking her to extra mathematics class 'just like everyone else', to a more 'democratic' approach: 'in high school they did not give me much pressure'. Jin's parents were not university-educated, but, according to Jin, her parent's changes followed her mother's 'reading a lot of books about parenting'.

From hindsight the benefits and limitations of the 'authoritarian' and 'egalitarian' elements became more clear and the parents in the interviews were able to make a reflective evaluation. However, the stated tendency towards non-authoritarian, non-hierarchical parenting style that emerged in the parents' interviews may have been inflated to some extent by the parents' wish to present themselves as 'open' and 'modern' parents in front of the researcher. Nevertheless, the fact that parents regarded a non-authoritarian style of parenting to be morally superior and politically correct demonstrates how well established the changed norms of parenting style in the middle-class Chinese families had now become.

Gender: A More Covert Divide

Undoubtedly girls in the one-child generation had greater access to university education than their mothers' generation. The Chinese female university enrolment rate has overtaken the male rate since 2000 (World Bank, 2006). The UNESCO's data[1] showed that in 2015 the percentage of females who graduated from a Bachelor's degree and a Master's degree in China was 50% and 52%, respectively. However, it is difficult to say whether this outcome is significantly associated with the one-child policy, because UNESCO also indicated that since the 1990s more women than men completed tertiary education in most countries. The gender gap is more ambiguous at the domestic level. There is no clear standard, such as education level, by which to measure the way daughters and sons are treated in the family. By comparing housework load between sons and daughters in China in 2010, Yang Hu observed that the increase of female employment had not effectively led to children's more egalitarian domestic behaviour (Hu, 2015). Nevertheless, as Hu noted, there may be a gap between egalitarian domestic gender role values and the actual translating of these values into behaviour. This section will focus on the gendered attitudes, rather than the behaviour, of the older and younger generations in terms of career and personality.

A crucially significant practical reason for the preference of sons in traditional Chinese families was the role of sons as the material supporter of the three-generation households (parents, the son and his wife, the son's off-spring). However, the material supporter role for parents became almost irrelevant as middle-class parents no longer depended on their off-spring for material support but were more likely to continue supporting their adult child(ren). In this context the directly-expressed parental expectation tended to be less about material returns (what the child can do for his/her family), but more about the child's own accomplishment.

The one-child respondents were either professionals working in the UK or postgraduate students in prestigious British universities. In the sample of six parents, two parents had sons and four parents had daughters. A widely expressed satisfaction was found among the parents about the career/academic achievement of their sons and daughters. However, in spite of the small number in the sample, a gendered difference emerged with regard to revealing their satisfaction to their child. Parents were more reluctant to reveal their satisfaction to sons than to daughters: 'Can't say that to him, because he may be arrogant about it, but in my heart I'm proud of him' (father of Tengfei, male, PhD student). Not showing satisfaction about the child's achievement is similar to the 'punishment instead of encouragement' parenting method used by 'authoritarian' parents. Parents were afraid that by showing their satisfaction to the child the child would stop working hard.

Furthermore, the view that 'career is more important for men than women' was more pronounced among parents with boys. Ran's (male, 27, software engineer) parents brought him up in an authoritarian way with high academic/career expectations; but their high demand was gendered:

> Ran's Mother: Even now I tell my son all the time that men are nothing without a career, you must work hard, you have no reason not to do well in your job.
> M.T.: What kind of expectation would you have had if your only child was a girl?
> Mother: Perhaps, we would want her just to be happy, not having to work so hard.
> Father: I wouldn't have such a high expectation on her… Just like the tradition goes, boys should be more career-oriented.

Ran's parents clearly maintained a traditional gendered attitude to career expectation on offspring. However, for some parents having a daughter is not a reason for low career expectation, but a reason to demand even *higher* precisely because of females' 'weaker' position in the job market. Beiyao's (female, process engineer) mother represents a parent of this type. We learned her story in Chapter 1.

While some parents' high career expectation for their daughters was influenced by the gender inequality they had experienced themselves (like Beiyao's mother), some parents' motivation was less gender-related: Bolin's (female, 38, export manager) father was a factory worker, his pursuit of higher education was ended by the Cultural Revolution: 'I lost my chance [to go to university], so when I had my child, I was very strict, I wanted my daughter to do well.' Zhaohui's (female, 23, Master's degree student) family came from a small town dominated by traditional culture which regarded it as shameful if parents could not keep their children near them. However, Zhaohui's father encouraged his only daughter to find a job in a big city in spite of the mockery from neighbours about the father's failure to keep his only child near him, because 'I had the chance to leave [the small town] when I was young, but I stayed for my parents, now I regret it.'

The above accounts demonstrate two different attitudes towards the traditional gendered expectation, with the greater emphasis on a male's career than a female's. There appears to be a gap with regard to the gendered role by only-son parents and only-daughter parents. Although Ran's parents thought they would not have such a high expectation if they had had a daughter, it is difficult to say whether they would hold the same opinion if they actually had had an only daughter. If Ran's parent's reduced expectation regarding an imagined daughter reflected the social norm of career-oriented male and family-oriented female, then the only-daughter parents' high career expectations could be said to reflect the parents' personal aspiration for their only child.

When it comes to career expectations for sons and daughters, parents' responses showed two levels of understanding: the micro-level (parental level) gender equality and the macro-level (society level) gender inequality. By placing high expectations on their only-children (regardless of gender), parents with sons behaved according to the traditional gendered norm, thus appearing to be the supporter of the traditional culture; while parents with daughters behaved against the traditional gendered role, thus appearing to be the promoters of gender equality. Therefore, the high parental expectations on both daughters and sons should not be considered as strong evidence to show gender equality in the society; rather it has more to do with parental personal aspiration transfer than the changing norm in the wider society.

Parental expectation is not limited to career achievements. In their words, about gender-associated personalities parents revealed a more covert gendered expectation on sons and daughters. In Chinese cities the public discourse has been dominated by pro-gender-equality propaganda since the implementation of the one-child policy in 1979 (Greenhalgh, 2008). Public remarks that favour men over women are likely to be judged as politically incorrect, especially among the educated middle-class Chinese. However, a gendered hierarchy exists in a more subtly covert presence. Gender stereotype differences are not exclusive to China. A cross-cultural comparison confirmed that women were more likely to be perceived as having openness, agreeableness, conscientiousness, anxiety and vulnerability; were less likely to be associated with impulsiveness, assertiveness, or to be excitement-seeking.

The findings were consistent across 26 countries (Löckenhoff et al., 2014). While the perception of gender difference and certain personal qualities may be universal the notion of a hierarchy of gender-related personalities is more likely to be influenced by the local society and local culture.

Zhaohui's (female) father and Bolin's (female) parents all had high career expectations for their daughters and claimed gender equality; meanwhile they also believed that certain stereotypically male-associated qualities were more desirable for their daughters. When asked whether he would treat a son differently, Zhaohui's father answered: 'No, I've always raised my daughter like a son.' Zhaohui confirmed her father's words, and she felt proud of his attitude on the matter attributed her early independency to her parents accordingly:

> They didn't treat me like a girl; they demanded that I must do what boys do. They didn't spoil me... People usually mistook my name for a boy's name. My Mum took my study to be a priority, she never taught me how to cook.

Keeping a daughter away from the traditional domestic 'female territory', like the kitchen, is only one way of suppressing the female-associated qualities in daughters. Bolin's parents showed another way to 'de-feminise' their daughter:

> Father: Now that we are only allowed one child, we never thought about 'if we had a son', we raised our daughter like a son. So our daughter has some boy's characteristics. I don't want her to be a spoiled child, we didn't allow her to dress up, have long hair, or wear a skirt.
>
> Mother: We never really thought about it before. I've only just realized it since you asked today! Indeed, although we have a daughter, we raised her like a son.

This association between the being a girl and 'being spoiled' reinforced the stereotype of a girl to be 'weak and dependent'. As Yizi's (female, 31) mother (55, teacher) put it, 'girls are to be protected, while men should have a greater sense of responsibility and be the leader of the family'. In contrast the parental concern of 'being spoiled' was less salient among male respondents and their parents.

Bolin's mother's attempt to blur her daughter's gender revealed the parental (sometimes unconscious) denial of a daughter and their everyday influence to define her into the boy they could not have without the daughter even realizing it. Bolin was in her late thirties and a mother of two at the point of interview, when talking about the ban on girl-like outfits in her childhood, she said jokingly: 'I was fat, short-haired and wore glasses. Even in university some people thought I was a boy [laugh]'. Bolin did not regard her situation as being unusual, but blamed the general plainness of material life in the 1980s.

However, without the comparison of the treatment of other children in the family as a reference group, gender inequality in one-child families tended to be covert; while respondents who had a sibling of a different gender were more exposed to openly gendered treatment in the domestic situation. The non-one-child sample in this research contains three women who had a brother and two men who had a sister. Although it is a small sample their perception of their siblings showed a sharp awareness of the gendered difference in terms of the entitlement for family resources and the assignment of family responsibilities.

Feng (female, 34, IT manager) grew up in a semi-rural town where 'it was normal to have more than one child' because most people 'wanted a boy'. Her mother was 'a typical Chinese woman' who thought that 'one ought to have a boy'. As we learned earlier in this chapter, Feng experienced some emotional struggle over the arrival of her brother. Fortunately for Feng her parents had enough income to fund both her and her brother's study abroad. However, as a boy born in an economically deprived rural family, Wenbin's (male, 36, entrepreneur) university education was made possible because of his older sister's sacrifice of her own education opportunities. Thus, although Wenbin was the younger child, the family directed all the resources to him instead of the older child. Respondents who grew up in urban two-children families also reported differences in the daily arrangements for the siblings but not as sharply obvious as the difference shown in rural families.

The gender inequality in two-children families was more overt, while that in the one-child families was more covert. The level of awareness of gender inequality among only-children was lower than children who grew up with opposite sex siblings. Therefore, while one-child urban families may have contributed to a seemingly more gender-equal environment for girls, the fundamental belief in a gender hierarchy still persisted. The limited number of children and the sufficient material provision blurred the underlying gender hierarchy in 21st century middle-class one-child families. In any case, we must not rush to the conclusion that there has been a fundamental gender value shift because of the one-child policy.

Education: The Usual and the Alternative

The transition from a planned economy to a market economy gave a greater level of freedom to the flow of resources and labour throughout China. The individuals in these transitions also found themselves in a crucial period where their former belief in a secure, egalitarian, long-term form of state employment was being challenged by a relatively uncertain, unequal and competitive employment system but one which also brought the opportunities for high income and social upward mobility. The changing demands of the labour market had a direct impact on the priorities of education for the younger generation. The competition for a good job thus started from the beginning of children's schooling.

China launched a '9-year compulsory education' law in 1986. By 2000, the middle-school education coverage reached 85% of the whole population (Ministry of Education of PRC, 2015). From the late 1990s, the state no longer assigned jobs for university graduates, and graduates were exposed to labour market competition. In the meantime the state initiated an unprecedented expansion of higher education. The level of university enrolment increased from 3 million in 1996 (Whyte, 2012) to 25 million in 2006; thus, transforming higher education from exclusivity to inclusivity (Yeung, 2013). It is believed that education as a means to gain middle-class membership was applied by the Chinese state from the top when the higher education expansion was carried out. An enlarged middle class 'is being created' through that expansion (Lin & Sun, 2010, p. 217). Such a state-planned phenomenon institutionalizes higher education as 'the most important criterion for middle-class status' (Lin & Sun, 2010, p. 238), which in turn is likely to re-enforce the belief that education is the only way to become a member of the middle class among the mass population.

The term 'key schools' in China refers to better quality state schools. As a result, key schools are seen as the early means towards a more promising future in the employment market. The admission to key schools was, in principle, based on merit. The 'key school system' was introduced in the 1980s. Key schools were given priority in the assignment of teachers, equipment and funds. They constituted 'only a small percentage of all regular junior or high schools and funnelled the best students into the best secondary schools, largely on the basis of entrance scores' (You, 2007). Nevertheless, a minority of key school students who did not meet the entrance requirement were able to study in such schools because their parents had social connections or/and paid extra money. The percentage of this cohort among all key school students is not clear. The percentage is likely to vary in different regions depending on local key schools' policies. It has been reported that students with a more affluent family background were more likely to be found in key schools (Yang, 2006). Therefore, the one-child generation's schooling consisted of academic competition among students alongside economic and social capital competition among parents.

In addition to the state school system the emergence of private schools since the early 2000s added to the diversity of schooling choices for the one-child generation. However, the percentage of students who attended private school remained small (7% in 2006 and 10% in 2014) (World Bank, 2015). In a more recent trend study abroad in secondary schools became another alternative to access education options without competing in the state system. Although the number of under-18 overseas students had been increasing since 2010 (Wang & Miao, 2013), such a choice was limited to a small number of families because of the high cost and the concern of the low age of the child (Table 1).

Table 1: State school system in China.

Age: 7–12	13–15	16–18	19+
Primary school	Key middle school Ordinary middle school	Key high school Ordinary high school Vocational or technical college	University

The one-child respondents in this research had an above-average level of schooling, especially so given that nearly half of the sample attended key schools. (In China the key school students make up only a minority of all school students.) This feature reflects the middle-class family background as well as the highly educated profile of the sample. However, a small number of respondents (four) revealed that their key school admissions were 'helped' by their parents' connections and extra money paid to the school (Table 2).

Table 2: The 33 respondents' school attendance history in China.

Pre-University Education	Male One-Child	Female One-Child	One-Child	Non-One-Child
State education ordinary school	6	7	13	5
State education key school	5	8	13	1
Private school	2	1	3	0

Because key schools were more concentrated in cities students out-side cities had fewer opportunities to go to a key school. However, this situation did not stop some parents using their social connections to bypass the state system. Zhaohui (female, 23, student) grew up in a town[2] in south China and was a top student in her local school. There was no key school in her town, so for students who wanted to go to a better high school, they had to go to a city. Because of the prior-ity given to the admission of local students, 'immigrants' like Zhaohui were in a disadvantaged position. Fortunately for Zhaohui, her 'uncle lived in ZH (initials of the city), he knew the headmaster of the key school, and the headmaster helped to get me into his high school. So I left my parents and went to ZH'. This kind of corruption was largely the result of unequally distributed education resources between cities and towns as well as the geographical discrimination in a key school's admission system.

The unequal nature of the key school system caused concern in the state administration and attempts were made to promote a more egali-tarian system (Ministry of Education, 2015, China.org, 2015). How-ever, this up-down approach did not fundamentally change the demand for key schools among Chinese families. The key school notion 'is taken for granted in a society conceived as a hierarchy', as an OECD[3]-led research observed in the 2000s: 'Parents do not question the existence of such a system; they only think how their own children might win the competition to get into key schools' (OECD, 2011, p. 95). This idea is congruent with Vanessa Fong's observation in the 1990s in Dalian, a north city in China: 'Poor students are more strongly motivated because they know a good education is the only way to escape their poverty' (Fong, 2004, p. 103).

Fong (2004) argued that such an aspiration found in economically disadvantaged students was partly to do with the not-yet-obvious social stratification in the 1990s. Furthermore, the pattern of student perfor-mance in the high school where Fong did her fieldwork appeared espe-cially hopeful for students from a financially deprived background: top students tended to come from poor families and rich children tended to do poorly in school. This pattern was contrary to what she found in middle schools. Soon she realized that the enrolment process to a high school was more flexible than that to a middle school. The latter was based on residency while a key high school could allocate a certain num-ber of places to rich students who had good exam results, but slightly lower than required exam scores, and were willing to pay extra to avoid 'falling down' to the ordinary high schools. This system acted as part of a 'screening device' (Ball, 2003, p. 15) where good students who could not afford the 'extra payment' were filtered down to ordinary schools, thus resulting in the pattern Fong saw in the ordinary high school where she did her fieldwork.

The majority of Fong's sample came from working class families, while the majority of my participants had a relatively affluent and educated family background. Their report on schooling choice showed more active parental awareness in generating various socioeconomic resources to secure a better education platform for their child. A few respondents mentioned the benefits they received during schooling because of their parents' social and economic capital. The reported benefits included the admission to a desirable primary school, starting school at an earlier age,[4] and the choice of studying with a preferred teacher. Shan (female, 32, post-doctoral researcher) attended both privileged primary school and a key secondary school. She said the admission to the key secondary school was 'based on my exam scores'; as for entering the desirable primary school, 'it all depended on who your father is. I've no idea how my Dad pulled the connections'. The majority of the respondents (both children and the parents) perceived the 'using connections' as something to be taken for granted; only a very small number of the respondents expressed a sense of embarrassment. Therefore, from a very young age, the one-child generation was not only involved in intense competition in academic performance, but they were also aware of the role of parental capital in their educational advance.

Another crucial change in education resources, namely the access to overseas education, was initiated from the top down. Following Deng Xiaoping's speech in 1978: 'We are going to send thousands or tens of thousands of students to receive overseas education' (Qian, 2009), the early groups of Chinese international students were state-sponsored. Compared to the state-sponsored students, the self-funded overseas education during the late 1970s and 1980s was limited to the elites who had the financial resources and overseas connections. In 1978 only eight self-funded students applied to study abroad. The number increased to over a thousand a year in the early 1980s (Dai, 2008). At the practical level two features slowed down the progress of migration: the complex bureaucratic process involved to obtaining a passport, and the undeveloped transport system to travel internationally (Skeldon, 1996).

In 1993 the state's principle of 'supporting pursuing studies abroad, encouraging returning to the homeland and free to come and go' was established; this subsequently led to the start of the self-funded study-abroad demographic (Zhu & Lou, 2011, p. 108). Of the students who went abroad, the percentage of private-sponsored students rose from 65% in 1996 to 90% in 2001 (Li, 2010, p. 283). In 1998 the state legalized the operation of study-abroad agencies (Dai, 2008); these agencies have played a crucial role in the expansion and commercialization of the study-abroad market. With more information, service, and facilities available (mainly provided by study-abroad agencies), study abroad was no longer a privilege limited to an elite of well-connected and well-informed individuals. The Chinese public rapidly became familiar with the notion of overseas study, and the newly-emergent middle-class families started to join this movement and to send their children abroad.

Study abroad remained restricted to university-level students, but recent years also saw a study abroad trend among much younger students. Nevertheless, during my participants' upbringing, going abroad for school education was relatively rare. Kai (male, 28, estate agent) was one of the teenage study-abroad students. He was born in 1986 in a small town outside of a southeastern city. Kai's father initially worked in a college and his mother was a nurse. His father started his own business in the 1990s and improved the family financial situation. Kai was sent to a private boarding school in the nearby city from the age of 10 until he finished middle school there at the age of 15. His father then decided to send him to a private institution in China which prepared young students to study an A Level course in the UK. Kai spent two years there before arriving at a language school in the UK in 2002. He then joined a private Sixth Form College and progressed to a Bachelor's degree and a Master's degree in a Russell Group University.

Kai's education path was entirely designed by his father. Kai described himself as a 'passive person', and that his father made 'three steps of mobility for him':

> Just like most Chinese people would think, 'wow, it [the private boarding school] is expensive therefore it must be a good school, my son will be one step further than others, we cannot lose at the starting line of the race'. In my Dad's words, I took three steps of mobility, one is from the small town to the city, one is from the middle school to the private institution, the final one is from China to overseas.

Kai revealed that in the early 2000s his father's business was not stable so the decision to break away from the Chinese state education system and send the 15-year-old Kai to a pre-A Level institution meant a long and expensive education journey ahead which entailed much uncertainty and great risk. Fortunately, his father's business grew and the education 'gamble' has achieved the expected result. It is hard to say whether Kai would have fared as well if he had taken the more usual route and studied in the Chinese state education system.

What Kai and Zhaohui had in common was that they were both from small towns in China where they were disadvantaged (compared with children born in big cities) in education resources, and that they were both, eventually, educated at the Master's level in a prestigious British university. However, the routes they took, and the parental resources involved, were very different. Zhaohui's familial social connections and Kai's familial financial resources played major roles in these two cases. Therefore, for students outside of cities, and who did not have social connections like Zhaohui's family did, private school and study abroad provided a channel for those with the financial resources to circumvent the unfair key school admission system. However, the decision to study abroad is not always as well planned as it was in the case of Kai's family. Chapter 3 follows the one-child generation as they left China to venture on an unknown path.

Notes

1. United Nations Education, Science and Cultural Organization. The data are provided by UNESCO Institute for Statistics. Available at http://tellmaps.com/uis/gender/#!/tellmap/79054752/3.
2. A 'town' in this study refers to a semi-rural, semi-urban area usually located between cities and countryside. Administratively, 'towns' are higher than rural villages and lower than cities. Usually 'towns' can be regarded as a transition period during the process of urbanization.
3. Organization for Economic Co-operation and Development.
4. The reason why some parents wanted their child to start school at an earlier age was said to be to get 'one step ahead of everyone else'. Sometimes it was also because parents were too busy to look after the child.

Chapter 3

One-Child Migrants in the UK: The Decision-Making Process, Mobility Trajectory and Parental Involvement

> Especially striking is the ability of these highly educated
> migrants to join the professional and business worlds of the
> settler societies while retaining a deep attachment in China.
> (Wang Guangwu in Kuhn, 2008, p. 357)

The migrants described above constitute part of what Wang Gungwu calls the 'upgrading' (Kuhn, 2008, p. 357) of Chinese migrants coming to the West, which includes student-turned-migrants from China. Growing up in a modernizing Chinese society, the one-child generation has experienced rising living standards and educational opportunities that were not available to their parents' generation in pre-reform China. The domestic change in China was accompanied by changes in the international sphere as well as China's relationship with the rest of the world. The opening of China's border not only facilitated domestic economic growth but also transformed the Chinese perception and participation in transnational mobility within three decades.

In Chapter 2 we learned Kai's story – a man from southeast China whose private schooling and study abroad was designed by his father from when Kai was a young child. Among the participants for this research there were only two migrants who came to the UK as A Level students and studied all the way up to a Master's degree. As I mentioned previously, this extremely expensive route was not taken by many families back in the early 2000s (although families increasingly opted for this path for their child after 2010).

The other migrant who also came to the UK at the age of 16 is Ying (female), a 29-year-old accounts assistant in London. Unlike the long period

Education, Migration and Family Relations between China and the UK:
The Transnational One-Child Generation, 73–106
Copyright © 2018 by Emerald Publishing Limited
All rights of reproduction in any form reserved
doi:10.1108/978-1-78714-672-320181005

of pre-departure training Kai had, Ying's study abroad sounded like an ad hoc decision, at least on her part. It all started one day when she was in the second year of her high school at a dinner gathering with her mother and her mother's friends. The adults started to chat about overseas education.

> So they were chatting and thought study abroad sounded like a good idea. Then my Mum turned to me and asked if I wanted to go. Neither my Mum nor me made the decision. We were just chatting and thought, why not?

Once the process started it seemed unstoppable; the next stage involved processing the paperwork to withdraw Ying from her high school; finding a study abroad consultant to identify a school in the UK or the US, and help with the school and visa application. At that time, whether it was the UK or the US did not seem to matter to Ying; she followed the advice of the consultant and came to the UK because 'the visa process is easier'.

Thirteen years later, Ying's migration decision pattern can be summarized by the temporary extensions made at each step of her education which eventually led to permanent residency (PR):

> I didn't plan long-term, I just thought I'd complete an undergraduate degree here. After that, I started to want a Master's degree. When I finished my Master's degree it [an overseas degree] seemed ordinary in China, so I thought I'd get some work experience before going back. After I started working, I felt the income level here is much higher [than in China], so [I remained in the UK].

As we were sitting in a café in London on 25 March 2014, Ying showed me her engagement ring – she was due to be married in May to an Englishman she first met through friends. She was full of plans for children and buying another flat in London so her parents could come and stay. 'I think I'm pretty much settled here,' Ying said with a tone of contentment towards the end of our interview. Nine months after our interview Ying told me that she had left her job as an accounts assistant at a small marketing company and had started a new job at a well-established bank.

In this chapter, we will hear more stories which connect migrants' upbringing, study abroad and the decision to remain. As I highlighted in the Introduction, migration can be treated as a *result* following a cluster of factors, a *process* which leads to certain consequences, or a *field* which contains interacting agencies and networks at all levels. Each decision a would-be migrant makes is connected to micro- and macro-level factors from the past and the perceived future. The participants were made up of members who were at different stages of their lives with different goals, obligations and priorities. Such diversity provides a unique opportunity for the researcher to capture whether, and how, the impact of parents (and other factors) may shift as the life of the migrant progresses over time. How are the post-study-migration decisions made? What are the decision-making implications on migrants' transnational mobility? These questions require a temporal context and a familial perspective.

Leaving China: The Changes in Sending and Receiving Countries

The second half of the 20th century and the first decade of the 21st century witnessed two extreme features of Chinese migration: from the closed border under Mao's government to China being the leading over-seas student-sending country. Family reunion migration, labour migra-tion and illegal migration also contributed to the growing migration wave after 1978. However, it was the study-abroad migration demographic that marked the most significant increase (see Fig. 8). In Mao's China,

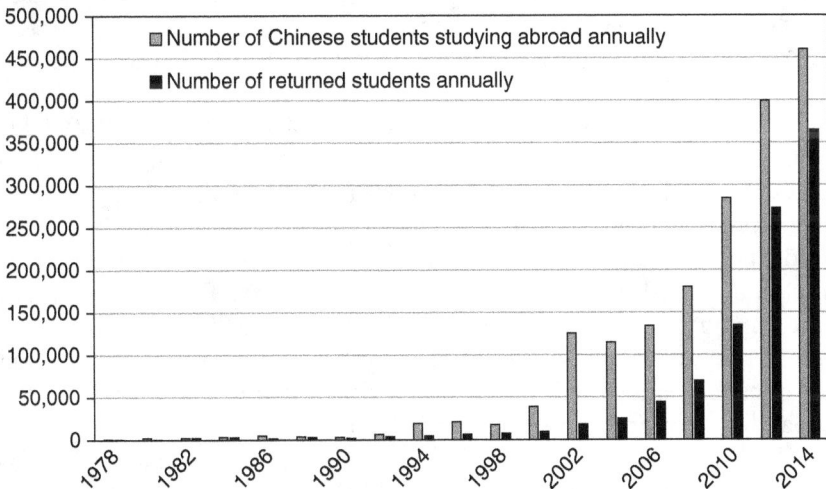

Fig. 8: Number of study-abroad population and return population. *Source*: National Bureau of Statistics of PRC (2015).

the public discourse of the West was associated with negative 'capitalist values' which opposed the state's communist ideology (Friedman, 1994). During the last two decades before the open-door policy, people in main-land China were neither allowed to go abroad nor were overseas Chinese allowed to re-migrate to China. Individuals who wanted to leave China remained silent for fear of being regarded as opposing the Chinese social-ist system (Liu, 2006). Legal migration from mainland China developed after 1978. However, emigration was strictly monitored by the state. Apart from those seeking family reunification (also called 'settler migrants' by Skeldon [1996]), a significant proportion of the early migrants were state-sponsored students who were sent to the US and Europe.

The turn of the century marked a significant increase in international students (see Fig. 8); it was also the time when the children born after the 1979 one-child policy turned into their twenties. The majority of overseas Chinese students have been postgraduate students. The percentage of stu-dents who went overseas for postgraduate degrees has remained higher than 25% of all Chinese postgraduate students for most years since 1994 (Li, 2010). Therefore, it was not uncommon for students who completed an undergraduate degree in China to continue into postgraduate educa-tion overseas. Meanwhile, fewer people in the later wave worked before they left China. In addition to the rapid increase, students who went abroad for undergraduate[1] and secondary school education increased rapidly (Wang & Miao, 2013, Dai, 2008). The average age of overseas Chinese students has become younger.

Accompanying the large volume of migration from China is the increas-ing number of returnees (see Fig. 8). In 1978, as a returnee who studied in Paris in the 1920s, Deng Xiaoping hoped that state-sponsored students would return after their education and contribute to the modernization of China (Xinhua News, 2004). However, from the period 1979–1990s, the approximate return rate was only 30%, and only one in five of the students who went to the US returned to China (Skeldon, 1996). This situation started to change from the late 1990s (see Fig. 8). The return rate remained lower than half until shortly before 2010. The increased return rate was largely the result of a tightened migration policy, limited job vacancies after the 2008 financial crisis in the host country, and the expanding economic opportunities in China.

The recognition of an international degree by the state and the poli-cies carried out to attract returnees added political and social value to the attainment of a Western university degree, which in turn helped returnees to transform their cultural capital to economic capital (Biao & Shen, 2009). However, in reality, the returnees' career prospects in China showed a mixed profile: on the one hand returnees were associated with privileged positions in both the private and public sectors; the state provided financial rewards to attract 'outstanding students' and supported their entrepreneurship in China (Biao & Shen, 2009); US and European returnees also made up 15% of the fifth generation of Chinese leaders (Liu, 2011).

On the other hand as more overseas degree holders entered the job market the advantage of an overseas degree perceived by employers lessened. Without any work experience in China or overseas, the graduate returnees' job-search process was as difficult as it was for their locally graduated counterparts. However, returnees who were waiting for a job were commonly labelled by the public as *haidai* (海带 seaweed); it is a pejorative reference that compared the returnees to seaweed washed ashore. Public media in China and abroad have been highlighting the 'over optimistic' career expectations among returnees since the early 2000s (China Central Television Channel, 2014, Fischer, 2014, Melik, 2012, Xinhua News, 2007, 2003).

In spite of the fact that the average starting salary for returnees remained significantly higher than for home-educated graduates (Zweig & Han, 2011), the large gap between study-abroad costs and the starting salary for returnees casts doubt on the value of overseas education. In 2013, for example, the annual study abroad cost in the UK was around £20,000, while the average starting salary of Chinese returnees was £9,675 in 2011 (Universities UK, 2014, Archer & Cheng, 2012). From a pragmatic

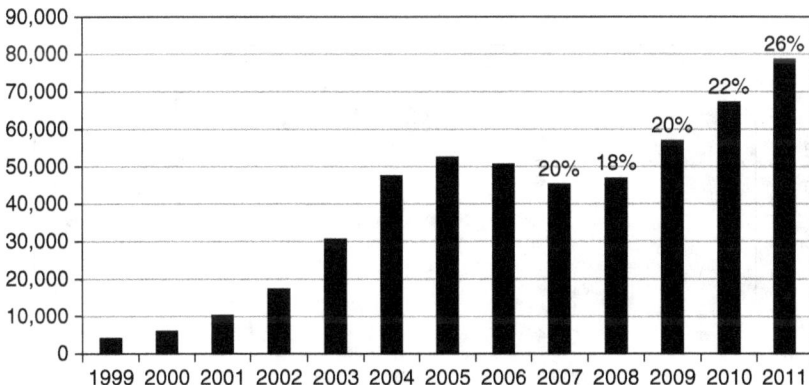

Fig. 9: Number of Chinese students in the UK. *Source*: Universities UK (2013) and Li (2010). The percentage shows the proportion of students from China among all non-EU countries after 2007.

investment-return point of view, studying abroad became a riskier investment for families in China.

As study abroad changed from an exclusively elite experience to a relatively common phenomenon, the quality of education, overseas experience, and the prospect for Chinese job applicants with an overseas degree, all added to the increasingly complex nature of the success in formal education and employment. Students in the host country were also subject to a cluster of impacts. Following the US, the UK is the second most popular destination for Chinese students, particularly for postgraduate studies (Ernst & Young, 2014, China Daily, 2013). By 2012, China provided the largest number of international students in UK universities (Universities UK, 2013, Home Office, 2013). In 2013, while China was the top UK-visa receiving country, 76% were student visas (Home Office, 2014, 2013).

In this study all respondents but one arrived in the UK after 2000. They were all below the age of 30 in the year of arrival (see Fig. 10). In fact only two respondents (Bolin and Qiaolin) were born before 1979 when the one-child policy was officially enforced. Most of them came to the UK as students (see Table 3). The minority who came to do an undergraduate or pre-undergraduate course eventually continued to complete a post-graduate degree. Only a third of the respondents worked in China before coming to the UK, ranging from one year to three years. The general lack of (or short) work experience reflects the young age of the arrivals. The respondent who came by marriage met her husband in China. One of the respondents who came with a work visa was recruited

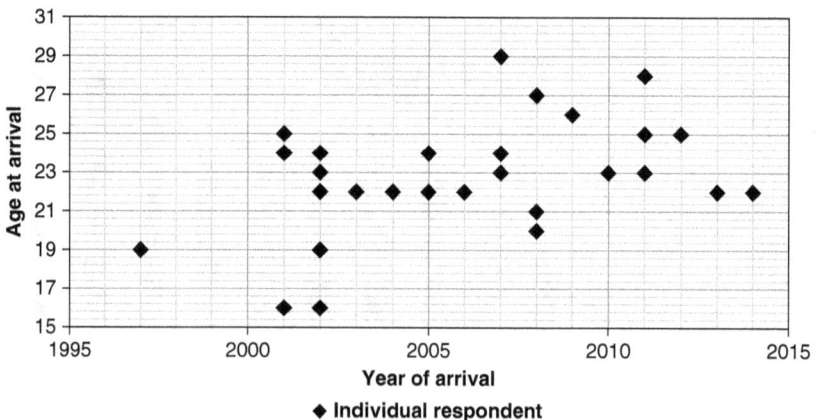

Fig. 10:   Year and age of respondents when first arrived in the UK.

Table 3: The route by which respondents entered the UK.

	Student		Work	Marriage
Post-Graduate	Undergraduate	A Level	2	1
18	9	3		

by a Chinese traditional medical doctor scheme based in the UK, and the other one was recruited by a British university as a post-doctoral researcher.

Most respondents in the sample had no direct connections in the UK before they left China. The lack of social or family connections in the host country adds to the difficulty of the extension of the new migrants' initial temporary visas, especially among most new post-graduate students whose visas lasted for only a year because of the one-year length of their Master's degree course. Apart from the minority who married a British citizen, for the overseas students who want to remain in the UK after their study, the most common way was to find a job that enabled the individual to switch to a work visa.

From 1995 to 2012; the work permits granted to the Chinese each year increased from 657 to 4873 (ONS, 2006, Home Office, 2013). Data from the 2007 and 2009 Chinese graduates' survey showed that 20% of the students who graduated in 2007 and 2009 remained in the UK for work (Archer & Cheng, 2012, p. 22). However, the level of difficulty for students switching to full-time employment in the UK has grown since 2007. Apart from the increasing competition in the British job market after the 2008 financial crisis, state policy has made the UK unwelcoming to non-EU job-seekers. Restrictions on work visas were introduced; most significantly, migrants need to obtain a certificate of sponsorship from the future employer before applying for a work visa. The employer would have to be a licensed sponsor recognized by the Home Office, and the job (if not on the shortage occupation list) offered to the migrant needs to have passed the Resident Labour Market Test as well as meet a minimum requirement in salary. For example, in 2017 the salary requirement was at least £30,000 per year, increased from £20,300 a year in 2013.[2] A change of migration policy is usually the most effective way to influence migrants' decision to remain or return in the short term. With the cancellation of the post-study work visa in 2012 the percentage of students who obtained a work visa after study immediately dropped by 87% (Universities UK, 2014).

The Home Office granted 'indefinite leave to remain' (ILR) to those who wanted to settle (also commonly referred to by migrants as 'PR').

The grant is based on different criteria, and the most common criterion is the length of residence, which requires applicants to have lived in the UK for at least 10 years (study and/or work) or worked and paid a required amount of tax for at least five years (Home Office, 2015). After being an ILR holder for a year individuals will be allowed to apply for British citizenship (Home Office, 2015). Based on this route a Chinese person who came to the UK as a degree student would need to work for at least five years before being granted an ILR.

The legal status of respondents in this study is shown in Fig. 11. The majority of the sample are temporary residency permit holders (student-visa and work-visa). This group of migrants is vulnerable to any changes in government policy. Under the current visa system, work visa holders are not allowed to work for a different employer unless the new employer is qualified to sponsor foreign nationals, and is willing to go through the complex process to apply for a work permit (certificate of sponsorship) for the migrant. This requirement has limited the job choice and also made current students' job searches difficult. However, the work restriction does not apply to ILR holders. Furthermore, ILR holders are entitled to welfare benefits in the UK, and their children are also entitled to enter the British education system.

Success in attaining long-term residency, therefore, broadens migrants' scope and security. It is viewed as the 'Green Card' for the UK. Although most non-settled respondents in the study desired an ILR, not many of them wanted to become a British citizen. The Chinese state does not recognize dual nationality: becoming a British citizen means giving up Chinese citizenship. As a result the majority of ILR holders (9 out of 10) in the study did not apply for British citizenship in spite of the fact that all these nine respondents were qualified to do so.

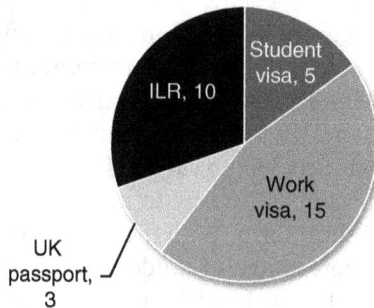

Fig. 11: Participants' legal status.

As the migration policy in the host country becomes stricter it is not surprising that an increasing rate of recent arrivals returned to China after studying, and hence the rising return rate (see Fig. 8). However, a significant number of the former international students remained. The 'student switchers' (Robertson, 2011) make up the majority of the sample. As the sample was *not* selected with a preference for former students, the high proportion of 'student switchers' suggests that the post-study migrants are likely to represent the majority of the new Chinese migrants living in the UK at the time of this research.

The sudden rise of international student mobility is a relatively new yet widespread phenomenon. The global cross-border student population increased by 70% between 2000 and 2008 (Robertson, 2011), which intensified the global talent circulation associated with 'brain gain' and 'brain drain' for different regions. The career outlook and post-study settlement of this highly qualified demographic thus became crucial for both the host country and the sending country. However, the understanding of the decision-making process of this highly mobile, highly qualified group of migrants, including the decision to study abroad, to remain in the host country or to return/re-migrate, is relatively limited. The next section explores the key factors involved in the one-child Chinese migrants' transition from international students to long-term residents in a transnational context.

From International Students to Working Residents: Changing Mobility and Personal Aspirations

International students have been treated ambiguously with regard to their designation as migrants. If the term *migrant* 'broadly covers everyone who leaves home without intending to return' (Wang, 2007, p. 167), then around half of the sample in this study could not be classified as a migrant; the respondents left China with different initial plans that ranged from a firm intention to return to China after study (12 out of 33), to a strong commitment to remain overseas (1 out of 33). The only participant who showed a strong commitment to remain overseas was Tao (female, 27, social media manager). She went to the county of Kent as a post-graduate student in 2010 and was determined to remain permanently. She married an English fellow student and has lived in the county since then. This is the only example of a planned settlement found in the research. A large number of the cases were between the two ends of this spectrum, with a significant proportion who either did not have a clear preference to return or to remain in the UK (15 out of 33) or who wanted to have some work experience before returning (5 out of 33).

The majority of the respondents who were working residents at the time of interview had experienced at least one major change in their travel plans. This kind of changing nature of post-study plans shows a flexible continuity from student to 'migranthood' (Wang, 2007, p. 168) which distinguished student-turned-migrants from traditional migrants. The blurring of boundaries in migrant types and decision-making stages requires a framework that captures an individual's evolving mobility trajectory as it unfolds with changing circumstances at different levels, and this takes place not only in a relatively more changeable period of a person's life (from education completion to career or family establishment) but is also embedded in a transnational context.

Studying abroad is not a decision made entirely by an individual as a one-off choice. It is 'an on-going interaction between micro-level and macro-level factors and considerations' (Mosneaga & Winther, 2013, p. 183). This description puts migration decision-making in both a relational and a historical perspective. The relational perspective includes the factors in an individual's family, affiliated groups and host or home countries, all of which directly or indirectly affect the individual's decision-making process. The historical perspective provides an understanding about how migration decision-making proceeds or follows other events (Carlson, 2013); it can be the outcome of previous mobility experiences, and it can also be the factor that influences an individual's mobility later in life.

The complex relationships of migration decision factors and their impact on the migrant mobility trajectory of the migrant are presented in the framework (Fig. 12). This framework was generated based on a diagram in Ana Mosneaga and Lars Winther's study (2013) about international students' career trajectory in Denmark. I borrowed the basic structure of their diagram but modified the content to reflect the Chinese cohort. For example, *migration policy* was added for its application exclusively on non-EU students; *parental factors* were highlighted given that the majority of the Chinese students were funded by parents, and hence the significance of parents in the decision-making process. Furthermore, the circulation of 'disposition to go abroad→ destination choice → extension of stay → disposition to return' was added to indicate the on-going nature of decision-making. The rest of the section will explain the framework in terms of its relational and historical structure; the focus will then turn to elaborating on the crucial factors that directly impact on the migrants' decision-making process.

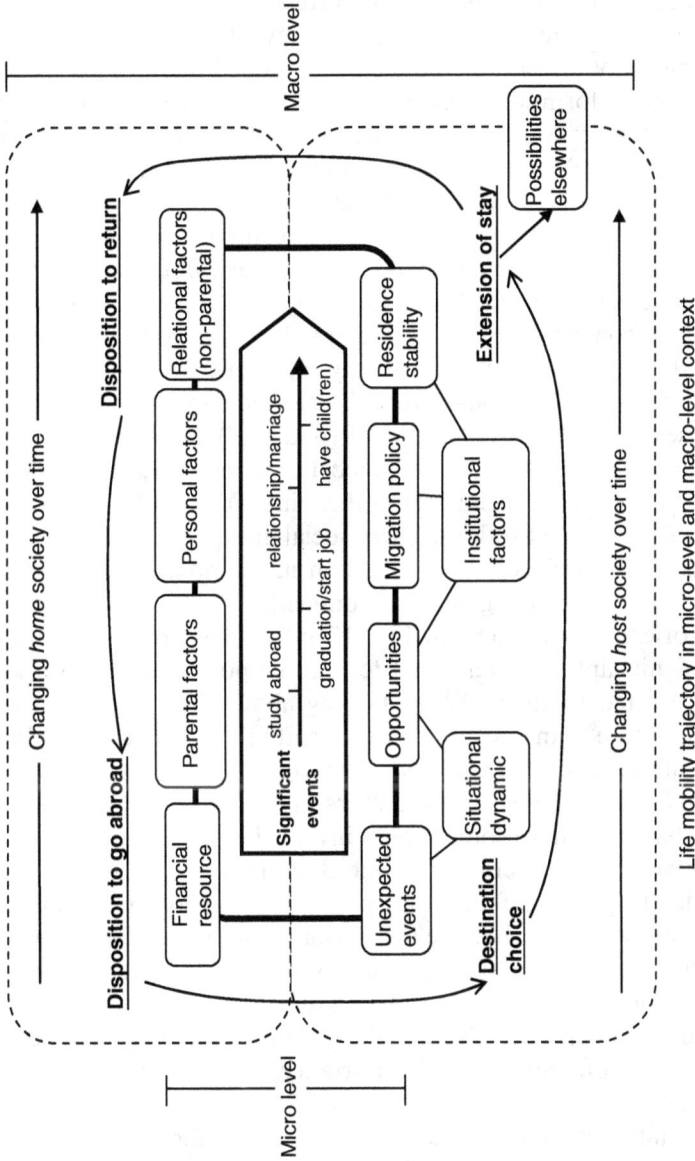

Fig. 12: Life mobility trajectory in micro-level and macro-level contexts. *Source:* Adapted from Mosneaga and Winther's (2013) study and reproduced here with permission from John Wiley & Sons.

The Structure of the Framework

The boundaries of the micro-level and macro-level factors are blurred; they have been referred to as 'individual-related factors' and 'setting-related factors'; the latter involves 'impetuses, events, persons or contexts that make mobility a workable possibility' (Guth, 2007, p. 1). Furthermore, based on the forms of an individual's relationship with other actors involved, the factors were also divided as 'relational embeddedness' (dyadic [pairwise] relations) and 'structural embeddedness' (structure of the overall network of relations) (Carlson, 2013, Granovetter, 1992, p. 33). These descriptions of the interactive relationships between individuals and their surrounding social elements reflect Bourdieu's concept of 'habitus' and 'social embeddedness' (1986).

Students are complex subjects whose life objectives go beyond higher education: they are simultaneously family members, friends, citizens of a particular country or in some cases (former) employees of an institution. Because of the multiple identities of (potential) migrants, their decisions are likely to be influenced by the local economic, social or cultural environment through the social groups these individuals are affiliated to: family, peer group or institutions. These social groups are also subject to the changes in the socioeconomic situation in the home country, host/destination country and the global environment.

The historical development in Fig. 12 introduces, in chronological order, the significant life events that tend to be points of decision and the factors related to them. When talking about their past decision-making and future plans, respondents' narratives usually evolve along significant life events: *study abroad, graduation/start job, relationship/marriage and have child(ren)*. The factors that operate at a micro-level or a macro-level are all, to some extent, involved in influencing the decisions. However, for different events the dominating factors may vary. For example, the parental factor may play a more important role in the decision to study abroad, but the institutional factors (in this case, job opportunities) may play a greater role in the decision to start a job in the UK. By looking at the framework in a timeline the factors related to the individuals are not static. Rather, they work dynamically in different conditions, with different levels of importance, at different life stages of the individual.

The importance of time in understanding the migration trajectory was also highlighted in Johanna Waters' longitudinal research about middle-class Hong Kong and Taiwan women in Canada (2011). Slightly different from this study, Waters' participants entered her research in 1999 as mothers with young children who migrated to Canada as 'astronaut wives' while their husbands worked in the home country. Eight years later these women's lives and outlooks changed with the growth of their children, the reunion with their husbands and their own changing sense of belonging to Canada and Hong Kong/Taiwan. Important life stages such as 'children becoming 18' and their own 'retirement' were significant marks in their future re-migration and settlement plans. Waters' research not only suggested that 'transnational migration is cyclical', but also indicated that the impact of the life stages of close family members can also shape a migrant's decision. In the case of Waters' research, her participants were largely influenced by their children's and husbands' needs. This research, with a younger cohort, explores the (potential) impact of parents as well as spouses and offspring on the migrant's decision-making process over time.

Similar to life events, which were most obvious to the respondents, the migrants' dispositions to go abroad, to remain or to return can also be better captured by looking through a developmental perspective. In the case of migrants arriving as students, their decision-making outcome usually started with the *disposition to go abroad* and *destination choice*. Their mobility trajectory continued with the *extension of stay* at the point of graduation, which may develop into permanent settlement in the host country or the decision to re-migrate. The latter option involves the *disposition to return* to the home country or going to another country. However, the trajectory does not end with return migration; individuals may decide to migrate again, and thus continue the cycle.

The stages of decision-making may overlap or take place simultaneously. For example, at the point of going abroad, some respondents planned to work for a few years after study in the UK before returning to China. Their initial plan may be shortened because of the lack of job opportunity or may be extended indefinitely because of meeting a partner and subsequently establishing a family in the UK. These variations of post-study migration phenomena (including return migration and re-migration) were found among the 30 respondents (who came as students) in this study. The highly diverse migration decision-making process found in a relatively small sample showed the heterogeneous profile of transnational mobility among these Chinese migrants.

Important External Factors in Decision-Making

Why did the diversity in migration patterns occur? To what extent is migration decision-making controlled (or not) by human agents as distinct from abstract factors, or bureaucratic institutions? Before focusing on human factors the rest of the section will explain crucial non-human factors (which are often overlooked by migration theorists), and how they impact on migrants' decision-making during their migration process.

Participants expressed different levels of passivity in their past migration decisions and future plans. The remarks that particular aspects of life were 'uncertain' and one could plan only 'one step at a time' were commonly found among new student arrivals and well-established migrants. The respondents' remarks referred to the ways in which various external factors shaped the migration process. If the *decision-making agents* are the key *motivators* for migration, then actions at crucial steps of migration cannot be completed without the non-human-agent factors, specifically, *institutional factors* and *situational dynamics*; such could be the facilitator or obstacle during the process that translates migration motivation into practice, thus leading to the variations of migration patterns.

Institutional factors influence migration decision-making through universities which provide courses, study-abroad agents who help with the course and visa applications, the host country's migration policies, as well as the employment opportunities offered by the host country companies. Institutional factors are particularly influential in destination choice. In this study, most respondents either initially wanted to go to the US or did not have a preferred destination country. More than half of the applicants chose to study in the UK mainly because both the course application and visa application were easier.[3] Study-abroad agencies were the most frequently mentioned information source for the respondents: more than a third of the respondents (12 out of 33) relied heavily on study abroad agents, including choosing the course and the university.

Furthermore, nearly half of the respondents who arrived as undergraduate students (four out of nine) came as part of the transnational education (TNE) programme,[4] spending the final one or two years of the undergraduate course in a British university was part of TNE programme. Two of the TNE students joined the programme *because* of the period they could spend abroad, while the other two were initially indifferent about the overseas study period; but they *became* motivated to continue their postgraduate study in the UK *because* of time they spent in the UK as undergraduate TNE students. Therefore, the causal relationship between taking part in a TNE programme and the aspiration to study abroad can work in both directions.

The above evidence suggests the importance of institutional factors in sustaining migration flow, redirecting the migration path or even generating migration aspirations. However, as the migration journey unfolds and migrants' needs change, institutional factors can become barriers to migration. Upon the completion of their studies the main reason for respondents to remain in the UK was being offered a job, and that is, for the migrants in this study, also the only legal way to remain in the UK, apart from marriage. Likewise, the limited job prospect a major reason for the graduates to return;[5] the possibility of finding a job was closely associated with the British migration policy, which directly affected the level of residence stability (i.e. type of residence permit).

In contrast to the relative stability of institutional factors in long-term migration planning, the *situational dynamic* represents the unexpected, uncertain elements in decision-making. Borrowed from Mosneaga and Winther (2013), the situational dynamic refers to the particular timing of specific opportunities and unexpected events. For example, Wenbin (male, 36) wanted to study in the US, but the 9/11 terrorist attack in 2001 resulted in the immediate tightening of the US visa policy, which also led to his doubting the level of social stability in the US. At that time Wenbin met a professor from a university in London in a study-abroad fair in China. After a conversation with the professor Wenbin decided to apply for that university in London instead.

These kinds of unexpected situational phenomena were usually ignored in the earlier theories of migration decision-making. Moreover, other than shaping the destination choice, situational dynamics can sometimes be the crucial factor that triggers or terminates a migration plan. The following example shows a change of study plan overnight triggered by a dinner conversation. Dahong (female, 27) was about to start her undergraduate course in fashion design in China when she met her relatives from France, who came to China for their summer holiday:

> They [relatives] said I should go to study in France, because it has the best fashion design courses. We were having a family dinner, everyone was there. So my parents decided, well, actually there was no need for discussion. That same night, [my parents] asked if I wanted to go. Because we have relatives in France, I can live with them, there is nothing to worry about. So the next day we started the process with a study-abroad agency.

This ad-hoc decision was made in the context that Dahong's family lived in a city where going abroad was popular, which to some extent helped to build a sense of security about the notion of studying abroad. The availability of study-abroad agencies in her city also facilitated the transformation of the migration decision into migration action within a short time. Furthermore, Dahong's parents also had enough financial resources to fund their daughter's immediate study abroad. Given all of the conditions the relative's words acted as a trigger that initiated Dahong's migration process. Dahong's example is very similar to Ying's which was described at the beginning of this chapter. However, in a different situation, circumstances can put a sudden halt to a seemingly smooth migration process.

For example, following her graduation from a reputable British university in 2010, Yizi (female, 31) started a highly paid job in London and was soon promoted. In the third year of her job, Yizi's mother was diagnosed with cancer. Yizi immediately went back to China to be with her mother and her family: 'I packed up everything of mine in London. I said to my friend "if anything happens to my Mum, post my stuff to me, I'll not return to England." That's what I decided to do at that time.' Fortunately, Yizi's mother survived the cancer and Yizi's overseas life resumed.

It could be argued that Yizi's limited attachment (thus flexibility) to the UK (single, temporary residency permit holder, not a property owner) made her commitment towards China stronger, in particular to her parents, thus reducing the impact of having to return to China unexpectedly. There is no parallel situation found among more established respondents (married, long-term residency permit holder and property owner). However, the latter group, especially those who had children, showed a clear commitment towards sustaining their overseas life for their own family in the UK (as opposed to their parents in China). Shifts in commitment towards their own nuclear families among married migrants are discussed more substantially in Chapter 5.

Having analysed how *institutional factors* and *situational dynamics* impact on the migrant's mobility trajectory, one can see how these factors functioned differently in the migrant's life over time in different social/cultural environments. What was also clear in the cases presented above was the role of personal aspiration and the involvement of parents in the decision-making process at different stages. The following sections will discuss 'human complexity' (Mosneaga & Winther, 2013, p. 183) in the migrants' mobility trajectory by focusing on personal aspirations and the role of family in shaping the migration process.

Changing Notions of Success: Career Development and Lifestyle Choice

As was shown in Chapter 2, the one-child generation grew up in a highly competitive environment and only-children were subject to the significant parental expectation: achieve success. However, what constitutes success? Before the completion of university-level education in China the standard of success was clearly marked by the type of school (key school or ordinary school) and the ranking of the university that the students attended in China. It is perhaps not surprising to learn that at the 'choosing overseas university' stage, university ranking and its prestige perceived by Chinese society featured as an important factor in participants' narratives. Data from the 2014 UK Higher Education Statistics Agency and the Higher Expectations Survey also confirmed the dominating role of university ranking in shaping university preference among Chinese international students in the UK (Cebolla-Boado et al., 2017).

However, the notion of *success* became blurred beyond university life. Although career advancement, measured typically by job type and income, still plays a significant role in defining 'success', a mixture of more abstract features became influential as individuals entered the wider society, thus shaping the idea of success. Such criteria included a sense of happiness, the level of freedom in life, and balance of career and family. These lifestyle-element choices represent non-economic factors in the respondents' migration decision-making. Furthermore, as migrants enter a different society and are exposed to a different culture, how will their personal aspirations change?

Life Stage and Migrants' Aspirations

The participants left China at different stages of their education or work (see Table 4): the most common point of departure was at the end of their undergraduate degree course and before starting a job in China, while a few left before or during their undergraduate course; a small number of respondents left even before the completion of high school. At the other end of the time line, a significant number of respondents left China after having worked for a short length of time (one to three years): among them eight came to the UK to do a post-graduate course, two came to work and one came by marriage.

Table 4: Migration point and work experience in China.

Level of Life Stage When Arrived In The UK	Never Worked	Had a High-Profile Job[a]	Had an Ordinary Job[b]	Total
Post-graduate study	10	4	4	18
Undergraduate study	8	0	1	9
A Level/language course	3	0	0	3
Marriage	0	0	1	1
Work	1	1	0	2
Total	22	5	6	33

[a]High profile here means jobs with a high social status or high income, or both (e.g. accountant, lawyer and doctor).
[b]Ordinary job here means a professional and semi-professional job (e.g. recruitment consultant, insurance salesperson or customer service operator) with less prestige, autonomy and income than 'high profile' jobs.

Given the difference in their age, life stage and experience in Chinese society, it was not surprising to find that the younger group's (undergraduate level students and A Level/language course students) study-abroad plan tended to be more parent-led, while the older group showed stronger personal aspirations including career development and lifestyle choice.

However, the career and lifestyle aspirations have different implications for different migrants. As reported by some respondents an overseas degree meant subsequently a higher income job or a wider choice in the future career path; for others, especially among new graduates, it was often mentioned as an excuse to avoid starting work 'so soon'. For some, study abroad satisfied a sense of curiosity about the 'world outside'; while for others, especially among those who had a job, it meant a 'long holiday' to get away from the 'pressure in China'.

While the majority of respondents reported a mixture of aspirations to study abroad, a significant number of study abroad plans in the sample were triggered, to a large extent, by *not having* a clear goal but having the desire to clarify it. Demin's (male, 33, lecturer, arrived 11 years previously) account about his study-abroad aspiration represented a commonly-found uncertainty especially among new graduates:

> I didn't think too much about it [study abroad] until I was about to graduate. What do I do next? I failed my postgraduate applications in China, I didn't know what kind of job

I wanted to do. So I had the idea to have a look outside (of China).

Distinct from respondents who applied for an overseas course straight after their education in China, were those respondents who had worked for a period of time (from half a year to three years) before going abroad; they showed slightly (but not significantly) less uncertainty about their career/life aspirations, and put more emphasis on their dislike of the social environment in China; particularly the complicated nature of many interpersonal relationships, the unfair treatment they experienced and the potential corruption that may disadvantage their career advancement.

Potential migrants with different life experiences in China may be influenced, at different stages, by both the 'pull' factors (such as the acclaimed value of a British qualification and the attraction of an overseas experience) and the 'push' factors (i.e. the negative elements of Chinese society). Likewise, the influence of different factors on the same person can be felt at different stages of her/his life. The two attempts of study abroad made by Tian (female, 31, lecturer, arrived nine years previously), first attempt at the age of 18 and second attempt at age 22, provided a good example of how various factors, at different times, can take priority in shaping an individual's decision-making concerning migration.

Tian's uncle went to study in the US in 1991, and she was also influenced by her father's pro-study abroad ideas. Tian was first motivated to study in the US when she was in high school: 'I could not see that far back then, I only knew an overseas degree had more value than a Chinese degree.' After her US visa was rejected Tian went to a prestigious university in China for her undergraduate degree and subsequently started working in a state-owned IT company. However, Tian did not enjoy her work or the social environment. After having worked for half a year Tian went to the UK for a postgraduate degree which then extended to a PhD course:

> I felt my life was like a stagnant pool of water...I wasn't happy. Why shouldn't I do something I really enjoy? Life is short. So you can say I was ambitious, or you can say I wanted to make my parents proud, or I wanted to escape from the reality in China. All of the above.

The comparison of these two stages in Tian's life clearly demonstrated the changing definitions of success, from a more 'valuable' overseas degree to the question about happiness in life. Similar to Tian, four other respondents who had 'high profile' jobs in China all expressed different levels of frustration about the negative social aspects in China and the desire to explore new possibilities in life. By giving up a 'successful' job in China these respondents showed the significant impact of non-economic elements in a migrant's decision-making.

The 'Devaluation' of a Western Degree and its Impact on Career Expectations

In her high school days, as shown in the case above, Tian took for granted that 'an overseas degree had more value than a Chinese degree'. It was in the 1990s and many people in China at that time, and around a decade following it, also believed in the *superiority* of a 'Western degree', which was reflected in the remarks among earlier arrivals.

Liwen (male, 30, engineer, arrived seven years previously):

> I had the idea of studying abroad for a Master's degree when I was an undergraduate student. Studying abroad looked good in many people's eyes. Although at that time, it was quite common and didn't prove [your ability], it was considered prestigious.

Meilin (female, 37, accountant, arrived 13 years previously):

> My Mum is from Shanghai, Shanghai people generally thought study abroad would gild a person with a layer of gold. She was supportive of me studying abroad...I also thought that an overseas degree would help.

The higher social status associated with study abroad clearly acted as an important motivator. The high social status was partly to do with the high-status jobs returnees were able to get when overseas degree holders were rare in China. However, as the returned graduates increased in China's job market the advantage of an overseas degree became less obvious. The level of expectations of economic return or career prospects among more recent arrivals has clearly dropped, the emphasis of a lifestyle choice increased, and the mention of high social status was absent:

Delun (male, 22, student, arrived two months earlier):

> I know I won't learn much professional knowledge in this one-year Master's course. I don't have much enthusiasm for study. I'm more interested in the overseas experience.

The shift from pursuing 'high-status' and 'employment advantage' to the emphasis on 'overseas experience' was also found in the interview with Yizi's (female, 31, advertising manager, arrived five years previously) mother (55, teacher).

> M.T.: Why did you support your daughter's studying abroad?
>
> Yizi's mother: I believe the younger generation is globalised. China is not the whole world for them. I think she should have a look outside, to experience life [overseas]. I didn't think too much. But it was never about the glory of being an overseas returnee.
>
> M.T.: Was there anything to do with the possible advantage of a British degree in the Chinese job market?
>
> Yizi's mother: No. I didn't think of it that way.

Yizi's mother did not deny the association of an overseas education and better career opportunity and status in China; however, she clearly wanted to distinguish her motivation from these 'popular' reasons for overseas education.

In her interviews in Beijing with university students from 2008 to 2010 who wanted to study abroad, Anni Kajanus discovered a sense of 'ambiguity' that her participants had towards the more concrete benefits (higher income and better career opportunities) overseas education may bring. Instead, studying abroad was viewed as a 'cosmopolitan project'. Some students and parents saw 'cosmopolitan competence' to be derived from the 'project' in utilitarian terms, while some cared more about its intrinsic value (Kajanus, 2015, pp. 9–10).

In this research the younger respondents' motives for studying abroad shared similarities with the 'cosmopolitan project' that inspired Kajanus's Beijing cohort. As the number of returnees increased, a Western degree alone becomes less competitive in a job market where demand for skills and talent becomes more diverse. It is less straightforward to convert cultural capital acquired overseas into economic capital in China without other forms of 'cosmopolitan competence'. Therefore, the respondents' emphasis on 'overseas experience' is, to some extent, a response to the changing demands in the Chinese job market.

The 'devaluation' of Western degrees in China not only changed the career aspiration of the more recent arrivals, it arguably led to the extension of the earlier arrivals' migration plan in the UK. In response to the possible difficulty of looking for a (good) job in China with *only* an overseas degree, respondents commonly expected that a certain length of job experience in the UK would give them a greater advantage over their fellow returnees.

However, as migrants decided to extend their stay in the host country for career opportunities, their adjustment to a British lifestyle was also a key factor in their deliberations. As individuals spent more time in the host society, with increased social connections established, and became more used to the host country's living standard and culture, many respondents found it increasingly difficult to leave their 'comfort zone' in the UK and go back to China. Thus the original career aspirations (to delay return) were replaced by a lifestyle choice (to further extension; to remain).

This kind of migration plan extension in order to advance education/career benefit was more likely to be found among the respondents who came as undergraduates or A Level students, partly because they were more likely to find a job in the UK than the Master's students who spent only a year here. At the beginning of this chapter we learned Ying's (female, 29, accounts, assistant, arrived 13 years previously) story. Compared to the smooth career success and the psychological impact of the financial security of Ying, Ran (male, 27, software engineer, arrived seven years previously) was aware of the migration extension's double impact on his future mobility. Ran was career-oriented and described himself as 'very lucky' in being offered a high-quality job in London after completing his Master's degree. In the third year of his job Ran expressed doubt about his changing states of mind:

> When I just started working I thought I'd return [to China] after 2 years. In fact the longer I live here, the more I am used to life here, the easier it will be for me to continue staying here, and the more difficult it will be for me to leave. I keep saying to myself that I won't stay here forever, but deep in my heart I am aware of the possibility of remaining where I am … but I know my thoughts may change, just like my circumstances change. The main point is not about what I will have to give up in the UK, it is about what kind of beginning I will have in China. How can you find a job in China that will promise you the same living standard like you have now in the UK?…I don't know. It's hard to tell.

Ran's struggle showed an awareness of the changing nature of living the reality of the migration decision; it also represents the combined impact of the job market in both the host country and home country on a migrant's career path. The desire to gain work experience in the UK in order to be better equipped in China was common among earlier migrants and more recent migrants. Those who successfully found a job after graduation tended to be the better qualified and more career-motivated ones.

Unlike the widespread problem of under-employment found among mainland Chinese migrants elsewhere (Teo, 2007, Gao, 2006), the majority of the respondents who remained to work had a professional job and income which matched their qualifications. Although a minority of Master's degree holders had a salary which cannot be considered high in their profession, none was found doing physical labour or low-skill jobs, as reported in the aforementioned research. This professional profile may be the result of several factors: the prioritizing of the professional experience of the job for individual job-seekers; the limited middle and lower-middle range jobs available to foreigners in the UK; the rising economy in China; and the generally well-off family background of the new Chinese migrants (the financial support from parents to migrants will be elaborated on in Chapter 4).

The factors to do with work experience at a professional level and the restrictive access in middle-range jobs for foreigners acted as micro-level and macro-level filters that limited the job choices largely to professional opportunities offered by established companies. The growing Chinese economy contributed to a wider job availability in the Chinese job market than in the UK. In addition to the benefits of parental social networks at home, working in China became a relatively easy (but not necessarily more desirable) alternative than in finding a job in the UK. Therefore, the career aspiration of this group of highly qualified graduates was influenced by personal, parental and institutional factors from a transnational field. Meanwhile, the on-going intra-personal negotiation of lifestyle choices also shaped the individual's response to the pressures or opportunities in the transnational career field.

The Diverse Parental Involvement in Migration Decision-Making

This cohort's migration pattern typically involved the child leaving home to go abroad for education, career or marriage while the parents remained in China. At no point in the initial stage of decision-making was it mentioned that the parents were to travel with the child, even among the respondents who came as teenage A Level students.

This feature distinguishes the cohort from the 'astronaut family' commonly found among Chinese and Korean transnational families as mentioned earlier. Furthermore, this cohort's domestic migration decision-making process is also distinct from the middle-class Hong Kong family's 'transnational family strategy' found by Johanna Waters, where the children's study abroad (in Canada) was the objective of the household migration (Waters, 2006, 2005).

Therefore, at the point of going abroad the majority of the respondents in the present cohort and their parents saw it as a temporary separation period. The subsequent extension of the migration plan, as shown in the previous section, was the outcome of the interaction between complex human agents and external factors. Parents are not a static element and their minds are subject to changes from their personal situation and surrounding environment. Therefore, parents' attitudes towards their child's overseas settlement may also change. How do parents respond to their child's migration, and to what extent have parents contributed to the shaping of the migrants' mobility trajectory?

Parental involvement has been strong in migrants' decision-making at the stage of leaving China. The one-child respondents reported significantly greater parental support than non-one-child migrants (Table 5 in Chapter 4). More than half of the one-child respondents had their migration plan initiated by their parents, while parental initiatives about going abroad were absent among the non-one-child respondents. Although the sample is small (especially for the non-one-child participants), the contrast in the narratives between these two cohorts cannot be overlooked. This contrast is arguably a continuation of the difference in parenting style found in the upbringing of the respondents. (One-child respondents tended to report more overtly involved parenting than non-one-child respondents, see Chapter 2.)

In the decision about studying abroad the limited initiative from parents with two children may be the result of financial pressure to fund two children as well as the largely rural origin of non-one-child families that limited parents' exposure to knowledge and promotions about study abroad. For example, Feng (female, 34, has a younger brother) came from a rural background and joined a TNE programme. Her father hesitated at the beginning of the programme although the family could afford Feng's study abroad: 'My Dad's business was going down at that time, he was concerned about money. He thought if I studied abroad, he must prepare for my brother's study abroad.'

The emphasis on equal opportunity for both children also created obstacles for the younger child's study abroad. Gaomei's (female, 27, has an older brother) wish to study abroad was opposed by her older brother, 'because he thought he didn't study abroad, why should I?' This kind of strict balancing of resources and emotional commitment towards both children does not apply in one-child families; such circumstances made the parents' initiation of study abroad more straightforward.

However, the two-children parents' relatively passive role in the study abroad decision-making process was not always the result of limited resources for both children. Instead of being a competitor of parental resource to study abroad (older), siblings could also be a supporter of their younger siblings. Thus, a sibling's role could mediate the level and nature of parents' influence over the decision to go abroad. One odd case that was not included in Table 5 is an extreme example of an older sibling performing the role of parent to the younger sibling. Qiaolin (female, 36, who had an older sister) experienced her parent's divorce and the loss of her brother when she was a young girl. Qiaolin's sister, who was eight years older, became Qiaolin's main carer and supporter since their mother became withdrawn after those events. The sister also initiated and funded Qiaolin's study abroad and looked after Qiaolin's post-study financial needs (see Chapter 5 for the continuing family support after education). Although such heavy financial support between siblings is rare, it was not unusual to find siblings who had supportive or indifferent attitudes towards the other child's study abroad.

Without siblings' input in the decision-making process concerning migration, the parent–child interactions were found to be a more intense two-way process (see Table 5). At one end of the spectrum parents were the dominant decision-makers in sending their child to study abroad; at the other end of the spectrum parental opinion conflicted with their

Table 5: Parental involvement in the study-abroad decision.

Parental Involvement in the Decision to Study Abroad	Non-One-Child[a]	One-Child
Initiated by parents	0	10
Ambiguous decision process	0	6
Initiated by child and supported by both parents	2	9
Initiated by child but opposed by at least one parent	3	2

[a]One non-one-child's migration was entirely planned by the older sibling, thus it is not included in the table.

child's migration aspirations. The small number of cases where parents were against their children's going abroad resulted in the compromise made by parents (hence the respondents being in the UK).

As is shown in Table 5, the majority of parents fully supported their child(ren)'s going abroad (in most cases study abroad). Acting as the financial resource provider for their child(ren)'s overseas study[6] was the most direct and common way for parents to support their child. There was a sense of taken-for-grantedness among child and parent respondents that parents should pay for the child's overseas education.[7] Parents who were the migration initiators tended to have a higher income and a higher level of education. Nevertheless, parents who were relatively less well-off also funded their child's study abroad in response to the child's initiative.

In the case of the least well-off one-child family where the parents were both factory workers, Bolin's mother recalled the day when her daughter said that she wanted to study for a Master's degree abroad:

> My first response was, how much money? We didn't have much savings. So how much was our flat worth?... I borrowed bit by bit from relatives...I just thought, if she wants to study, then I must support her education ... my daughter always knew I'd support her study no matter what.

The possibility of a student loan from banks or other institutions was absent from this cohort's decision-making. This was partly to do with the lack of an established student loan system in China and the lack of student loan experience among Chinese families. Moreover, the emphasis on education in the traditional Confucian culture has been to place the family as the prime supporter for its members' education (Bodycott, 2009, Fong, 2004, Mazzarol & Soutar, 2002).

The willingness of parents to invest in their children's education was not exclusive to Chinese parents. Students from other East Asian countries like Japan and South Korea, funded by their parents, also make up a significant part of international students in Western universities. Although education has been perceived as important for an individual's socioeconomic mobility in most countries, the Confucian Asian societies place a particular emphasis on the value of education for the family. Thus, gaining entrance to a high-status university is not only the individual's achievement, but it is also a success for the family and the failure to obtain such value would bring shame to the family. Therefore, the 'practical and economic value of education, in conjunction with the value placed on family success, has traditionally provided a strong motivation for families to invest heavily in the education of their children' (Choi & Nieminen, 2013). Following this argument parents are *expected* to support their children's education as much as they can in order to meet the culturally assigned obligations.

Such cultural factors are likely to contribute to the taken-for-grantedness of the parental financial role found in the study abroad decision among the respondents. However, it is difficult to show something which may covertly be influencing people's decision-making processes. Nevertheless, the absence of any parents suggesting that the child look for funds elsewhere, including the small number of parents who were initially opposed to their offsprings' study abroad, shows the continuity of such a culturally defined role among 21st century Chinese parents.

Apart from financial support, and perhaps less directly, some parents positively contributed to their child's migration motivation by providing a sense of security and freedom. This kind of parental support was well summarized in Yizi's (female, 31, advertising manager) response to the question about why she was motivated to leave her high-profile job in China and come to the UK:

> It's difficult to say ... I haven't really thought about it. To some extent it was because of my family, my parents had given me a great sense of security. That is to say, even if I have failed I could always go back home, they are always there for me.

However, it cannot be said that parents and children in these families explicitly negotiated the decision to study abroad; rather, the negotiation process was embedded in daily communication, and sometimes throughout the child's upbringing. Respondents from these families described an 'ambiguous decision process' where they could not recall any specific points of 'decision making' (see Table 5). Rather, the disposition to go abroad, as Shan (female, 32, post-doc researcher) said, was 'always there' and was almost taken for granted. Therefore, for potential international students like Shan (and her parents), study abroad was a natural outcome in her life. Whereas in families where parents initiated the process, study abroad was more of a life-changing event for the child. Likewise, in families where the child initiated the study-abroad idea, parents were under pressure to respond to the new proposition. As a result, some one-child families were better prepared for the long-distance separation than others.

It is perhaps not surprising to find that respondents from the 'better prepared' families were also more likely to have reported an 'egalitarian parenting' experience in childhood (see Chapter 2). However, it is worth noting that half of the 'authoritarian style' parents were also liberal and supportive towards their child's wish to study abroad.

The tendency towards a more egalitarian parent–child relationship in the study-abroad decision-making process found in this study is in sharp contrast to the findings of a mixed-method (questionnaire and interview) research conducted among mainland Chinese students studying in universities in Hong Kong. Peter Bodycott and Ada Lai's research (2012) showed an overwhelmingly parent-dominated decision-making process and a frustrated student demographic that was being pressurized into doing an undergraduate degree in Hong Kong. The authors found that '100% reported and described parents using strategies ranging from gentle cajoling to heavy-handed coercive approaches during family discussions' (Bodycott & Lai, 2012, p. 262). The parent–child relationship in their research was regarded as following 'Confucian cultural roles':

> On the one hand, we see the adolescent child, often in contradiction to his or her own desires, adhering to the cultural values, expectations, and choices of his or her parents. On the other hand, we see how parents use their culturally derived status and power to manipulate decisions in order to achieve what they believe is the very best education for their child and in so doing ensure their own and their family's longer-term status and security.

However, in this study only two respondents reported a similar regime, as quoted above, where their parents entirely decided and planned the study-abroad decision following the child's high school completion. Furthermore, three respondents who came to the UK to do a postgraduate degree course reported that they had rejected their parents' advice to do an undergraduate degree course overseas as they felt they were not ready to go abroad back then. Finally, among the two cases where parents opposed their only children's wish to study abroad, the respondents emphasized their 'only children' status as the reason why parents 'couldn't do anything about it'. This sense of entitlement and privilege among only-children, which was also found in their upbringing (see Chapter 2), was absent from the reportedly submissive profile of young Chinese students observed by Bodycott and Lai (2012).

What motivated parents to encourage their child to go abroad? The findings revealed reasons beyond the scope of a calculated return on an overseas education. A common feature found among the six parents respondents, who initiated or actively supported their child's study abroad, was the belief that Western countries were better and that their child's life experiences could be broadened by studying and living overseas. However, what did the parents mean by 'better'? The parental response showed a variable focus, and different levels of understanding about the 'West':

Yizi's mother (55, teacher):

> I went to Canada for a training course the year my daughter entered university in China, so I truly felt the world outside was different... I always had doubts about the higher education system in China. What I saw in Canada confirmed my doubts... So I wanted my daughter to have a look outside, too.

Ran's mother (51, businesswoman):

> I have a good friend who went to the US. Every time she visited China, she'd say how good life in the US was, and that we should send our son to the US. I saw her two sons who were brought up in the US, they seemed like decent, well-behaved boys. So I thought she was right, if I can afford my son's education overseas, why not?

Tengfei's father (58, retired accountant):

> I've never been abroad, but I don't randomly support my son's decision. If he wants to go abroad, it has to be a country much better than China. Better technology, better policy, better economy. Maybe the US and some European countries are decades, even hundreds years more advanced than China. Some people went to Russia. Russia is not any better than China, what's the point [to go there]? US or UK is much better, something to learn from there.

These selected responses demonstrate an individualization of parents' understanding about the 'West' and the sources of their information. Such findings contradicted the widespread uncritical acceptance of the notion that Western countries are 'paradise' (Fong, 2011, p. 10) found among the Chinese citizens in Vanessa Fong's research. Fong blamed the Chinese state's propaganda which portrayed Western countries as 'the imagined community of the developed world', and the limited information resource her cohort had access to for this unrealistic assumption. In contrast parental understanding about the 'West' in this study contains different degrees of rational (and non-rational) interpretations from a variety of information resources. Notwithstanding the small number of the parent sample, such a diversity of perceptions indicated the complexity of the parental motivation in supporting their children's study abroad.

The largely pro-migration perspective of these parents was reflected here in the sample recruited among children who were already in the UK; thus it does not represent parental attitudes more generally in China. However, what the parental involvement profile showed is that different levels of agreement and conflict take place at the start of the migration-decision process. As the migration-decision-process developed parental attitudes and influence were subject to negotiation and changes from different sources.

The Changes in Parental Involvement Over Time

When Bao (female, 31, purchasing manager, arrived seven years previously) finished high school in Shanghai in 2002, 'following the study abroad trend', her parents asked whether she wanted to go to study abroad. Bao did not want to go 'because I thought I was too young.' Instead, Bao went to a university in China far away from home to get away from her parents who 'wanted to control every aspect' of her life. She came back to work in Shanghai after graduation and lived with her parents. Two years later she decided to do a Master's degree abroad because of the pressure of living with her parents. 'I wanted to stay abroad for a couple of years, as a long holiday.' Her parents were strongly against Bao's idea because they thought she 'shouldn't give up a secure life in Shanghai', but she 'insisted for a long time, and they couldn't do anything about it, I'm their only child, so they compromised'. Funded by her parents, Bao came to the UK as a postgraduate student and found a job as a purchaser afterwards. In the third year of Bao's stay in the UK her parents changed their minds and encouraged Bao to remain overseas:

> Because something happened in my family, my grandparents passed away, the relatives turned into enemies. Also the

pollution and corruption going on in China during the last couple of years were really bad. The situation at home was nothing like this before I went abroad, now the big environment [Chinese society] and small environment [extended family] both changed, so they don't see the point for me to return.

Bao's case showed the kinds of multi-level changes which could shape intergenerational negotiation. The first level is the *individual pathway* of the migrant (or potential migrant). In this case Bao's university experience far away from home and her growing independence since she started working, contributed to her confidence in making a significant decision about her commitment to going abroad. The second level reveals how parental opinions changed in response to the micro-level and macro-level factors around them (in this case family issues and problems in Chinese society). Finally, intergenerational conflict (or agreement) became manifest at the decision-making point of the migration process. In this case Bao and her parents experienced the first (mild) conflict in opinions at the end of high school, the second (strong) conflict at the decision to study a Master's degree abroad, and, finally, at the point of visa extension, Bao and her parents were of the same view about her future plans (to remain in the UK).

Children's motivation to study abroad can be directly or indirectly influenced by parental involvement at earlier stages of the child's life. In Bao's example, her parent's suggestion of overseas undergraduate education later became part of the reason that inspired Bao's decision to study abroad. However, some parents had the idea of sending their child abroad much earlier when the child was little, or even before birth. When pregnant in the 1980s, Beiyao's (female, 30, process engineer) mother (55, teacher) started to read 'self-help parenting' magazines which were largely based on American experience: 'from those magazines I realised our country was underdeveloped. So even before she was born, I thought of sending her abroad to have a look outside.' Consequently, Beiyao grew up under her mother's pro-study-abroad influence. She described her route to study abroad as something 'designed by my parents, they wanted me to go abroad, they urged me to go forward'. Having experienced a successful education and career development, Beiyao was appreciative when referring to her mother's 'push'. Beiyao's case showed how far back in time the source of an individual's study-abroad aspiration can be traced.

Moving forwards along the migration timeline, the three levels of decision changes (individual pathway, parental opinion change and intergenerational interaction) were found in most respondents' interactions with parents with regard to post-study migration plans. However, the content of the changes and the level of influence of the changes on the child's migration trajectory varied. A strong influence of parental involvement still existed, especially among respondents who were single.

Delun (male, 21, student) had an 'open, democratic' relationship (see Chapter 2) with his parents, and they were supportive of his plans to study abroad. However, Delun decided to return to China upon graduation in response to the demand of his parents that Delun 'must return to his home town, not any other city in China, but the city where they [parents] live, as near as possible'. The near-authoritarian insistence of Delun's parents upon their son's return was a distinct change in their otherwise open and supportive attitude towards their son's other important decisions. Delun reported to me that he had responded calmly to this demand; he believed the anxiety of his parents was triggered by the death of the only child of his parents' friend.

He was, at the point of interview, understanding about the impact the incident had had on his parents and emphasized the fact that looking after his parents was his filial duty. Furthermore, he listed a number of advantages of living in his home town, such as the help of parental social connections on his career, the relatively cheap cost of housing and the less hectic lifestyle (compared to major cities). Therefore, having no strong preference about a place to settle, Delun showed no resentment about the insistence of his parents that he return to be near them. He presented the case in a calm manner even though his attitude may have been the outcome of rationalization, even resignation.

In sharp contrast to Delun's experience was that of Liwen (male, 30, telecommunications engineer). He had a strong desire to return to China after his PhD but his father, who was initially supportive of the son's study-abroad decision, persuaded Liwen to remain in the UK:

> If it was up to me to decide, I'd be in China now. But my Dad didn't want me to return, because he thinks the social environment in China is not good for me.

While the changes in the opinion of Delun's parents appeared to be motivated by both concerns about their son's well-being, as well as a 'selfish' desire to have him near them, the parental perspective, however, in Liwen's case seemed entirely about wanting the best for their son. However, Liwen expressed a high level of frustration about obeying his parent's wish to remain in the UK, a place which he found 'boring'.

The cases of Bao, Delun and Liwen showed the potentially multiple changes in parents' attitudes and feelings about their children living abroad. The main causes of parental attitude changes could be macro-level (e.g. the unfavourable Chinese social environment) or micro-level factors (e.g. worsening extended family relations, or a friend's loss of child). Such seemingly distant factors or events in China indirectly but profoundly shaped the migrant children's post-study migration plans.

The changing influence of parents was accompanied by the spatial changes and relational changes caused by migration and the growing independence of the child. The analysis showed that the transnational location between parents and only children had a different effect on the intensity of family connection, and any conflict in the decision-making process depended on the childhood parenting style, gender and children's marital status. However, parental involvement in their migrant child's overseas life went beyond their advice and exhortations at crucial decision-making points. Apart from funding overseas education parents continued to provide financial and emotional support for their children. Chapter 4 investigates the financial and the care transfers from the older to the younger generation.

Notes

1. A higher number of undergraduate students came under the transnational education (TNE) scheme (cooperation between operating or management of higher education institutions in China and foreign countries). According to a Universities UK briefing in 2013, British universities were behind 25% of all Sino-foreign joint degree programmes which makes the UK the largest provider of joint degrees in China (Universities UK, 2013).
2. The information about visas can be found on the website of UK's Home Office: https://www.gov.uk/browse/visas-immigration.
3. Participants compared course and visa applications to the UK with the US. The US was generally the preferred destination. But the postgraduate course application to a US university is more complex, and the rejection rate of visa applications made to the US is also higher.
4. A TNE is a cooperation scheme between operating or management of higher education institutions in China and foreign countries. A report in 2014 indicated that approximately 60% of the Chinese undergraduate students in the UK came under a TNE scheme (Ernst & Young, 2014).
5. Four out of the five students in the sample attempted to find a job in the UK but failed; they all returned to China shortly after the interviews were

conducted. The only one who remained was the PhD student who was later offered an academic job in his university.

6. Among the 30 respondents who arrived as students, 27 were funded solely by parents, 1 received a full PhD scholarship and 2 non-one-child respondents were funded jointly by their parents and sibling.

7. This notion changes among PhD course applicants who tended to turn to scholarships rather than parental funding.

Chapter 4

The One-Child Family as a Transnational Dynamic Field: Money, Childcare and Aspiration

> [L]iving together did not necessarily mean living in the same physical locality. Living 'in' the family (in the sense of one's obligation and expectations) was not compromised because one was living 100, 1000 or even 10,000 miles away. And living 'separately' might mean living in the same compound but cooking on a separate stove. (Kuhn, 2008, p. 25)

Philip Kuhn identified the 'space continuum' feature in the Chinese family across the past five centuries. The family members referred to here were, historically, largely male inheritors. However, in the 21st century, when traditionally big families had been reduced to one-child families, the implication of such a 'space continuum' is focused on the three members of the family: the parents and the child. Kin support has been regarded as a migrant's 'most valuable asset in the country of origin' (Vertovec, 2009, p. 63). Unlike former Chinese migrants whose family at home depended on their remittances from the host country, middle-class Chinese migrants were likely to receive financial support from China.

Chapters 2 and 3 revealed the one-child migrants' life paths from their upbringing in China to their arrival in the UK as students and their transition from student to migrants engaged in professional-level jobs. This chapter focuses on 'the present', in particular the current support dynamic between migrants and their parents in China. As the migrants' journey continued to unfold in the UK, the parents' roles were changeable as the two generations led their separate lives as part of a transnational family. However, what was consistent before, during and after the

Education, Migration and Family Relations between China and the UK:
The Transnational One-Child Generation, 107–136
Copyright © 2018 by Emerald Publishing Limited
All rights of reproduction in any form reserved
doi:10.1108/978-1-78714-672-320181006

child's migration was the resource transfer from the older to the younger generation.

The matter of money was briefly mentioned when discussing parental support in the study-abroad decision process. Parents were the main financial providers for the students' overseas education.[1] However, following the completion of degrees, parental support typically became more complex and ambiguous. When the one-child migrants left university new challenges emerged, such as securing a job, becoming a property owner and establishing their own family. Substantial post-education financial support from parents was reported by the majority of one-child migrants in the sample. The support included informal subsidies and help with buying a property. Furthermore, all the migrants who had children benefited from their parents, who came to the UK to provide childcare.

Chinese students' financial contribution to British higher education as well as to related industries (e.g. accommodation, tourism and catering) has been highlighted (Universities UK, 2013, Nania & Green, 2004). However, post education, migrants' continuing contribution to the UK's economy, backed by continuing support from their parents, has been overlooked. Unlike most previous Chinese migrants who sent remittances home, this study shows not only a reverse direction of international money flow, but also the large amount of the (continuing) financial and resource transfer from the older to the younger generation.

What were the financial arrangements between members in the one-child transnational families, and how were these arrangements made? This chapter continues in three parts: the first part elaborates on the monetary transfer between parents and children; the second part throws light on the 'flying grandparents' who travelled between China and the UK to provide childcare support; the third part analyses the attitude and justification of such intergenerational monetary transfers, from the parents' as well as from the children's perspectives.

Parents' Continuing Giving and Children's Continuing Receiving

Much of the research concerning money flow in migration has largely focused on the financial support from migrants (in developed countries) to their family members at home (in developing countries).[2] Based on this observation Levitt and Sørensen (2004) categorized three types of migration experiences: those who actually migrated, those who stayed behind but received support from migrants, and those who did not migrate and had no support from outside. Jørgen Carling (2008) has suggested that the second type misleadingly described the role of 'those who stay behind' as a passive reception; rather, he proposed to name it 'non-migrants who are engaged in transnational practices' (Carling, 2008, p. 1455) to highlight the social interaction between migrants and non-migrants.

However, the financial flow from the people who 'stayed behind' to the migrants has been overlooked. The direction of money flow from the sending country to the host country is not new, and evidence has been largely recorded in education-related migration. For example, the Chinese 'astronaut families' and Korean 'Kirogi (wild geese) families' tend to operate in a model where the fathers' work in the home country is essential in supporting their children's education and wives' maintenance in the host country (Waters, 2012' Kim, 2010). However, the family financial flow in these families, after the children grew up and the parents retired from work, was seldom discussed. The one-child transnational families in this study showed a curious feature: parental financial support continued in spite of the fact that most post-education migrant children had a professional-job-level salary. Financial support here refers to direct money-giving at an informal level and family wealth transfer at a more significant level (i.e. parental contribution in buying a property in the UK). The next two sections will elaborate on the two forms of intergenerational financial support: informal finance-related activities and UK property purchasing.

Apart from the five one-child migrants who were full-time students and the one respondent who did not wish to reveal her income, the 21 one-child migrants who had a job had various levels of income (see Table 6). Among the working migrants, 20 respondents were working in full-time jobs, and 2 mothers opted for working part-time in order to look after their young children.

In 2014 the gross income required for reaching an 'acceptable minimum standard of living' in the UK was £17,000 for a single person and £20,000 each for couples with two children (Davis et al., 2014). The majority of the sample exceeded the required income level. However, when talking about their finances, none of the respondents reported any difficulty in making ends meet nor did they express anxiety about their current or future financial situation. Evidence from lower-income migrants revealed a secure financial purchasing capacity, including owning a house and annual holidays to China and European resorts. Although married migrants were believed to have benefited from their spouses' income to a certain extent, the most commonly reported (potential) source for extra financial support of one-child migrants was from parents.

Table 6: Respondents' income level.

	Lower-Income (£15k–25k)	Middle-Income (£25k–35k)	Higher-Income (£35k–45k)
Number of one-child migrants	6 (2 part-time)	8	7

Notes: See Appendix for the details of each respondent's job and income level.

The majority of the working one-child migrants expressed their confidence about parental 'financial back-up'. For example, when asked about whether her parents would fund her PhD course if she failed to secure a scholarship, Tian (female, 31, higher-income) said they would: 'They would borrow money from relatives if necessary.' Similar responses also showed that one-child migrants believed their parents would be willing to help financially and that parents would be prepared to give full support: 'If I ask [for money], my parents will definitely give all they can' (Zhimin, male, 31, lower-income); 'It feels like they have money prepared for me, whenever I ask, they are ready to give' (Jiayi, female, 36, middle-income). In all three cases the financial transfer did not actually take place; Tian was granted a scholarship for her PhD course; Zhimin had savings from doing part-time jobs, and Jiayi was able to manage her household finances with her fully employed husband. Nevertheless, in all three cases where there was confidence in the parental capacity and willingness to fund their financial needs, a similar belief was common among the sample.

The 'financial safety net' acted as an insurance between parents and child migrants. The actual financial transfer did not necessarily occur frequently; only a minority of the participants reported having asked for money. Sending subsidies to children in the UK was informal; the amount of money, the time of the need or the condition of spending were not established. These elements usually remained unknown until the child's specific financial needs arose. The areas of the reported extra spending included paying for a wedding, paying for a flight ticket to China, buying new furniture and helping with maintenance when the child was living on an unstable income.

The 'financial safety net' played perhaps a greater role as a psychological comfort rather than an immediate funding source to meet practical needs; this comfort helped to explain why little financial anxiety was felt even among the lower-income migrants. Examples of money giving in everyday life was reported on a small scale, among which recipients of the subsidy were found among low-, middle- and higher-income groups. Gender did not make a significant difference in this kind of intergenerational transfer. Although more affluent parents tended to give more money to their child, less affluent parents were also found contributing to their child's daily expenses. The money-giving pattern did not entirely depend on the income of the children or the parents, nor was it to fill a gap in a crisis or for basic needs. This pattern suggested a symbolic rather than a pragmatic basis in money-giving among middle-class families. However, the next section shows a type of more substantial financial transfer.

Property Purchasing in the UK and Parental Involvement

The majority of the sample did not have British citizenship. Certain restrictions were applied to non-EU citizens in the mortgage market in the UK. Restrictions vary slightly with different lenders, but the general rules are clear: the migrant must have lived in the UK for more than two years to build a traceable credit history; he or she must have a permanent resident permit or a work visa and have a permanent job.[3] In spite of being restricted by such requirements (five respondents were students), 17 of the 22 eligible migrants either had a property or were planning to buy a property in the near future, as shown in Table 7. The majority of the property owners and potential property owners were located in the more expensive regions of England (10 of the 17 properties were in London or near London). Furthermore, the fact that four property owners had bought, or were planning to buy, a second property also indicated a high purchasing capacity among the one-child property buyers.

The respondents who bought their property either outright or by getting a mortgage made their purchases between 2009 and 2014, which was also the period when most British people had difficulty buying a property as a result of the 2008 financial crisis. On average these respondents became property owners after having worked for three years (from less than a year and up to seven years). While the average savings period

Table 7: Property ownership among 27 one-child migrants.

Property Owners			Non-Property Owners	
Mortgage	Outright payment	Owned by spouse	Has plan to buy	No plan to buy
5	3	5	4	10 (including 5 students)
	Total: 13		Total: 14	

for a single English young person to get a mortgage was predicted to be 14 years (12 years for young couples with children) in 2013 (Shelter, 2013), these young Chinese migrants clearly had had a much shorter transition period from graduation to property-ownership capacity.

The above features indicated this sample's upward mobility on the host country's property ladder. However, they do not tell the stories behind such a property-owning profile. The longer length of stay in the UK and being married had a positive impact on the migrants' decision to buy a property. Why did the one-child migrants buy property in the UK so relatively soon? How could they afford it? If parents helped, then what were their family financing arrangements? Apart from one respondent who got a mortgage by himself, the rest of the property owners (including the married ones who bought a property with their spouse after their marriage) and those who planned to buy a property at the time of interview all mentioned forms of parental assistance.

This finding echoes a study by Guiqi Tomba (2004), in which he found relatively low-income young couples living in a wealthy neighbourhood of Beijing. These young couples were able to benefit from their parents' various resources (accumulated during the 1990s) to secure upward mobility during the transition in China's housing market. Middle-class families in Tomba's study experienced a parallel situation to the one-child families in this study; the difference is that in the latter case parental resources made an impact on their child's mobility outside of China.

Of course, parental help in children's property purchasing is not limited to the Chinese. The notion of the 'bank of mum and dad' (Hosking, 2015) is not unfamiliar to British first-time buyers, especially after the 2008 financial crisis. In 2009 around 85% of first-time buyers under 30 had to turn to their parents for help to pay for a deposit (compared to 8% in 1997) (Kuvshinov, 2011). However, according to an HSBC survey on the British first-time buyers and their relatives who helped in financing the purchase in 2012, the majority of those families who were willing to provide family financing expected to be repaid with charged interest (Solomon, 2012).

Parental financial help that the one-child migrant respondents received for property purchasing was not offered as a loan: it was an outright gift. The most common way for parents to contribute was to pay for the deposit (or part of it if the child's spouse also contributed) and leave the child to pay the mortgage. The only respondent who mentioned a 'lend-borrow' relationship was Zhipin (female, 33, middle-income, London). The financial arrangement between Zhipin and her parents was slightly different from the others:

> Zhipin: My husband and I had enough savings to pay for the deposit, we exhausted our savings for it. But there were still costs for solicitors, furniture, and daily expense, we couldn't live with two empty bank accounts, so I borrowed some money from my Mum
>
> M.T: Did she ask you to pay her back?
>
> Zhipin: I said I'd pay her back before the end of the year, I've paid back half of it by now, but if I don't pay the rest, she won't say anything about it.

In the later part of the interview Zhipin revealed that her father had started a small business in China; he hoped to help her pay the mortgage so that she would 'have more freedom in life'. Zhipin's account, in which she described her parent's help as a 'loan', but then said that full repayment was not really expected and 'more help' from her father was 'on the way', may appear contradictory, but it is not. Some parents and children may feel more comfortable with the ritual of children asking for a 'loan', even if neither side really expects the loan to be repaid in full. A similar scenario was highlighted in Anni Kajanus' research (2015) about Chinese students in Europe. She found that it was common for students to talk about repaying parents the money spent on their overseas education, but these words were not likely to be realized: neither parents nor children really expected such a loan repayment.

Kajanus interpreted what she called a 'game of money return' as 'the tension between the idealization of independence and the actual reliance'. Such tension may also partly explain Zhipin's claim of a borrow–lend' relationship. Compared to Kajanus' cohort, this study's participants were, on average, older and had more income. Most parental financial support in this case was aimed at the 'betterment' of the child's material life in the UK; helping the migrant children not just to survive in what Vanessa Fong referred to as a 'First World' country, but to help them live a 'middle class' life according to the 'First World' material standard. This financial support objective can be seen in the choice of housing and method of payment, which are analysed in the following section.

Although the majority of property purchasing could not have happened (or have happened so soon) without parental help; not all the respondents needed their parents' money to buy a property. Some respondents could afford a relatively modest property, but wanted a more expensive one. In this kind of situation parental financial help enabled the upgrading of the property of the child. These cases occurred among married respondents whose spouses also contributed to the purchase. Shan's (33, higher income) parents helped her and her husband to buy a small house in London in 2009:

> Back then my husband and I could afford a cheap house, but if my parents helped with the majority of the deposit, then we could afford a better house. They were happy to do that. In this way, we paid less for the mortgage each month, we had a better living environment, and when my parents came to visit us, they also lived in a more comfortable place.

Three years later Shan had a son and, as he grew up, Shan and her husband decided, in 2014, to sell the house and buy a bigger one:

> We bought a new house recently. This time my parents also helped. It's the same principle as last time. We could afford an ordinary house, but my parents thought with their help we could buy a house in a better location, near a good school.

In another case, Jiayi (36, middle-income, Somerset) and her husband both worked full time in the UK for seven years to save for a house purchase. When they bought their house in 2014 Jiayi's parents made a contribution. Rather than 'upgrading' to a more desirable house like Shan did, Jiayi and her husband 'upgraded' their payment method; instead of getting a mortgage they were able to buy the house outright.

The way parents contributed money to their children's house purchasing showed a motivation which more than fulfilled the basic housing requirements of the children; parents sought to enhance their children's lives and status in the UK as well as that of their grandchildren. Similar to the way parents provided subsidies to a migrant's daily life, the parental contribution towards buying a property helped to establish their children's middle-class status in the UK.

Arguably parents were likely to help their only child with house purchasing regardless of the location of the child (in China or overseas) (see Wang, 2010, Tomba, 2004). This study shows a high level of transnational capital flow; it was essentially inspired by intra-family transfers mainly to do with the well-being of the younger generation. In the context of the transnational family, this capital flow led to the emergence of a group of well-off property buyers who had a greater upward mobility in the British property market than the average British nationals, especially after the British property market was negatively impacted following the 2008 financial crisis. The outcome of the financial flow also revealed how family financial activities led to an impact at the transnational level.

Making Sense of the Asymmetrical Intergenerational Transfer

There was no clear point when the money flow from parents to children would be expected to stop; nor was there a clear point planned for when children were expected to start to pay back any funds to parents (if at all). In traditional Chinese families it was generally understood that sons were the main, life-long supporters of elderly parents, while daughters were expected to contribute to their natal families until they married, at which point daughters' support was redirected to the in-laws (Song et al., 2012). However, traditional convention did not indicate exactly when sons or unmarried daughters should start reimbursing their parents' expenses, nor did convention provide a financial solution to those parents who did not have a son.

The reality of the family financial dynamic is more complex than the rules recorded in the traditional practice. Chinese family conventions were largely derived from agrarian society (Fei, 1992). Urbanization challenged the big family cohabiting tradition and resulted in more dispersed nuclear families. Furthermore, compared to the seasonal rhythms in a rural society, the less flexible urban working hours, longer travel distance from parents, more intense competition for resources, and a relatively better pension system meant that the younger generation in general had less time, money and financial need to care for their parents than had been the case for their parents' generation. A large population of adults in Chinese cities from both working class and middle-class backgrounds were found to be still receiving parental support, which ranged from helping the child to get a job, buying property, to providing childcare, and everyday housework assistance (Wang, 2010, Tomba, 2004).

The types of parental support in this research were similar to those found among families in China, and the timing and nature of parental support were relative to the life-cycle of their families. The 27 one-child migrants were at different life stages, ranging from postgraduate students who had recently arrived in the country, to those who came more than a decade ago and had established their career and family here. The findings showed a predominately parent-to-child intergenerational flow of money and care regardless of the child's income level and age. However, the repayment from child to parents was currently very limited. Clearly transnational one-child families have a new set of intergenerational expectations that have helped the family to function (successfully) in the global context. To make sense of the asymmetrical transfer we discuss this matter from the parents' perspective as the providers and the child's perspective as the beneficiary.

Why Do Parents Continue to Support Financially Independent Children in the UK?

To provide support for their adult children, parental financial ability and willingness was required. As is shown in Table 8, the majority of the parents were affluent or medium-affluent. Although a small number of parents were relatively less wealthy and had offered less financial support to their migrant child, they were self-sufficient and had not indicated any need for financial support. The majority of parents had had a college or university education and a professional and/or a managerial job.

The willingness of parents to continue transferring a significant part of their wealth to their child should not be taken for granted. Among the less affluent demographic family tensions about parental assets and children's filial duty is more intense. Danning Wang (2010) observed such conflicts among some working class families in Tianjing (a north city in China) and described these families' financial behaviour as a *game of power*: the older generation in the family 'maintain legal ownership rights over family real estate and other property' so that 'they can maintain a measure of prestige and power within the family structure' (Wang, 2010, p. 966).

In Wang's research, parents used their property ownership as a leverage to achieve what they believed to be the maximization of the family fortune during a time of economic transition. The families in Wang's study were mostly working class parents with two or more adult children, and such a 'power' strategy was more overtly practised among those families who also had working class children. With a scarcity of resources (and less economic security) between both generations, 'the parental authority still plays a crucial role and has been further consolidated by the rapid growth of the urban Chinese property market' (Wang, 2010, p. 978).

However, although a very small number of parents in this study were less affluent, they have only one child, and that child had qualifications and a professional job. The legal ownership of the family assets (mainly in the form of property) among all families in this study was not a priority

Table 8: Parents' job and income level.

Parents' Level of Affluence[a]	Less-Affluent	Medium-Affluent	Affluent
Job description	Office clerks or factory workers	Professionals and managers	Medium business owners, professionals in higher management
Number of households[b]	3	14	10

[a]'Affluent' is a relative term. Different societies have different notions/standards of being 'affluent' In China a family can be referred to as affluent if it owns more than one property and that the child's overseas education was not a financial pressure on the parents.
[b]In households where parents had different levels of jobs and incomes the more affluent parent's job was recorded.

in the parents' family financial plan. Instead, *how the assets could better benefit the child* was the primary parental concern (see also Tomba, 2004). Therefore, the social stratification of Chinese families not only meant a difference in resource possession, but was also likely to result in a difference in parental attitude about family resource transfer. In this way, the gap between middle class children and working class children will become wider.

After having funded her daughter's Master's degree course in the UK, Beiyao's mother (medium-affluent) was faced with the possibility that Beiyao might not get a scholarship for her PhD course:

> M.T: Would you have funded her PhD if she had not got the scholarship?
> Beiyao's mother: Yes, I would. I bought two flats when the house price was low. If she had not got the scholarship, I would have sold one flat to fund her.

Given the limited means of investment in China during the rise of the market economy, buying property was a common way for more affluent parents to secure their newly-gained wealth. Middle class parents, like Beiyao's mother, had spare money to invest in a second or third property. The less-well-off parents in the study were also property owners, but did not have separate investments. For example, Bolin's parents lived in a three-bedroom flat near the centre of Shanghai when I visited them in 2014. The flat was inherited from Bolin's grandparents and was worth a large sum of money, but it did not make Bolin's parents well-off as they did not have the level of savings to allow for flexible spending. Rather than using their own property to fund a more comfortable retirement two less-well-off parents decided to transfer all their assets to their child even before their death.

For example, Tengfei (28, PhD student) perceived his father as an authoritarian figure in the family. The father (58, retired accountant) also presented himself as a firm-minded head-of-family in the interview, but he was prepared to give up his independence:

> I have made up my mind. If my wife died before me, when I am all alone, I will sell the flat, give all the money to my son, and I will follow my son.

Bolin's (female, 30, lower-income) parents (both retired factory workers) were in their late sixties, and at the point of the interview they were living in the father's deceased parents' flat, having sold their own flat:

> We are going to buy a house near Bolin under her name. It doesn't matter if we eventually manage to move to the UK or not, we are leaving the house to Bolin... We definitely won't use this flat to pay for a care home scheme, this is the only asset we have, we are leaving it to Bolin, to our grandchildren.

Clearly, 'leaving it all to the child', was what parents in the study intended to do with their property. However, while inheritance normally happens after a parent's death, many one-child parents brought the process forward to a much earlier stage when parents were alive and sometimes only in their middle age. While the inheritance process in the family was usually focused on the distribution of parental assets among children, such a concern was irrelevant in the one-child families. One-child families skip the stage of negotiating the amount of inheritance (i.e. who gets what) and can progress directly to the decision about *how* and *when* the assets should be transferred. Such an advance in the family inheritance process gave a higher level of flexibility in the ownership of certain parts of the family assets between parents and the child; which also explained why the substantial financial support from parents tended to be in the form of an outright gift, rather than as a repayable loan.

Moreover, such concentrated, substantial and early asset transfer gave the one-child migrants significant socioeconomical upward mobility compared to their middle-class counterparts in Western countries; the parental wealth passed on to the younger demographic, generally speaking, is diluted and relatively late. Middle-class parents in the United States and European countries were reported to be giving money to their children to fund education, housing and urgent needs (Reeves & Howard, 2013). However, the average amount received by each child was significantly reduced by the number of children in each household (average number of adult children being 3.3 in the US households and 2.4 in European households in 2006) (Zissimopoulos & Smith, 2010).

In her study on inheritance and financial transfer in families, Janet Finch (1996) highlighted the matter about the timing of inheritance. The longevity of the older generation meant that few could expect to inherit from parents until they themselves were near retirement, thus significantly reducing the effect the inheritance can have on an individual's quality of life, whereas a wealth transfer at an earlier stage of the beneficiary's life would make a substantial contribution to enhancing an individual's potential in the housing market, employment and education opportunities.

By helping with the child's financial needs in the UK, parents' savings and assets in the sample were also transferred outside of China. As far as most parents were concerned, assets under the child's name were still the family's assets regardless of the physical location of the assets. Such a principle of family wealth redistribution was similar to the way a transnational commercial corporation organized its capital to maxmize its global advantages. However, what made the 'transnational family corporation' different was that rather than generating a profitable return to the parents, the objective was to maximize the development of the next generation of the 'family corporation'.

Gary Becker's (1993b) family economic model suggested that while selfishness dominated market transactions, it was altruism (pace Danning Wang, 2010) that dominated family economic behaviour. Parents gave more to children than children to parents because the investment in children was more productive than that investment to parents; children had a longer remaining life and had not accumulated as much capital. This model reflected the 'parental sacrifice theme' in research into economically disadvantaged Chinese families where parents gave up their personal needs for the education cost of their children (Leung & Shek, 2011, Fong, 2004, Song, 1999).

Becker's economic model is also consistent with parental support for financially independent children in the study. Parents saw children as an extension of themselves (Birditt et al., 2012). In middle-class one-child

families, parents were able to maintain financial self-sufficiency, acceler-
ate their child's education, career and personal development, by flexibly
redistributing their savings and assets to balance family wealth towards
the child's advancement.

Children's Response: A Sense of Entitlement

How did the one-child migrants feel about being at the receiving end
of the asymmetrical intergenerational financial arrangement? What did
they do in response to their parents' support? Although the 27 one-child
migrants in the study were largely from middle-class families, their socioeconomic status in the UK varied depending on their age, career stage and
marital status. The sample included individuals ranging from Master's
degree students in their early twenties with no employment income, to
one-child parents in their late thirties with a stable household income, and
a property. Respondents at different stages of their life received different
amounts of support from parents. In general married migrants received
more accumulated financial support from parents than unmarried ones;
the need for money rose with the process of establishing a family (e.g.
wedding expenses, property purchase, childcare costs).

I did not ask the respondents directly about their *feelings* towards
parental support; rather, the related question in the interview was: *In
what way have your parents supported your life in the UK?* However, after
reporting various forms of support from their parents, most respondents
continued and spoke about their feelings, as if they felt obliged to evalu-
ate, explain or justify their position as the recipients of their parents' gen-
erosity. A large number of respondents were appreciative, while a small
number of respondents reportedly felt 'embarrassed' about using their
parents' money while still having an income. Nevertheless, the most commonly expressed feeling was a sense of entitlement towards parental support. The sense of entitlement was either directly expressed or indirectly
suggested in their financial expectations of their parents when talking
about their future plans.

Nearly a third of the sample was explicitly aware of their status as the
sole recipient of parental support and their absolute priority in their parents' resource allocation. In this study female participants expressed their
sense of entitlement more directly than males. Men reported themselves
as 'the passive receiver', whereas women, especially married women,
were more prepared to show their financial bond with parents, and some
respondents even enjoyed this sense of 'being spoiled' by parents.

Baiwen (33, lower-income, affluent parents) was a mother in Leeds; she reported various instances of parental support, including their purchase of her house outright:

> I actually don't need their financial help, but I'm the only child. Aren't all only children's parents like this? They'd say 'if we don't give money to you, who do we give money to?' If I didn't accept their money, they'd be upset. So I usually just keep my mouth shut and accept their money.

For Baiwen, showing her 'entitlement' to her parent's offer was a sign of emotional closeness, while the similar 'entitlement' for Shan (32, higher-income, affluent parents), a mother in London and the beneficiary of parental support on two house purchases, meant something slightly different:

> Because I'm the only child, I feel all [my] parent's money is mine, and that's also how they [parents] always made me feel … I'm living the kind of life my parents want me to have. In fact, this was the kind of life they wanted for themselves, they live vicariously through me.

For Shan, intergenerational *financial* transfer was also a form of inter-generational *aspiration* transfer, where the parents lived their unfulfilled dream vicariously through their children. In most cases receiving parents' money was justified in terms of the parents' aspirations for their only-child: for the child to be better equipped to achieve what the parents had not been able to achieve. The parents' generation was found to have a great admiration for the developed 'West' (Fong, 2004) as well as anxiety driven by the future and rapid social stratification in China (Biao & Shen, 2009). The one-child migrants' continuing establishment in the UK consolidates the parents' desire to participate in the 'First World' (Fong, 2004) affluence and security. Therefore, in addition to class reproduction at a transnational level, aspiration reproduction is also an important feature of one-child transnational families[4] (Tu, 2017).

In a study about Indians in Australia, Supriya Singh et al.(2012) noted the remittances sent from Indian parents to their children who were studying, or who had just finished studying in Australia. These students saw the money they received as 'family money in terms of family obligations', not in 'contractual terms as an investment that needs to be repaid'. Singh et al. (2012) highlighted money as a medium of care in the transnational family context:

> '[T]ransnational family money' is a 'special money' in that remittances, gifts and inheritance are the medium of care and belonging across the physical and cultural distance of national borders. (Singh et al., 2012, p. 487)

In spite of the similar attitudes that Chinese students and Indian students shared about parental financial support for their overseas education, some Indian students, in Singh et al.'s research, sent money back to support their family in India. It was not clear how affluent these Indian students' parents were. Nevertheless, Singh et al. (2012) did not indicate parental financial needs as a factor; instead, they pointed out that the difference in Indian students' money-sending behaviour, was in the different 'value students are placing on self-reliance and their questioning of their previous financial dependence on their parents' (2012, p. 487).

Compared to the Indian children, Chinese one-child migrants showed a stronger sense of entitlement, especially to do with their identity as 'the one and only' in the family. Although a very small number of (mostly male) respondents felt guilty about being financially dependent on their parents (like the Indian students), the pursuit for greater mobility overshadowed the slight sense of guilt. In most cases, receiving parents' money was justified in terms of their parents' *aspirations* for their children – for the child to be better equipped to achieve what the parents had not been able to achieve.

A similar theme can be found in the parents' interviews, where many parents mentioned 'the lack of opportunity and material condition' when they were young; therefore the ultimate goal, to let their child take the opportunity and live a better life, overrode the matter of money. Beiyao's (female, 30, middle-income) mother (55, teacher) recalled how she had to persuade her daughter to accept her financial support:

> She [my daughter] didn't want to do a PhD after the Master's degree. She said she didn't want to spend my money any more, she knew it wasn't easy for me to earn money. I said 'you are young, you should carry on studying' ... I took her to my home town, a very poor mountain village. I told her how I studied and worked my way to the big city... I said 'you are now standing on top of me, you shouldn't turn back'.

With parents also encouraging the idea of financial transfer, it was easy for the children to take their access to parental resources for granted.

Two respondents reported that they became aware of their 'financial privilege' through the comparison with their peers who had siblings. Bolin (38, lower-income, less affluent parents) was born three years before the one-child policy was officially enforced, and so some of her peers had siblings. Bolin observed that:

> Because you are the only child, parents give all their resources to you. This kind of support can continue even after you finished university. Among my peers, those who had siblings tended to be more calculating. Especially among girls who had a brother, if there is only one portion of resource in the family, she'd know from a very young age that the family resource was more likely to go to the brother, therefore, she'd learn more quickly about how to keep her eyes sharp and take advantage for herself.

Yizi (31, higher-income, medium-affluent parent) also compared her sense of financial security in the family with her Malaysian friend who had three siblings:

> She [Malaysian friend] was jealous of me, she said 'you don't need to think much when you spend money, you can choose to save your income or to spend it all, because your parent's money will sooner or later be yours. But I can't. Even when my parents did give me some money they had to do it in secret so that my brothers and sister didn't know … My parents said their property would go to my brothers, there will be nothing left for my sister and I.' She said the issue of money was something the only child took for granted. I think she was right, I never had to worry about such things.

The awareness of entitlement through comparison with non-one-child peers was found only among females. Gender inequality still existed in the parents' generation but it was much less evident in the one-child families in this study. Male only-children were less likely to express awareness of their financial privilege when they compared themselves with other male non-only children because the latter were also in an advantaged position in the family resource distribution. This factor may partly explain the fact that the male respondents did not articulate a sense of entitlement; it is also possible that they did not feel as comfortable about expressing their sense of entitlement to the researcher.

Slightly fewer than half of the respondents expressed certain levels of financial expectations from parents, which included some who had received informal subsidies after education or help in buying a property, and some who had not (yet) received parental financial support beyond education costs. However, regardless of whether the money had been transferred, when talking about the need for parental financial help to achieve their plans respondents used the phrase '*Jia li de qian*' (家里的钱), meaning 'money from home' or 'my family's money' rather than saying 'money from parents' or 'my parent's money'. Furthermore, there was an absence of the need for a negotiation process when it came to including parental financial support in the respondents' spending plans; respondents spoke about their spending plans with 'money from home' being already incorporated in their plans, regardless of the level of seriousness of their plans.

Quan (male, 26, lower-income, affluent parents) had just applied for a self-funded PhD course at the time of the interview. His parents had a successful business in China; their wealth formed an important foundation for Quan's future plans:

> China's economy has been good lately, my parents made some money, so my PhD cost is not a problem ... I had a problem with visa extension last year, otherwise my parents could have come and bought me a house as soon as I got my visa extension ... I still need to go back [to China] and inherit my parent's business, so I will return in the future. If I had a sibling ... I don't know.

Quan clearly took his parent's money for granted, while Yongan (male, 35, middle-income, medium-affluent parent) relied entirely on himself when he bought his property in Buckinghamshire. However, Yongan thought that he also 'owned' his parents' flat in China. When talking about his future settlement, Yongan said, 'I have properties in both China and the UK, so I can settle in either place.' When asked to explain, he said: 'The property in Shanghai belongs to *my parent's side*, I can go to live there whenever I want. It's all the same (emphasis mine).'

The high rate of entitlement in the sample did not differ significantly in terms of gender,[5] one-child's income level or parental income; all these categories were expressed by the other cohort members with a high level of entitlement. This finding revealed three features about the one-child migrants' sense of entitlement to family wealth. First, unlike the traditional belief that mainly sons had a claim to family wealth, both daughters and sons in the sample felt equally entitled to parental wealth. Second, even the more economically advantaged one-child migrant felt as much sense of entitlement as the less economically advantaged one-child migrant. Likewise, the one-child group from less-well-off families felt as much entitlement as those from well-off families.

This evidence suggests that parental financial support for their children should not be understood as an instance of charitable behaviour from a more well-off family member to a less well-off member, nor was the amount of the financial support consistent with the child's level of financial need or parental ability to give. The dominating principle existed beyond the individual family members' financial circumstances and needs.

The Symbolism of Money and Its Implications for the Child-To-Parent Transfer

Apart from the four Master's degree students in the sample, the other 23 one-child migrants had an income, and the majority of them had never given parents any money, while the minority who gave money to parents did so on special occasions as a sign of gratitude. When asked why they did not give money (or did not give more money than just occasional gestures), most one-child migrants' immediate response was, 'they don't need my money'; for the others it was not necessary given that their parents had a secured pension and medical insurance in China, while a few others simply said, 'they have more money than I do'.

The respondents who recognized that their parents' financial transfers were a 'significant sum' expressed little negative emotions associated with it; they did not show or express any sense of pressure to pay back that 'significant sum'. Such an attitude and lack of pressure to reimburse their parents was in sharp contrast to Vanessa Fong's findings about working-class one-child Chinese migrants: 'children of factory workers' who went to study in developed Western countries 'often had to use their parents' entire life savings and proceeds from sales of their family homes' as well as loans from relatives. The loans and desperate financial situation 'put a lot of pressure on the transnational student to earn enough money abroad to pay back those loans as soon as possible' (Fong, 2011, p. 78).

Interestingly, the three respondents in this sample who worked part-time during their study in the UK came from affluent and medium-affluent families. Their motivation for doing part-time jobs was not because their parents could not afford to pay for their expenses, but from a sense of achievement generated from 'using my own money'. Overall, this study's sample was more financially affluent than Fong's sample, and it was clear that the parental level of affluence made a significant difference in the psychological impact of parental financial help and the one-child's economic behaviour in the host country.

Although most respondents saw the giving money to parents as a 'symbol of gratitude', a small number of male respondents saw the 'symbol' as inappropriate in relation to their emotional closeness with their parents. Liwen (30, middle-income, medium-affluent parents) and Kai (28, lower-income, affluent parents) were dismissive of the idea of 'sending/giving money to parents' and commented that it was 'weird' and 'false'. Demin (33, higher-income, medium-affluent parents) said, 'giving money is only a symbol, and such a formality is not required between parents and child'. Although this kind of opinion was not widely shared, it suggested different implications of money transfer from child to parents in different families.

Furthermore, given the traditional emphasis of the adult son's role as the supporter of the family, these three one-child males clearly felt that the traditional obligation element in the family was irrelevant in today's context. The absence of a sense of financial obligation was not a feature of previous waves of Chinese migrants, especially among migrant sons, whose priority was to send remittances back home. In the new middle-class migrant cohort, the direction of international as well as intergenerational money flow has been reversed.

Comparison with Non-One-Child Migrant's Perception

The six respondents with siblings added another dimension to the family's financial arrangements. Respondents from non-one-child families reported a significantly different financial family dynamic. The intergenerational financial transfers took place in an emotionally less intense context. No respondent mentioned parental support (or the expectation of it) in buying a property in the UK. Furthermore, there was an absence of the sense of entitlement to parental wealth. Nevertheless, instead of an intense exchange with *parents*, for some respondents the financial exchange with their *sibling* became the priority (Table 9) shows the emotional and financial relationship the six non-one-child migrants had with their siblings redundant.

In the emotionally and financially close group, the two respondents both had an older female sibling, but they had a different inter-sibling

Table 9: Six non-one-child respondents' relationship with siblings.

Emotionally and financially close	Qiaolin (36, female), Wenbin (36, male)
Emotionally close but financially separate	Feng (34, female), Chuanli (31, male)
Emotionally distant and financially separate	Gaomei (27, female), Qianqian (27, female)

financial relationship. Wenbin (male, 36, higher-income) grew up in a financially deprived rural family. His parents were both low-income farmers, and they had had to borrow money to raise two children. Wenbin's sister was six years older than him. She had had to give up high school and started working from a young age to help with the family finances as well as to help fund Wenbin's university education in China. When Wenbin decided to come to the UK to do an MBA course his parents and sister supported him both financially and emotionally. At the point of interview Wenbin had a successful business in both China and the UK and had become the main financial supporter in the family. He was the only migrant in the sample who reported sending money to parents regularly: 'They don't need my money, but I transfer money to their account each month anyway. It's their decision whether to use it or not (laugh).' When speaking of his sister, Wenbin was full of appreciation and gratitude; he also revealed the financial closeness between him and his sister: 'We are close in many aspects, even finance, we haven't separated our assets … she is part of my company, she also has her own business now'.

Qiaolin (female, 36, middle-income) grew up in a medium-income urban family. She experienced her parent's divorce and the loss of her brother when she was a young girl. Qiaolin's sister, who was eight years older, became her main care support since their mother became withdrawn after those events (see Chapter 3). The sister and her husband funded Qiaolin's study abroad and continued to support her financially after Qiaolin started working in the UK, including house purchasing and informal subsidies. Qiaolin was aware and was very appreciative of the extraordinary amount of support her sister had given to her: My sister is more like a mother to me…They say 'you have such a good sister, [we've] never seen any sister like that'… it is very rare to have such a selfless sister.

Qiaolin later emphasized that her sister frequently offered to give her more money without her asking and described herself as 'lucky'.

These two cases show that financial transfers could be between a more well-off family member and less well-off family member, and that a sibling sometimes replaced the role of parents as supporters for the other sibling. Furthermore, the role of receiver and supporter in the family could change over time.

However, it was not clear to what extent the sibling financial transfer was a loan or an outright gift. Qiaolin, for example, called the financial transfer from her sister 'subsidies'; while Wenbin shared his business asset with his sister, to some extent, as a way to 'pay back' his sister's support earlier in their lives. Nevertheless, although there was no clear 'lend–borrow' feature found among sibling exchange in the small sample, there was also a much less felt sense of entitlement of sibling's financial support than the kind of entitlement only children felt about parental support.

The sense of entitlement was much weaker among non-one-child respondents in terms of the actual financial support they received and financial expectations from parents. However, gender inequality became more obvious as it appeared to be a governing rule of family resource distribution in some families, especially in Wenbin's case. In spite of the deep appreciation for his sister and parents, Wenbin did not indicate in any way that the matter was unfair for his sister in the sacrifice of her own education. At the time of the interview, Wenbin's business had expanded in both the UK and China. His sister benefited financially as she was in the management team. Wenbin was also prepared to provide a base for his nephew if his sister wanted to send her child to the UK for education. Perhaps, by sharing Wenbin's success, the sense of 'unfairness' to the sister was reduced in the family. Nevertheless, how each party felt before the gendered family strategy became successful was obscured in this retrospective account.

In terms of giving money to parents, apart from the regular financial transfer in Wenbin's case, the other five non-one-child migrants showed a similar pattern to the one-child migrants; two out of five respondents gave a small amount of money to parents on special occasions as a sign of gratitude. Chuanli (male, 31, middle-income, less-affluent parents) had a younger sister and he saw himself as the sibling with more responsibilities; he separated 'giving money to parents' from '*asking* parents if they needed money', and regarded the former as a sign of gratitude and the latter as unnecessary:

> It's my *own parents* we are talking about. No need to ask!
> They *definitely* won't accept my money. Usually I don't ask
> such things, I think it being *too polite*, it doesn't even sound
> like we are a family [emphasis original].

Therefore, a similar awareness of parental financial self-sufficiency, lack of pressure to support parents financially, and the disputed opinion about the implications of the symbolic nature of money-giving were found in non-one-child transnational families. However, having a sibling brought more diversity (and complexity) to the financial dynamics in such families; similar to the dynamics of care in non-one-child families, there was a level of flexibility in the supporter/receiver roles. Nevertheless, one-child families have more flexibility in terms of parent-to-child asset transfer, which was frequently used, and sometimes taken for granted in the allocation of transnational family resources.

By taking advantage of the global-financial and social environment, the transnational one-child families were able to maximize investment with the younger generation's interest as its priority. Such a strategy was based on the condition of parental financial self-sufficiency. The parents in the study were largely the beneficiaries of the 1978 economic reform, which led to a rapid income increase and business opportunity. Additionally, the high saving rates of parents also resulted in wealth accumulation at different levels. Therefore, as the research here has shown, the traditional money-giving activity from child to parents no longer constituted an essential income for parents: it had primarily become a symbolic formality, which became a way of bonding in the transnational family.

The Continuing Care Provision from the Older to the Younger Generation

Given the relatively young age of the cohort, the 27 one-child-migrants sample contained only seven participants who had become parents. Apart from one mother who gave birth to her son in China, the rest of the parents all had their child(ren) in the UK. To distinguish the three generations in the analysis, the seven one-child migrants here are referred to as 'one-child parents', the children of one-child parents are referred to as 'grandchildren' and the parents of one-child parents are referred to as 'grandparents'.

The average age of the grandchildren was three years, and the majority were below the age of four at the time of the research in 2014 (see Table 10). In the UK children's full-time schooling starts at the age of five (gov.uk, 2014). Children in England aged between three and four are entitled to free early education or childcare of around '15 hours each week for 38 weeks of the year'.[6] Therefore, for parents with children under the age of five, state-provided service played a minor role in day-time childcare support. All of the seven one-child parents in the sample had substantial childcare help from their own parents (and sometimes parents-in-law).

During the research the majority of one-child parents had the grandparents living in to provide childcare. Because of the visa restrictions grandparents were allowed to stay in the UK for no more than six months per year. In situations where both husband and wife were Chinese the common arrangement was that both sets of grandparents took turns to come to the UK for half a year each so that the rotation could guarantee all-year childcare support. The arrangements among inter-ethnic (e.g. Chinese/White British) couples varied depending on the availability of the husband's parents (in this study all inter-ethnic couples were ones with a Chinese wife and non-Chinese husband). For example, Ying's (29, account assistant) English husband was also an only child, and his mother had agreed to help with the other half of the year's childcare were the young couple to have a baby; whereas Bolin's (38, export manager) English parents-in-law passed away before she and her husband had children.

In general, the non-Chinese grandparents spent significantly less time providing childcare than the Chinese grandparents, in spite of the geographical closeness of the former. Nevertheless it cannot be assumed that the British grandparents are less committed to childcare. The fact that Chinese grandparents usually lived with the couple and spent extensive periods of time in the UK (to make the most of their temporary visa) reduced the need for British grandparents to help with childcare. Therefore the British grandparents may have contributed care in a more episodic fashion. Furthermore, for the Chinese grandparents there was the extra benefit of being reunited with their children while also spending more time with their grandchildren. 'Looking after grandchildren' clearly has different implications for Chinese grandparents and British grandparents. The Chinese grandparenting arrangement and the negotiation process are elaborated on in this section.

There was no significant gender division among grandparents in providing childcare. While grandmothers were reported to be 'more involved' than grandfathers, both grandmothers and grandfathers showed a commitment to coming to the UK to give childcare support, which was

Table 10: Three-generation caring situation.

One-Child Parents	Grandchildren	Grandparents Childcare-Provider
Bolin (female, 38)	Older son aged 8, younger son aged 7	Parents
Meilin (female, 37)	Son aged 7 (born in China, came to UK aged 1)	Parents
Jiayi (female, 36)	Older son aged 3, younger son aged 4 months	Father, mother-in-law
Baiwen (female, 33)	Son aged 4, daughter aged 3 months	Parents
Shan (female, 32)	Son aged 2	Parents and mother-in-law
Beiyao (female, 30) and Demin (male, 33)	Son aged 1 month	Wife's mother and husband's parents

traditionally regarded as the job for female relatives. The choice of grandmother or grandfather in childcare was usually the result of practical rather than cultural reasons. Jiayi (female, 38, sons aged 3 and 4 months) had her retired father as the main childcare provider because her mother was working full-time in China. Beiyao's (female, 30) son was only one month old. Her father was too ill to come to the UK for the birth of the grandson, so her mother came to care for her and the baby for five months, while Beiyao's father was looked after by his own aged parents in China. In most cases grandparents were involved in childcare together. These findings suggested that the traditional gender role of care-providers in the transnational family was being overridden by the more urgent practical needs of the next generation.

What was unusually absent from the childcare arrangement among one-child migrants was the alternative: the 'sending grandchildren back to China' to be looked after by grandparents. This arrangement was common among earlier Chinese migrants. Children (usually the first-born) were left in Hong Kong with their grandparents while parents were busy with their catering businesses in the UK. The child(ren) later joined their parents in the UK for education, sometimes to help with the family business or to look after younger siblings who were born in the UK (Song, 1999, Watson, 1977). Similar arrangements were also found among highly educated parents who migrated from mainland China to Australia in the 1990s. Newborn children were sent to China to be looked after by their grandparents; children returned to Australia when they reached school age (Da, 2003). Compared to having parents living in the host country to provide childcare, this kind of arrangement appeared to be less costly, and was more convenient to both the migrant parents as well as the grandparents.

However, among the seven parents in the study there was no report of any form of negotiation between the grandparents and one-child migrants with regard to whether grandparents should come to the UK, or whether the grandchild should be looked after in China until reaching school age. It appears to have been taken for granted that the grandchild would be raised in the UK with the one-child parents. As Demin (male, 33, lecturer) recalled: 'It [childcare arrangement] was like a mutual understanding, we did not need to sit down and talk about it, it was natural.' A similar response was made by parents. Bolin's (38, sons aged 7 and 8) mother (66, retired factory worker) recalled:

> We never asked whether she [daughter] needed our help [in childcare], we just took it for granted that we should look after her children. She never asked us whether we wanted to do this. It was like, your daughter is having a baby, **of course** you should go and look after the baby [emphasis original].

The first time Bolin's mother realized her dedicated care for her grandchildren was somehow 'different' was during one of her entries into the UK at the British Border Control. She was asked by a Border Control officer a routine question: 'Why do you come to the UK?' With the help of an interpreter, she answered: 'To look after my grandchildren.' The officer responded, pointing to the visa page of her passport: 'Then you should have applied for a work visa, not a family-visitor's visa.' Bolin's mother was so shocked at the incomprehension behind the officer's interpretation of her relationship with her daughter's family that she felt it necessary to tell me about the incident from 'several years ago'. Bolin's mother thought the officer's question was evidence of the 'lack of cohesion in British families' and felt proud of the 'closeness' shared by Chinese family members.

Like Bolin's parents, grandparents did not get paid for their childcare; on the contrary they were reported to be contributing to grandchild-related spending and in some cases paying for their own flights to and from the UK. In most cases grandparents were well-off enough to afford the cost. In addition to their financial capacity, grandparents expressed the pleasure of being with their offspring and felt 'useful' in their only child's household. For many grandparents (and potential grandparents), the period of looking after grandchildren in the UK was usually the only time they could be reunited for a long time with their only child. To some extent providing childcare became a *valid reason* for parents to come and live with their long-missed only child, hence the grandparents' willingness to come. Once the grandchildren reached school age and the grandparents' intensive childcare was no longer needed, their visiting time in the UK was accordingly significantly reduced; the one-child family then often went back to a situation involving global separation.

The phenomenon of 'flying grandma' was not new to migrant families from Hong Kong and other Asian countries in the UK, but the extent of grandparents' involvement was different. Mabel Lie (2010) found that compared to other Asian countries, where women's freedom to travel was largely determined by the Islamic practice of purdah, Chinese grandmothers were more likely to travel from Hong Kong to provide childcare. However, unlike the Chinese families in Lie's research, where the common transnational childcare arrangement was for paternal grandmothers to come for a few months, in this study both paternal and maternal grandparents from China were actively involved, and the time the grandparents dedicated to childcare was significantly longer.

Although the childcare arrangement findings were based on only seven one-child parents and two sets of grandparents, the 'flying grandparents' found among all seven cases revealed the overwhelming shift of transnational childcare location from China to the host country. Only one participant (male, 31, single) mentioned the possibility of a China-based childcare arrangement, but such an idea was absent among the others who had not become parents. The fact that these one-child parents did not seem attracted to the possibility of having children raised in China, with their children's grandparents, suggested not only practical considerations but also normative commitments to staying together as a family unit in the UK.

Furthermore, the one-child parents' being professional, middle class afforded them such a choice; which was not usually the case for previous cohorts of Chinese migrants who worked extremely long, anti-social hours, and who lacked various forms of human and cultural capital in Britain. Living together in the UK was certainly more beneficial to the one-child migrants and their children than having to be separated. Even among parents in China who had not yet become grandparents, there was already an indication (especially among mothers) that they would come to the UK to help look after their future grandchildren.

The Challenges for Grandparent Childcare Providers

Physical and mental exhaustion have been reported among grandparent childcare-givers in China (Lo & Liu, 2009, Goh, 2006). For grandparents who came to the UK, in addition to highly demanding daily childcare duties, the combination of a lack of English, a change of diet, and a disruption of their daily routine in an unfamiliar place formed a potential threat to their psychological well-being. The majority of grandparents in this study had had a university education and professional jobs. In spite of being highly educated in China, most of the grandparents did not speak English. They were faced with the language and cultural barriers in the host country – similar challenges for any non-English-speaking migrants.

In general, grandmothers showed a better ability to adapt to the new environment than grandfathers. This outcome was partly to do with the gendered family role grandparents had in China; women were more involved in domestic affairs than men. As most grandparents came to the UK to provide childcare and help with domestic chores, grandmothers were more 'at ease' with such routines, while it usually took grandfathers a longer time to get used to them. Although three respondents reported their father's frequently expressed dislikes about life in the UK, they came nonetheless. Grandparents who came *together* as childcare-providers benefited from each other's support in terms of their own psychological well-being.

Bolin's parents had provided the longest childcare in the sample. They had a five-year visa[7] and lived in Birmingham from 2006 to 2011 to look after their grandchildren. The grandparents were both retired factory workers who did not have much education and no English. Fortunately for them Birmingham has a relatively large mainland Chinese population; grocery shops and community activities cater to the Mandarin-speaking residents. Bolin's parents managed to familiarize themselves with the local environment and made some friends with other Chinese. However, they had a clash of opinion with their son-in-law (white British) with regard to childcare[8], and their daughter had to act as a mediator.

Different attitudes towards childcare between two generations were not uncommon; other families with professional and highly educated grandparents also acknowledged disputes of opinions, but they expressed them in a milder manner. It was not clear to what extent the grandparents' class background was significant in the nature and scale of disputes about childcare. Therefore, while childcare for their migrant child was a significant resource for the young parents, and gave grandparents emotional comfort, childcare could also be the source of family tension.

At the point of the interview, Bolin's parents had returned to China after their grandchildren started school. In their retrospective account of their years as full-time childcare-givers in Birmingham, they highlighted their emotional and social difficulties in the UK:

> Our life in England was okay, very quiet. But the most important thing was that we were *both* there. If today we are suddenly allowed to go to England, it would be better if we can go together. One person will be lonely. If there was only one of us left, I'd rather stay in China. In China I can chat with neighbours, phone my friends. Who do you chat with in England? Our daughter needs to go to work, she can't accompany you all the time… Our neighbours were friendly to us, they said 'hello' to us, but we could not communicate because we didn't speak English [emphasis original].

Bolin's parents clearly valued each other's company and feared the possibility of losing such company and support in the UK. In comparison to Bolin's parents in Birmingham, Jiayi (38, sons aged 3 and 4 months) lived in a small town in Somerset where access to Chinese-related outlets was extremely limited, and her father came to the UK to provide childcare without her mother. Jiayi described her father's frustration:

> My Dad said 'coming here for a short holiday is ok, living here is unbearable. Such a small place, no proper food to eat, no place to socialise with people, no language I can understand, nothing is interesting at all'.

Nevertheless, Jiayi's father still came to the UK and alternated childcare with Jiayi's mother-in-law.

In spite of the challenges grandparents were faced with in the UK, their decision to come nonetheless showed their dedication to helping their children and to enhancing the well-being of their child and grandchildren. Without other offsprings' families to look after, parents of one-child migrants became the most reliable and committed childcare providers to the younger generation. One-child parents frequently expressed their gratitude about parental care help; as Jiayi said: '…childcare is tiring and involves great responsibility. Apart from family members, who else is willing to look after your child for free?' This study cannot claim to have discovered a major childcare arrangement pattern for the whole sample, as the majority (two thirds) had not yet become parents. Nevertheless, the existing cases of transnational childcare indicated a largely taken-for-granted child-centred arrangement in the transnational one-child family.

Notes

1. Apart from two women who came to work and one man who came to study on a funded PhD course, the rest of the 27 one-child sample came to the UK to study on a self-funded basis. The courses ranged from pre-A Level Language schools to a Master's degree course. The initial tuition fees of the self-funded students came from parental savings. In most cases parents also supported full living costs while their child studied full time. Only three respondents reported having had part-time jobs during their studies; the part-time jobs were not essential; their parents had provided cost-of-living funds.
2. The remittances were found to be sent from adult migrant children to their parents and spouse at home. For example, the previous Hong Kong migrants in the UK (Benton & Gomez, 2011, Watson, 1977); or from migrant parents to their children at home, for example, from Filipino mothers working in Europe to their young adult children (Parreñas, 2001).
3. There is no governmental resource which provides a clear account of mortgage restrictions on foreign nationals; the information used here is compiled based on data provided by private mortgage companies in the UK. For example, G Force Mortgages UK Ltd: http://www.gforce mortgages.co.uk/ForeignNationalMortgages#citizen. Accessed 2 March 2016.
4. I do not mean that aspiration transfer exists only in one-child families, but that having only one child makes intergenerational transfer more intense. Vanessa Fong (2004) demonstrated such intensity in her ethnographical account of one-child families in China.
5. Males expressed their sense of entitlement less directly than females, as discussed earlier in the section.
6. As shown on UK government's website on 21 September 2017. For more detail see https://www.gov.uk/help-with-childcare-costs/free-childcare-and-education-for-2-to-4-year-olds
7. A five-year visa was rare among parent visitors. Bolin's parents were granted their visas when visa policies were less strict in 2006.
8. The disputes were the outcomes of both cultural difference and the generational gap. For instance, the son-in-law regarded the grandmother's constantly holding the infant as potentially spoiling the child, while the grandmother thought that holding the infant was essential for the psychological well-being of the child.

Chapter 5

Between Space and Time: Long-Term Home-Making in the UK and in China[1]

> The master said, 'The service which a filial son does to his parents is as follows: In his general conduct to them, he manifests the utmost reverence; in his nourishing of them, his endeavour is to give them the utmost pleasure; when they are ill, he feels the greatest anxiety; in mourning of them (dead), he exhibits every demonstration of grief; in sacrificing to them, he displays the utmost solemnity. When a son is complete in these five things (he may be pronounced) able to serve his parents. (Classic of Filial Piety, 1988, p. 480)

Qingmin Festival, also called Tomb-sweeping Day, is an ancient Chinese festival dedicated to the remembrance of one's ancestors. Traditionally, filial piety is applied both to when parents were living and dead. In feudal China an official had to resign in order to mourn the death of a parent (Wolf, 1984). Such a posthumous filial piety requirement is unrealistic in contemporary society. Nevertheless, the Chinese government dedicated a three-day public holiday during the first week of April for Qingmin Festival, so that the living can pay tribute to their ancestors at their family's grave.

The importance of ancestor worship partly explains the 'son-preference' phenomenon among couples, even after the one-child policy was enacted in 1979; posthumous rituals were traditionally performed only by sons. The gendered role of posthumous ritual no longer applies in most cities, especially given that each family could have only one child. However, having an only child settled overseas would mean that there would be no offspring left in China to sweep the older generations' tombs after parents pass away. Thus, this form of filial duty has been discontinued.

Education, Migration and Family Relations between China and the UK:
The Transnational One-Child Generation, 137–156
Copyright © 2018 by Emerald Publishing Limited
All rights of reproduction in any form reserved
doi:10.1108/978-1-78714-672-320181007

When the only child's permanent settlement in the UK became closer to a reality, practical problems and their implications, such as the tomb-sweeping ritual, became something that could not be avoided. In the Prologue, we learned that Bolin's long-term settlement in the UK was understood by both generations. Although subjects such as what to do after a parent's death are not common in family conversations, Bolin's family seemed to be more open about it. Bolin revealed to me, in a light tone, her mother's plan for the future:

> My Mum said, 'Don't bother burying me or your Dad anywhere in China. Who will sweep our graves? Your uncles? Then will our nephews remember to do that? It's too much trouble for you to travel from England. Even if Jason and Tommy [Bolin's children] manage to remember their Chinese grandparents, will their children know anything about us?' My parents know it is difficult for them to migrate and spend the rest of their days here in England. So my Mum asked me to cremate her body and cast her ashes in the sea. In this way, she said, she could flow to the east coast of England. If I want to pay tribute, all I need to do is go to the coast and talk to her.

We do not know if Bolin's light tone was to ease her sense of guilt, nor do we know how serious Bolin's mother was about such an arrangement. What was clear was the crude reality of distance and time in overseas children's discharge of filial responsibility to their parents. Parental investment in their children's upbringing and well-being in exchange for old-age care from those children is a basic principle of reciprocity between the two generations within a family. At the end of Chapter 2, we discussed the compromises the parents' generation made in looking after the older generation and the emotional struggle they felt about such compromises. In this chapter, we will focus on how the one-child generation and their parents come to terms with the gap between the culturally embedded filial duty and the transnational reality.

The Chinese Family Contract in a Changing Society

The economist Gary Becker pointed out that both parents and children would benefit more if parents invested more in children for a commitment by the children to care for parents in return. But can children's commitments to their parents be enforced? 'Economists and lawyers usually recommend a written contract to ensure commitment, but can you imagine a society that will enforce contracts between adults and ten-year-olds or teenagers?' (Becker, 1993a, p. 14). Instead of a formal negotiation, Becker described how parents could help determine the value of the children by making their children feel a sense of indebtedness and/or create a 'warm' atmosphere in their families to increase their children's willingness to reciprocate (Becker, 1993a).

However, the formation and modification of a family contract is more complex than superficially rational and/or normative interactions between parents and children. Instead of explicitly agreeing upon a set of expectations and responsibilities, family members are *socialized* into pre-existing contracts (Göransson, 2009, Song, 1999, Walker, 1996, Finch & Mason, 1993). These contracts have been shaped by factors beyond the family level from above (state policy) and from below ('culture logic') (Göransson, 2009, p. 85, Finch, 1989, Lewis & Meredith, 1988).

While children's support to parents may have been motivated by a sense of 'indebtedness' or affection, it was also significantly influenced by a socially constructed set of rules which apply specifically among family members. This unwritten 'contract', and its 'rules', act as the fundamental principle that shapes each member's understanding of resource distribution as well as responsibility allocation within the family (Song, 1999, Walker, 1996, Finch & Mason, 1993, Lewis & Meredith, 1988). Unlike any contract in the legal sense, family contracts are developed over a long period of time, shaped by internal and external factors, and often found to be taken for granted by family members.

The concept of a 'family contract' provides a framework to examine intergenerational relationships in general. In Chinese families, filial piety, as a form of 'family contract', has dominated intergenerational relationships for centuries. Children were expected to support parents when parents became elderly. However, this reciprocal relationship was made based on the principle that elderly parents still relied, materially and practically, on their offspring for old-age care.

After the growing social stratification during the post-reform period (see Chapter 2 for family stratification pre- and post-1978), expectations and responsibilities between parents and children varied among different regions and economic backgrounds. Compared to their rural counterparts, elderly people in urban areas rated psychological needs (such as leisure activity and close company) as being more important than material needs in their life (Sun et al., 2015). In this research, middle-class parents did not need financial support from their children, but had continued to transfer money and sometimes had been the care provider for their child's family (see Chapter 4). With parents being more financially and physically independent, the child's role as the material supporter for the older generation has been reduced (or delayed); meanwhile the emotional care from the only child became even more valued.

It is widely acknowledged, both in China and in the West, that emotional care is an important part of parental care. Niky James has proposed a formula of care: 'care = organization + physical labour + emotional labour' (1992); Hilary Graham (1983, p. 28) called caring 'a labour of love' which consisted of the carers' 'affection and service'. However, filial piety requires more than that. The required conduct or behaviour needed to fulfil parents' psychological needs, and the social pressure to do so, are the two features of filial piety that distinguished the Chinese intergenerational relationship from the West's idea of care responsibility.

The consistent condition in filial piety prescribed obedience and respect from the younger to the older generation regardless of an individual's age. The general pattern of obedience and respect to parents is maintained throughout the child's life (Keller et al., 2005). At the point of the interview, a few migrant children as well as all seven parent respondents, explicitly emphasized the importance of *shun* (顺, meaning obedience/respect) in their understanding of filial piety. Therefore the role filial piety plays in middle-class families may be less observable; but it would be too simple to assume the erosion of filial piety based on the decline of more observable filial acts, such as material and practical support.

Moreover, the implication of 'being a filial child' for an individual's reputation in Chinese society has blurred the boundary between domestic care and public opinion, thus making filial piety a socially enforced obligation. An individual's 'filial demonstration' is associated with being 'a reliable, trustworthy and honourable person' (Ikels, 2004, p. 5); thus it is 'a central measure of their moral worth' (Whyte, 2004, p. 106). An individual can gain social capital outside of the family by being filial to his/her parents; likewise, an individual's reputation (social capital) can be harmed by not being filial. In this sense, the implication of filial piety goes beyond the domestic sphere; it has become a social issue in which both the general public and the state have a role to play.

State Intervention in Reinforcing Filial Piety

As Ikels has asserted, 'the practice of filial piety was everybody's business' (2004, p. 5). Other members in the community were given the right and responsibility to inspect, monitor or even interfere with how the younger generation should care for the elderly. In response to the belief that there was 'no offence greater than lack of filial piety', the pre-Tang dynasty (pre-AD681) law stated that 'parents (or even other persons) might accuse children of unfilial behaviour of any kind and have them punished by the authorities' (MacCormack, 2002, p. 141).

In 21st century China, the state has encouraged families to sign a Family Support Agreement; a voluntary contract, validated by legal institutions, between parents and adult children to provide support to parents (Chou, 2010). In order to carry out the contract, according to *The Law of the People's Republic of China on the Protection of the Rights and Interests of the Elderly*, 'a grassroots self-governing organization and organization of the elderly or the employer of the supporters shall supervise the fulfillment of the agreement' (The State Council of PRC, 2012). The law was considered 'educational' and served as a starting point of a lawsuit (Hatton, 2013).

While promoting filial piety through legislation and propaganda, the Chinese state was reluctant to develop a more sophisticated welfare system for the elderly in need; this can be observed from its pension system and state care provision. The establishment of the Chinese pension system has been uneven between the employed and the unemployed (and self-employed) as well as between urban and rural areas. Urban employees, especially those working in state-owned institutions, have had a secured pension scheme for decades (Qu, 2010) (see Chapter 3 for the work unit welfare process).

However, a systematic pension scheme for rural residents and unemployed urban residents was carried out only from 2010, and pension scheme coverage did not reach a national level until 2012 (Wang & Tian, 2015). A national survey conducted in 2009 showed that rural citizens preferred to rely on themselves or their child(ren) for old-age care, rather than rely on social welfare (Yu, 2012). Whether this nation-wide pension system will bring financial security to the impoverished elderly, especially in rural areas, is not yet clear.

The long-term care institutions have a mixture of standards and policies. Government-funded care institutions accept only the very desperate elderly, and turning to such institutions is usually associated with stigma (Wu et al., 2008). The emergence and quick development of private services has taken place since the mid-1990s (Zhan et al., 2008). However, high-quality care homes cater for only affluent clients. The high cost of these institutions contributed to a shift of attitude from stigma to privilege (Zhan et al., 2008). The gap remains for the vast group in the middle: 90% of the elderly still relied on familial care in 2012 (Zhang, 2012).

In China in 2014, there were more than 36 million bedridden or semi-bedridden elderly people but only 356,000 care-staff and 50,000 certificated carers for the elderly (Wang & Tian, 2015). Meanwhile the state has reduced its funding towards maintaining elderly care institutions in order to make them become financially self-reliant as part of further economic reforms (Feng et al., 2011, Zhan et al., 2008). The shortage of staff in the caring provision, and the reduced government subsidies are likely to pose long-term care problems even for middle-class urban residents. Staff shortages in the long-term care sector have become one of the major issues in the UK and other Western European countries (Royal College of Nursing, 2010, Hussein & Manthorpe, 2005). Chinese families have become more geographically dispersed as a result of massive internal migration,[2] and the demand for non-familial care assistance is likely to increase across the country. Parents and children in this research expressed the tendency to rely on paid carers or 'high quality' care homes for parents' future long-term care. However, the current underdeveloped professional care provision still has a long way to go before becoming an alternative to familial care for the majority of the middle-class elderly population in China.

The support from the state for the elderly is believed to undermine family obligations (Ikels, 1990). By minimizing the state's role in providing welfare for its citizens, the family will remain the main source of support for the very elderly (and the very young), thus enforcing filial piety in intergenerational relationships. On the other hand, by establishing a welfare state, like the British did in the late 1940s, the principle that a citizen has the right to a claim upon the collective resources of the state (as an alternative to family) has emerged (Finch, 1989). However, the 'familial contract' strategy has also been found in 'nearly every society in the east, south and southeast Asia' where family support significantly subsidizes contemporary Asian development (Croll, 2006, p. 478, see also Lee, 2010, Park et al., 2005, Sung, 2001). Therefore, the relationship between economic development (modernization) may not necessarily lead to weakened family contracts.

In order to investigate how contemporary Chinese family contracts are reconfigured and renegotiated, the rest of the chapter will move back to a micro-level observation by focusing on one-child migrants and their parents (while keeping in mind the influence from the macro-level culture and policy changes). Most research has focused on contemporary Chinese intergenerational relations, but the transnational one-child family comprises the most challenging change since the founding of the People's Republic of China in 1949.

The Practical Difficulties for Transnational One-Child Families

Long distances constituted the main fear for migrants when talking about possible 'emergency cases in China'. By 'emergency cases' respondents meant a sudden major illness or accident that could happen to parents. Migrants in the UK faced a much longer travel time and less frequent flights than children who lived in China. Compared to migrants who had a sibling living in China, one-child migrants showed significantly greater concern and pressure about this practical matter. As Ran (male, 27) emphasized: 'I need to be able to go back within a few hours' time, not the next day. In some emergency situations it would be too late.'

In comparison, Chuanli (male, 31, who has a sister) found that his sister's physical proximity to their parents gave him 'a sense of peace of mind'. The issue of distance affected both sides. Although some parents have travelled to the UK on a regular basis (see Chapter 4, 'flying grandparents'), for some other parents, because of their chronic illnesses, long flights were physically and psychologically challenging. A small number of respondents reported that their parents had never visited the UK because of the fear of the long flight.

British migration policy is the most direct barrier for parents to come to the UK for family reunification. At the time of the study all parents who had been to the UK came under the short-term visitor's visa (see Chapter 4). None of the parents had attempted to apply for a long-term visa to the UK. The primary reason was the strict migration policy concerning an 'elderly dependent relative'; applicants must prove that they have no means of survival in China and that joining their child in the UK is the only option.[3] Because of the parents' physical mobility, financial independence and the company of their spouses, no parent in this study met such basic application criteria. It was understood by most respondents and parents that the chance for parents to be granted a long-term visa was very small.

Apart from the visa policy, the lack of overseas medical insurance for parents was another problem. Under the short-term visa, parents were not entitled to free medical care provided by the NHS in the UK. As parents are more likely to become ill as they age, the potential cost of private medical care imposed a great financial burden on both parents and children. Furthermore, living in the UK for parents entailed giving up the benefit of their medical insurance in China. The contrast between the medical expense in the UK and in China added another barrier to any likelihood of long-term parental care in the UK.

Finally, even if parents were granted a long-term visa and free medical care in the UK, their lack of English would make any parent's daily activity difficult and would increase his or her dependency on the child, thereby reducing self-mobility. More than half of the parents (21 out of 33) in this study had never been to the UK, or only came briefly as tourists. Furthermore, among the parents who came to look after their grandchildren, it was found that the lack of English, together with lifestyle changes, formed a potential threat to their psychological well-being. Therefore such a psychological challenge posed a dilemma for parents' future settlement; they may suffer from loneliness as 'empty nest' parents if they remained in China; but they may also suffer from loneliness and a sense of alienation if they were away from their familiar social environment in the UK.

Given the difficulty of parents joining their child in the UK, in order to ensure parents' emotional well-being, the most viable and practical way would be for migrant children to return to China. The 'Report on Employment & Entrepreneurship of Chinese Returnees 2017' presented the following statistics: in 2016 nearly 300,000 graduates returned after studying abroad. In a multiple-choice survey, 70.6% of them chose 'to be near parents' as one of their main reasons to return (63% chose cultural reasons and 47% chose the stable economic development in China as an important reason to return) (CCG, 2017). These figures indicate a close relationship (interdependency) between parents and the one-child graduates.[4] Furthermore, the figures show that parents may be the most significant factor for return migration, but not necessarily the only factor, as career opportunities and lifestyle in China were also major considerations.

It is perhaps not surprising to find the confirmation of the only-children's felt responsibility towards their parents was among those who had already returned. The only-children who remained in the UK represented the cohort that was not included in the report. However, just as returnees went back to China for a variety of reasons, the one-child migrants also remained in the UK for a mixture of reasons (see Chapter 4), and the decisions to return or remain were not made based solely on the needs of parental long-term care. Therefore, it cannot be said that only-children who remained overseas were necessarily less filial than those who returned. Chinese families have become so diverse that filial practices need to be assessed against their specific circumstances, rather than following a homogeneous standard of filial piety. The next two sections will discuss the commitment shift faced by adult children staying overseas as they grow older, as well as the practice of 'long distance intimacy' and its implications on a changing perception of filial piety.

Home-Making in the UK and Responsibility Shift

The longer the children remained in the UK, the more established their families and careers became, which meant that migrant children had more to lose when returning to China. In other words, the economic and social capital one-child migrants accumulated through overseas education and post-education experience may decrease following return migration. Unlike a Western university degree, whose 'value' is transferable across borders, other forms of 'capital' were not always transferable, including (some aspects of) work experience, professional/social connections and the quality of the migrant's family life in the host country.

As a result married respondents generally expressed a stronger wish to settle in the UK; unmarried respondents (single or in a relationship) tended to speak in favour of returning to China. While career prospects were an important factor in respondents' decision-making, two single men and one single woman saw parental needs as the dominating factor and had planned to return to China solely because of it. By contrast, the married migrants, especially those who had offspring, generally lived in the UK for a longer period and were more established in the host society. They regarded the next generation's well-being in the UK as their primary responsibility.

It cannot, however, be assumed that unmarried respondents were 'more filial' and married respondents were 'less filial'. Behind the differences in settlement choices was the shift (and compromise) in family responsibilities that migrants experienced before and after marriage. Compared to the unmarried respondents, married respondents had a very different way of seeing their role in migration decision-making: responsibilities not only expanded from the natal family to their own nuclear families, but sometimes also to the in-laws (especially if the spouse was also a one-child migrant). As Demin (male, 33, lecturer, arrived 11 years previously) put it:

> Any decision you make, is the result of compromises after taking all aspects into consideration: not just your parents, but also your spouse, your child and your spouse's parents. All of them.

In this complex decision-making web, as described by Demin, the influence of parental needs had clearly (temporarily) lost its once dominating position. It is worth noting here that the married women and men in the sample showed a similar pattern of commitment transfer from parents to their own nuclear family. However, with 10 married one-child women and only 2 married one-child men (in spite of attempts to recruit a gender-balanced married sample), it was difficult to make any meaningful gender comparisons in terms of the impact of marriage on a one-child migrant's sense of filial piety.

The one-child migrants' parents were relatively young, which enabled migrants to focus on their own child(ren) rather than on the care needs of their parents. By the time parents are elderly with decreased mobility (in their 70s and 80s), migrant children will be in their late 40s to 60s with grown up child(ren). This useful spacing was mentioned by a number of one-child migrants (married and unmarried) as a justification for making parental care responsibility secondary to the needs of their own family (or career) at the current stage of the respondents' lives. The relative youthfulness of Chinese parents avoided the caring 'squeeze' which is more commonly found in British families, in particular among the higher educated women whose childbearing is delayed and who are more likely to face the expectation of 'two-way' ('downwards' to children and 'upwards' to parents) care (Agree et al., 2003).

This child-centred support flow put one-child migrants at an advantage in terms of socioeconomic mobility in the host country. However, for adult children, not being able to reciprocate parental investment in a direct and tangible way can result in serious frustration. In interviewing older Taiwanese migrants (aged above 60) who came to the US when they were young, Ken C. Sun (2014) found that these migrants' care duties to their elderly parents in Taiwan were shared by their siblings. However, in spite of sending regular remittances to their parents and siblings, these migrants believed they still had unfulfilled moral obligations. In a similar study, Italian migrants in New Zealand were found to relinquish their claims to inheritance in order to compensate, financially and morally, for their sibling's larger share in parental care (Baldassar, 2007).

However, unlike the Taiwanese and Italian migrants, as we learned from the previous chapter, the one-child migrants I interviewed did not have siblings to share their parental long-term care responsibility, nor did they send remittances regularly. On the contrary, financial transfer from parents to children was based on the mutual understanding that the only child was the sole beneficiary of parental assets. The oldest female respondent in the sample, Bolin (38, export manager) was the recipient of continuing financial and childcare support from her parents. While emphasizing her commitment to settling in the UK and the priority of her children, Bolin also expressed a high level of emotional and moral pressure:

> They [parents] want to give everything to me, but they fear to trouble me with anything. I'd rather they loved themselves more than they loved me, I'd rather that they have asked something from me … this love is too heavy.

Co-existing with the sense of guilt and indebtedness, respondents also expressed different levels of reflexivity on the more abstract elements of filial piety as a justification for choosing career/family development in the UK. Making parents proud, as explicitly expressed by four one-child migrants (two women and two men), was also highlighted as essential to being a filial child.

> You need to ask yourself: 'What do parents want from you?' Do they want you to be with them, or do they want you to be independent with your own career and life? I used to think filial piety was to be near your parents and look after them. Now I realise the importance of successfully managing your own life, not to let parents worry about you, and make them proud. I think this is also a form of filial piety. (Wen, female, 33, married, legal assistant)

Such an understanding was in accordance with the traditional concept of filial piety that 'a child's achievement is not only a matter of personal success, it brings honour to the family' (Göransson, 2009, p. 119). However, other aspects of filial piety, such as physical closeness and material support, are compromised in the transnational one-child families. It is not yet known whether one-child migrants' responsibilities will shift towards parents in the future. Both parents and children in this study were struggling to come to terms with the new family contract in a fresh geographical setting. While the only child felt the practical and moral dilemma of remaining in the UK instead of returning for their parents, parents also had mixed emotions about the asymmetrical intergenerational support.

Parental Ambivalence Towards the New Family Contract

In chapter 2 we learned about some of the unsettled emotional struggles parents experienced with regard to balancing the new competition of a modernizing China and adhering to the traditional requirements of a filial child. If the 1978 reform marked the beginning of modernization of China, then the parent cohort in this research arguably represented the more 'modern' group in their generation; they emerged as the new middle class. In the meantime, this feature made them the 'modern minority' in comparison to 'the more conventional majority' in their community.

For example, parents with whom I talked promoted 'modern elements' of family relations, such as a more egalitarian relationship and a less dependent older generation (i.e. themselves), in contrast to their observation of more 'traditional' families around them. One mother cited a colleague's 'half-joking' comment against the idea of the transnational one-child family to show that by letting her daughter remain overseas, she became the 'different' minority among her peers. While parents may have promoted their 'modernness' in front of the researcher, or were taking pride from it to justify their transnational relationship with their child, the following case showed the serious struggle between the 'more modern individual' and the still-conservative social norms in the local community.

Zhaohui (female, 23, student) came from a small town in South China, and she reported that some parents in her home town prevented their child from going to university so that the child would not leave the parents. After her mother was paralysed several years ago, instead of being a 'filial daughter' and taking up the role as her mother's carer, Zhaohui came to do her Master's degree in London and was determined to get a distinction:

> In our small town, everyone knows what everyone's children are doing, they'd compare with each other. I want my Dad to be able to tell others with pride when he was asked about me ... I know he suffered a great deal from the gossip.

Zhaohui's father's (56) story was briefly mentioned in Chapter 2. He became semi-retired from his job as an accountant in order to look after his paralysed wife and his aged mother. When asked for his opinion about his daughter's being far away, he replied:

> I had the chance to leave [the small town] when I was young, but I stayed for my parents, now I regret it ... It's a different time now. It's not good to tie your child to you. I know some parents want their child near, but I have let the kite go loose. She can fly as far as she wants.

This more sharply-felt parental struggle with peer group pressure was more likely to be found in more conservative regions in China, while parents from big cities did not report direct social pressure. However, in spite of the predominantly positive feelings parents reported about the 'generational leap' (Göransson, 2009, p. 52), there was still a sense of disappointment and perhaps some sadness among parents. Mothers were more likely than fathers to show an ambivalence towards the asymmetrical intergenerational support.

Ran's (male, 27, married) mother (51, businesswoman) thought such a generational difference was 'unfair':

> Sometimes I said to my husband, that we are more or less the last generation that need to materially support our parents for filial piety. We do not need the next generation to materially support us when we are old and we are also left alone by the next generation (laugh). My generation is the most exploited. We need to look after the previous generation, but the next generation is not going to look after us.

Fathers indicated their opinion more indirectly. For example the two fathers who were interviewed with their wives nodded while the mothers talked of their disappointment about the asymmetrical intergenerational transfer. The fact that I was a young female may have been a factor for such a gendered response. Moreover, the one-child policy and the increased job competition in cities had a more negative impact on women than men; two mothers had to have an abortion when they were pregnant after their child was born, one because of the policy, the other one because of the lack of time to look after two children.[5] It was unclear to what extent parents felt negatively about the generational difference. Nevertheless, the evidence from the interviews showed the parents' emotional struggle to come to terms with the generational changes compared to their relationship with the previous generation, as well as compared to their peers in the same generation.

Distance, Intimacy and Changing Perception of Filial Piety

'Distance lends enchantment' (or 'absence makes the heart grow fonder')[6]; such proverbs describe how interpersonal attraction may be enhanced by individuals being away from each other. While a study of 63 dating couples in the US supported such a claim (Jiang & Hancock, 2013), there is no similar research about parent–child relationships. Nevertheless, evidence in this study suggested that both parents and children were *aware* of the role distance played in smoothing their relationships. The majority of both child and parent respondents indicated the importance of *not living together* under the same roof. Both generations' wish to live independently is not new. Surveys in the 1990s indicated urban Chinese residents' support for parents and children to 'live close by but not necessarily together' (Ma et al., 1994, Hu & Ye, 1991).

Different levels of tensions with parents were reported among the migrants who for some reason shared a house with their parents over a substantial period of time (e.g. when parents were helping to look after of grandchildren or when migrant children went back to China for a long holiday). The causes of arguments ranged from everyday petty squabbles to serious disputes about child rearing. Conversely, not being able to see parents often made co-presence more precious.

Ran (male, 27, software engineer) had authoritarian parents and reported difficulty in communicating with them when he was a child, yet he felt much closer to his parents during each home-visit: 'When you meet only two weeks a year, you tend not to argue with each other, you tend to feel closer.' Chuanli (male, 31, post-doctoral researcher) who has a sister, also articulated a similar feeling regarding parents: 'When you see parents on a daily basis you won't treasure that feeling [between parent and child]. I appreciated filial piety more after I left China.' Overseas children were likely to develop a romanticized outlook on the parent–child relationship, therefore increasing the likelihood for them to support the notion of filial piety. Migrants' emotional support for parents was a significant element of the changed meaning of filial piety for them following overseas settlement.

Although the long distance between China and the UK limited the migrant children's practical support for their parents, they showed emotional support by practising 'long distance intimacy'. The term 'long distance intimacy' was developed by Rhacel Parreñas (2005) to describe the transnational intergenerational relations between Filipino migrant mothers and their young adult children left at home. As migration literature on transnational intergenerational relationships tends to focus on the migrants' relationship with their younger family members, such as children, research rarely addresses 'intimacy' with older generations of families who are also separated from the migrants. Even less academic attention has been paid to middle class migrants' relationship with their middle-class parents living in the home country.

'Empty nest' middle-class parents showed a significantly higher demand for emotional than material support. The development of International Communication Technology (ICT) in the 21st century has been celebrated for 'generating new ways of living together and acting transnationally in the digital era' (Nedelcu, 2012, p. 1339). Migrants in this study reported using ICT to maintain 'long distance intimacy'. Both parents and migrant children could message, talk and video-chat with each other on a 'smart phone' at a very low cost. Apart from a small number of respondents whose parents sometimes had to work at a weekend, the majority kept a routine of video-chatting/telephoning with parents at least once a week at the weekends. The length of video-chatting/telephoning typically lasted for around one hour each time, as reported by respondents. Video chatting happened more frequently among migrants who had child(ren) as the parents also wanted to 'see' the grandchild(ren). Furthermore, other means of communication, like messaging (text or photo), took place even more frequently; in some cases respondents reported daily communication with parents.

However, not *all* the respondents *enjoyed* this kind of frequent communication with parents; a small number found such communication with parents psychologically demanding or practically difficult to balance. For example, Zhaohui (female, 23, student) found it difficult to express intimate emotion to her father; Ran (male, 27, software engineer) felt guilty: 'If my Mum don't call me, I'd forget to call her, then she'd be unhappy about it.' Dahong (female, 27, market analyst) kept daily messaging with her parents, but said the content of the exchange was sometimes 'boring' and 'trivial'. Nevertheless, in spite of the negative experience, these respondents still felt morally obliged to fulfil their parents' emotional needs by committing time and patience to long-distance communication.

Long-distance intimacy did not only manifest itself in how often the child and parents talked, or what they talked about, but it also had to do with what was *not* said by parents and children. Respondents rarely contacted parents for their own emotional support; that is, when they felt sad or anxious, they tended to rely on their spouse or friends (in the UK or in China) for emotional support. 'Only tell parents good news' was the 'golden rule' mentioned frequently by respondents; any emotional distress expressed by the migrant child would also bring anxiety to parents; thus it was felt to be wiser not to reveal negative emotion to parents.

The 'golden rule' of 'only tell good news' was also practised by some of the parents of one-child respondents. For example, the incidences of a close relative's death or parents' own illness was not revealed to the child until a few months later. The earlier remark from Bolin (female, 38, export manager) that 'they [parents] fear to trouble me with anything', also indicated the parental tendency to look after their child's emotional well-being by not becoming an emotional (and practical) liability. Because of the limited parent sample it was not clear how common, or to what extent, parents hid from their migrant child their negative emotions in their communication. Nevertheless the existing cases in this study showed the delicacy of long-distance intimacy: because of the lack of alternative means to learn about each other's life (e.g. physical visits), what parent and child chose to include, or not to include, during their communications was likely to have a greater psychological impact on each family member than in families who are not separated by distance and borders.

How do parents perceive the implication of long-distance communication with their child? Bolin's parents regarded frequent telephone contact as a sign of their daughter's filial piety to them. Bolin's mother cited an occasion as an example of her daughter's care for parents: Bolin shortened a Sunday family outing with her sons in order to get back on time to video chat with her parents. Although Bolin's parents took emotional comfort from the indication that they were their daughter's priority on that occasion, they had tried nevertheless to 'push Bolin away'. Bolin reported in her interview that sometimes while she was online chatting with her mother, her mother would ask her to stop the conversation and spend more time with her own children; thus, Bolin felt a sense of 'selfless care' from her parents.

In this way the international daily communication became a 'dynamic of intimacy'. It was important for children to contact parents *in spite of inconvenience* to show their filial piety, while it was also appropriate for parents to reject their child's 'sacrifice', and not to impose parental emotional needs on children. Nevertheless, the children's failure to keep up with frequent communication caused parental anxiety or disappointment; as a result the children's *availability* for international communication was vital to parents' emotional well-being. Thus, the cycle continues: between one-child migrants and their parents, it was the two parties' 'sacrifice' and 'anti-sacrifice' pattern that drove the dynamic of the intergenerational intimacy.

Dai and Diamond observed in the 1990s that, compared to American culture, which regarded limited responsibility from children to parents as the norm, Chinese culture encouraged unlimited responsibility and devotion to parents or family (1998). However, *how* parents and children perceive and discharge 'unlimited responsibility' is clearly changing in the 21st century. An increase in investing in the younger generation and a decrease in the taken-for-grantedness of care-in-return of the older generation has been consistent across Asian societies (Lee, 2010, Göransson, 2009, Croll, 2006, Park et al., 2005). In the context of the middle-class one-child transnational family, children had very limited material responsibilities towards parents, and future care expectations were unclear. For now, it is the *willingness* to commit oneself to caring for parents' well-being, not necessarily the *observable* filial actions, which has been regarded by both generations as the priority of being filial.

Home, Belonging and Future Migration

> I don't think people like us have a sense of belonging to China or to the UK. I consider myself highly flexible and have cross-border mobility. Nevertheless, I sometimes feel that I also belong to both sides. (Zhimin, male, 31, sales manager, arrived 12 years previously)

Zhimin's remark reveals both the advantage and the limitations of transnational embeddedness: the more established their life had become in the UK, the more difficult it was for migrants to return to China. However, with the continuing financial and emotional intimacy with parents, the difficulty in balancing overseas aspirations and family relationships became inevitable. In one-child transnational families, narratives from both generations revealed an ambivalence towards the child's possible settlement in the UK.

Yizi's (female, 31, advertising manager, arrived 7 years previously) mother was a high school teacher and was proud of her daughter's career achievement in London, but this sense of pride was also mixed with a sense of loss:

> Mother: When children grew up and suddenly left, parents would feel lonely. We are 'empty-nest elderly', just like those 'left-behind children.'
> M.T: Do you want Yizi to come back?
> Mother: No, because there is a lot of pressure to face in the Chinese society, food safety and air pollution … I don't want Yizi to face these many kinds of pressure in China. However, for us, we certainly want her to be near us. If she is in the same city, at least I can see her every day, unlike now, she is 12 hours' flight away. This is such a dilemma. It's really difficult to find a point of balance.

In their reluctance to articulate their 'selfish' hope for family reunion to their child, middle-class parents clearly prioritized their only child's progress to greater success. Zhaohui's father compared his long-distance parenting to flying a kite, 'now I let the kite go loose, she can fly as far as she wants'. It is not clear whether the parents' attitude would change when both generations become older. Nevertheless, there was an unspoken mutual understanding of the intergenerational dilemma between parents and the overseas child:

> Parents know your life and career will be better if you remain overseas. But gradually their wish for your return will develop as they get older. From last year my Dad started to hint at the possibility for me to return, but he will never say it out, like 'you should come back'. (Dahong, female, 27, market analyst, arrived 6 years previously)

Shared ambivalence is common among one-child migrants. It reveals the emotional cost of the family capital accumulation project, and more specifically, the frustration of not being able to fully discharge *guan*[7] and *filial piety* from both generations. Accompanying the migrants' inner struggle was an emerging fragmented sense of belonging through complex attachment and detachment to parents and home society. The majority of migrant participants expressed a sense of belonging (feeling of home) which obtains between China and the UK, with parents being the central focus, and sometimes the only reason, to identify China as home.

Bao (female, 31, purchasing manager, arrived 7 years previously) was single and a house-owner (purchased with the financial help from parents). Although she did not have any return migration plan, and expressed her love for the lifestyle she had in the UK, she defined her home as the bonding of nuclear family members: 'as the only child, I regard home as where my parents are; and my parents regard home where their daughter is. We are a solid triangle'.

A married woman, Meilin (37, accountant, arrived 13 years previously), who has a son in the UK, reported a similar emphasis on parents as a definition of home:

> China is home because I have parents there. Actually I asked myself before, if one day my parents are no longer there, then home is where my husband is, my family here. Now because my parents are still there, I feel there is a home in China.

Meilin, like many married migrants, acknowledged the association between emotional attachment to family members and to the place these members live, while Demin (male, 33, lecturer, arrived 11 years previously), a father and a house-owner, rejected the necessity of forming emotional attachments to a particular physical space in his definition of home:

> It is meaningless to talk about a sense of belonging to *China* or to *the UK*. The key is where your family members are. My parents are in China, so I feel I belong there. Likewise, I have my wife and son here in the UK, so I also feel I belong here. I attach my sense of belonging to micro-level individuals, not places like China or the UK [emphasis original].

The three respondents have different levels of establishment in the UK (e.g. length of residence, property ownership, marriage and parenthood), but their expressed sense of belonging does not necessarily shift from China to the UK according to their level of establishment. Demin's conflicting remark resembles a transnational community constituted of the highly mobile, flexible 'global citizen' (Ong, 1999) for whom notions of the 'nation-state' have become irrelevant (Yang, 2011). However, in reality, the level of migrants' flexibility is severely limited by practical reasons such as migration policy and the needs of the migrants' new family in the UK.

This study is, in part, a response to Johanna Waters' (2003) argument that when examining transnational family accumulation strategies, the family's mobility should be viewed in conjunction with migrants' acculturation and 'rooted' influence in the host society. Among Hong Kong children who went to Canada as secondary school students, the earlier assumption of adult children's return migration, after their education, was challenged by the grown children's desire to remain in Canada (Tse & Waters, 2013). However, compared to the clearly articulated identity shift from home to Canada among the Hong Kong cohort, the one-child migrants in this study experienced a more diverse, uneven change in their sense of home and belonging.

Apart from the fact that migrant 'children' in this study left home at an older age, the sense of the one-child family as a 'solid triangle' (see Bao above) arguably contributed to the cohort's stronger identification with China. However, the migrants' articulated close emotional attachment to parents (and to China) forms a sharp contrast to their hesitance and reluctance to return to China, which was also accompanied by their lack of commitment to settle in the UK. Therefore, under the seemingly steady process of establishment in the host country, migrants in this study revealed a high level of uncertainty as a result of the on-going interaction between the self, transnational family relationships and space.

Notes

1. Parts of the content in this chapter were previously published in 'Chinese one-child families in the age of migration: Middle class transnational mobility, ageing parents, and the changing role of filial piety'. *Journal of Chinese Sociology* (https://journalofchinesesociology.springeropen.com) and 'The transnational one-child generation: Family relationships and overseas aspiration between China and the UK'. *Children's Geographies* (http://www.tandfonline.com/toc/cchg20/current).
2. According to the Chinese Census in 2010, among the country's 1.3 billion population, 26% were internal migrants. Compared to the previous census in 2000, the number of internal migrants had increased by 81.3% (National Bureau of Statistics of PRC, 2011).
3. The wording from the Home Office is: 'You must prove that: You need long-term care to do everyday personal and household tasks; the care you need is not available or affordable in the country you live in; the person you'll be joining in the UK will be able to support, accommodate and care for you without claiming public funds for at least 5 years.' See https://www.gov.uk/join-family-in-uk/eligibility, as checked in September 2017.
4. According to the Report, 80% of the returnees in 2012 were aged between 24 and 30. Therefore, it can be inferred that they belong to the one-child generation.
5. In the latter case, the mother had her first child in 1976, and was pregnant again in 1978. The one-child policy had not been enforced, but because she and her husband were working full time without extra childcare help, she had to abort the child. Both the mother and the father revealed deep regret about the abortion in the interview.
6. Both sayings are recorded in the Bible; the Book of Proverbs.
7. See Chapter 3, *guan* literally means 'to govern', with positive connotations of 'to care for' and 'to love' (Tobin et al., 1989, p. 93), which equates to parental concern and involvement (Chao, 1994).

Conclusion

The Migration Decision-Making Process and the Family Life-Cycle

> The lives of increasing numbers of individuals can no longer be understood by looking only at what goes on within national boundaries. Our analytical lens must necessarily broaden and deepen because migrants are often embedded in multi-layered, multi-sited transnational social fields, encompassing those who move and those who stay behind. As a result, basic assumptions about social institutions such as the family, citizenship, and nation-states need to be revisited. (Levitt & Glick Schiller, 2004, p. 1003)

This book is partly a response to Levitt and Glick Schiller's call to revisit how family and migration impact upon each other. The discussion from an 'analytical lens' recognizes migrants as individuals in 'multi-layered, multi-sited transnational social fields'. Migrants in this study are primarily examined as the only adult children in transnational families. But as the migrants' human stories unfolded, the scope of the analysis extended beyond the 'current host country' experience. Migrants' former, current and future identities in China, in the UK or in another (potential) country, all have different levels of impact on migrants' settlement decisions; these decisions in turn shape the intergenerational relationship between migrants and their parents as well as the establishment of the migrants' own families.

The personal life-cycle and family are both important in influencing decisions concerning migration and its aftermath. 'One's emotional and material needs are strongly linked to stages of the individual's life-cycle'

Education, Migration and Family Relations between China and the UK:
The Transnational One-Child Generation, 157–165
Copyright © 2018 by Emerald Publishing Limited
All rights of reproduction in any form reserved
doi:10.1108/978-1-78714-672-320181008

(Bryceson & Vuorela, 2002, p. 17). Findings from this research showed that one's sense of responsibility is also strongly linked to one's life stage, which involves changes in the content of responsibility, and towards the people to whom one was responsible. More specifically, as shown in the accounts presented in this study, marriage, and the forming of one's own family, was a significant point where one-child migrants' spouse and offspring became the priority of their 'family responsibility', while their 'filial duty' towards parents became secondary. This is also the period of life when a migrant may become committed to remaining in the host country. However, as a migrant's offspring grows up and the migrant's parents become elderly, the migrant's sense of responsibility may shift to parents (if they were still alive), and hence the disposition to return to China.

The migration pathway was based not only on the migrants' life-cycle but was also substantially shaped by the life-cycles of the individual's close family members, that is, parents and offspring. Therefore, by combining the influence of family and life-cycle, the family life-cycle model provided another approach to help clarify the factors shaping the migrants' long-term migration decision. This finding was consistent with Johanna Waters' longitudinal research on Chinese mothers from Taiwan and Hong Kong living in Canada (2011). Her participants' disposition to settle, to return or to re-migrate was largely associated with their offspring reaching adulthood, their spouses' retirement, or their own point of retirement. The dominant factor of an offspring's life-cycle in a migrant's decision could also be found in, for example, Korean mothers who accompanied their children to study in Singapore (Kim, 2010); the time of return entirely depended on the children's completion of education.

However, what is absent from most studies that have taken the family life-cycle into account is the influence in the life-cycle of the older generation. This was perhaps because migrants' siblings shared the responsibility towards the older generation, and so the impact of parental needs on the individual migrant was diluted and became relatively insignificant compared to the migrant's own nuclear family's needs in the host country. Without the dynamic of a sibling, this study of transnational one-child families brought out the profound impact of the parents' life-cycle on the migrants' decision-making process in terms of both benefit and responsibility. More specifically, the material and childcare contributions provided, where parents were reasonably young and healthy, were concentrated on the only-child; so were the needs for emotional and practical care when parents were elderly and vulnerable. The lack of parental influence in other transnational families, however, indicated the impact of a sibling in reducing parental influence in a migrant's long-term migration pattern.

Re-Examining 'Traditional Chinese Family Values' in 'Modernization' and 'Globalization'

The opposition of the 'traditional Chinese' and the 'modern West' has been the dominant discourse about China's journey to 'modernization' since 1978. The family can be regarded as a social field for observing the progress of 'modernization'. It would be difficult to find a family cohort that experienced more radical changes from 'traditional Chinese' to 'modern West' within two generations than the experience of the one-child families studied in this research. The macro-level ideological changes and the micro-level family dynamic changes are both powerful factors that have challenged 'traditional Chinese family values' in the context of 21st century 'modernization' and 'globalization'.

In the discussion about how the one-child migrants understand and negotiate their responsibility to their parents, this research has demonstrated an uneven change in the interpretation of filial piety as perceived by parents and one-child migrants. The unevenness has mainly resulted from a separation of the individual's filial behaviour and filial feelings. For example, the material and practical exchange between the two generations demonstrated a reversal – a transfer from the older to the younger generation which went against the traditional sense of filial practice, but neither party felt such a reversal to be unfilial. However, although the majority of one-child families did not expect the child to provide practical care when the parents were elderly, more children than parents were found to be resistant to the idea of a paid care service in replacement of the care from offspring (nevertheless, whether their opposition will remain as steadfast when their parents come to need such care in the future is an open question).

The sense of 'traditional Chinese family values' was found to be pervasive among one-child migrants. However, the moral awareness of family responsibility did not necessarily translate into clearly prescribed forms of action. A variety of factors interfered with or encouraged the discharging of filial piety between family members. In the case of transnational one-child families, distance, finance, communication technology, and migration policy all acted as barriers or facilitators in the fulfilling of filial obligation (Tu, 2016). Therefore, the lack of observable filial actions did not mean that filial piety did not exist as an implied abstract notion among family members.

There is no obvious or easy solution for one-child migrants to balance their aspirations in the UK and their filial responsibility in China. Participants showed different levels of physical and psychological struggle speaking from different stages of their migration experience or cycle. The 'family value' and 'filial duty' perceived by various families manifested itself in complex forms, shaped by factors within and outside of the family. Having experienced life in a Western society, intergenerational expectations and responsibilities in these transnational families did not simply become 'Westernized'. Instead, the 'contract' between the two generations showed a reconfigured reciprocity as an outcome of family adaptation.

This book proposes a new approach to the examination of the Chinese family in the 21st century's key phenomena of 'modernization' and 'globalization' beyond the East/traditional versus West/modern debate. Families are versatile; household members are found actively adapting in extreme practical and psychological conditions such as the one-child families in this study. Perhaps the sudden transformation of the domestic environment in China, and the engagement with the global community, are not to be seen as 'threats' to Chinese families. Instead, these changes have provided the possibility of choices for a great number of families in China. The essential elements of the family have not changed, but the changing environment has enabled families to evolve sometimes sharply distinctive configurations, which were formerly restricted because of economic, political and social conditions.

'Middle Range' Migrants and the Overseas Chinese Heterogeneity

Previous research into mainland Chinese migrants has been largely focused on migrants from a deprived background living a marginalized life in host countries. Illegal migrants from Fujian Province, for example, have been a main migrant cohort for public and academic concern. At the other end of the spectrum, the international investment of the wealthy mainland Chinese became a headline focus especially after the 2008 financial crisis.[1]

This research brings attention to the 'middle range' mainland Chinese migrants. These migrants possess a certain amount of capital resources in China and in the host country. These resources opened up more choices in terms of education, career and lifestyle. Meanwhile, having such resources and choices has also meant uncertainty and risk. 'Middle range' migrants have more to lose than the working class and/or illegal migrants, but less transnational mobility compared to the 'affluent elite'. Therefore, the 'middle range' migrants are sensitive and vulnerable towards political and economic changes in both China and the host country.

However, the 'middle range' Chinese migrants are not homogeneous; within the cohort there were subdivisions of migrants with different levels of mobility and affluence. This research produced a close comparison with Vanessa Fong's research, which is also about one-child migrants in Western developed countries. Fong's longitudinal study started as an ethnographic research about one-child Chinese families in Dalian (2004). Her participants were drawn largely from middle-income or lower-middle-income families and had an average or below-average academic attainment. Fong (2011) followed her one-child participants as they grew up and went abroad to study. Both groups of participants from this research and from Fong's research went to school in the 1990s and went abroad between 2000 and 2010. Notwithstanding the shared macro-level environment, the micro-level difference in family background and the academic attainment of the two groups of one-child migrants, there was a distinctively different migration strategy and socioeconomic outcome.

In the decision-making process to study abroad, Fong's participants chose to study mainly in Japan and Ireland because these countries were cheaper and had lower language or academic requirements. A common route of migration, for Fong's research cohort members, was to 'buy a visa' by entering a course in the cheapest language school in the host country. Parents usually exhausted their savings to help with this initial stage. During their time in the language schools, the students had to support themselves and save money for a university degree course by doing extensive part-time jobs. The urgency to earn money and the little time to study, weak language skills, and below-average academic attainment, in addition to the pressure to fulfil their parents' expectations (hence the reluctance to return to China), all formed a vicious circle and limited many one-child migrants' upward mobility in the host country, as well as their career advancement.

In comparison, most one-child migrants in this research came from above-average income families, and the majority were above-average or top students in China. These students had much less financial pressure with regard to overseas education costs; their priority was to get into a high-ranking university. Half of the sample entered a Russell Group university, and the majority were postgraduate degree holders. Following their graduation most one-child migrants, with the help from their parents, had a relatively smooth transition into professional jobs, property ownership and parenthood in the UK. Between Fong's participants and this research's participants, there was a shared aspiration for 'Western' affluence. However, the profiles of one-child migrants generated from these two separate studies clearly demonstrate that the difference in the transnational mobility trajectory resulted from a difference in parental income and the child's academic performance in China.

More and more young people from China's middle-class families are likely to join the migration wave and pursue their transnational aspirations and exploit the associated social and professional mobility openings.

As most Western countries have tightened their migration policies, apart from the most affluent and the illegal migrants, becoming an international student is likely to be a popular route of entry chosen by future migrants, thus adding to the diversity of the 'middle range' migrants as well as complicating the transnational mobility profile associated with international students.

Ronald Skeldon noted the year 1978 as the turning point of the Chinese migration history with the incorporation of China into the global community as well as the global spreading of highly diverse 'new' migrants from mainland China. Skeldon pointed out that 'Chinese Overseas' is 'a highly heterogeneous phenomenon and essentializing it into a transnational community of Chinese Overseas is not doing justice to the real situation' (2007, p. 45). The sketch of one-child migrants in this book, especially in comparison to Vanessa Fong's findings, contributes to the complex picture of 'the real situation'. However, the emphasis on heterogeneity certainly does not imply a lack of shared features between these different Chinese migrant cohorts. The point here is that migrants are multidimensional individuals, and no single dimension should be over interpreted to imply a similarity (or difference) of the other dimensions. In other words, when using categories such as 'Chinese migrants', 'students' or 'middle class migrants', the other aspects of the migrants' lives should neither be taken for granted nor ignored.

The Continuing 'Migranthood'

By now readers are probably familiar with the names such as Bolin (female, 38, export engineer, arrived 13 years ago), Ran (male, 27, software engineer, arrived six years ago), Yizi (female, 31, advertising manager, arrived five years ago) and Zhaohui (female, 23, postgraduate student, arrived one year ago). Some of their parents' hopes and ambivalence were also presented in the limited scale of a few chapters. As I kept in touch with the majority of the participants after the research in 2014, news about decisions to return to China, changes of jobs and purchase of properties were reported throughout the analysis and writing stages of the book. The continuing life changes of participants acted as a constant reminder that each interview account was only a snapshot of a living person in a certain place at a certain stage of his/her life.

The year after I visited Bolin at her home in 2014, she moved to a new house so that her children could go to a good primary school which would lead them to a good state school. Bolin's parents had sold the flat that I visited in Shanghai and had helped with the deposit on Bolin's new house in Birmingham. They used the rest of the money to reserve a small flat in an old people's home and planned to move there in a few years' time should their health deteriorate. Bolin and her parents had not seen each other since 2013. The parents' visit to the UK was being planned for following year (2018). 'They want to visit us as often as possible before they had to move into a home.' Bolin told me in a text message in September 2017, 'but I quietly hope that I can go back to China to be with my parents, after my children are independent'.

Ran is now in his third job in London. He switched from the IT department in an investment bank to a technology-investment company and continues to advance in his career. 'I want to establish more connections with China. As a first-generation migrant I find it easier to do business with people from China.' However, he does not intend to return to live in China, at least not in the near future. He now owns a one-bedroom flat at the financial centre of London, and he plans to apply for permanent residency as soon as he is qualified in 2018. Ran became a father last year. 'My wife and daughter are still living in China, but they will join me soon. And we hope to buy a house outside of London.' As for the future education for his daughter, he became hesitant: 'I'm not sure, I want her to receive at least primary education in China, otherwise she may forget her Chinese identity.'

Yizi's past three years have been mainly about work. She too had a major advancement in her career. She now manages a team of more than 10 members – a role which requires her to travel regularly between London and other European countries. 'I don't even need to unpack my suitcase because I know I'd be on the road again soon.' At the point of our interview in 2014, she was in the process of buying a flat in London. The following year she moved into her new flat and has enjoyed a rich social life. Yizi sees her parents at least once a year: either a holiday in Europe together or a visit to China for a family reunion. There was no mention of a relationship or marriage in Yizi's updates.

When I interviewed her in 2014, Zhaohui was about to complete her Master's degree course and was in the middle of a summer internship with a company in London. She had a strong wish to work in the UK for about a year before going back to China. Unfortunately, she failed to find a full-time job and returned to China with her long-term boyfriend, who was also studying in the UK with her. Zhaohui did not return to her father, who was looking after both his paralysed wife and aged mother. Instead Zhaohui returned with her boyfriend in Shanghai. They got married in 2017. Zhaohui told me that her parental grandmother had passed away, and her mother was 'still the same'. Zhaohui and her husband are now living with her husband's parents in Shanghai. The domestic 'migrant' life continues.

As briefly mentioned in the beginning of the book, Wang Gungwu distinguished student-turned-migrants from traditionally defined migrants who leave 'their home without intending to return'. Students are not migrants. But being a student may lead to 'delayed' migration. 'Migranthood' is the condition of a migrant in the space 'between that of a student and that of a migrant' (Wang, 2007, p. 167). Migrants' stories, including Bolin, Ran, Yizi and Zhaohui, in this book, have shown that an individual's decision to study abroad and the decision on migration can have a time lapse ranging from months to years. The switch from student to the status of highly-skilled migrant in a professional occupation largely depends upon the individual's aspiration for education and career advancement at a transnational level. In this respect, this book confirms this relatively underdeveloped term, 'migranthood', which describes post-student migrants as 'the product of economic and technological globalisation' (Wang, 2007, p. 176).

Nevertheless, Wang did not indicate when, or whether, 'migranthood' ends. These migrants' experiences point to the possibility that the 'migranthood' will not completely end among the first-generation migrants and that migrants are likely to invoke their 'migranthood' in order to justify or help their settlement in the host country. For example, the strongly expressed commitment to look after parents in China (in the future) reduces the sense of guilt of migrants being unable to be with their parents (now), which justifies the migrants' choice of (temporarily) focusing on their life in the host country. At a nation-state level, the Chinese state is actively fostering its transnational ties with skill-bearing, overseas-educated migrants. Instead of calling overseas Chinese to return to China and work, the state's narratives have shown a shift towards keeping the cohort's 'migranthood'; it views overseas Chinese as a socio-political asset which may be of long-term benefit to China. Therefore, at the individual, familial and nation-state level, 'migranthood' is a significant concept which deserves more academic and social attention.

Re-emphasis of key points and notes of caution will not sufficiently demonstrate the complexity of intergenerational changes in Chinese migration nor is any research capable of accurately predicting individuals' responses to the socioeconomic changes in their immediate, as well as global environment. As the world becomes more closely connected, and our investigations into various aspects of this world continue, it is almost impossible to cover the full spectrum of subject, cohort or phenomena in a single research project. This book focuses on the family as a social field to observe cultural and value changes across time and space. In this sense, the family acts as an intermediate unit between individual

mobility and the global society. But it is certainly not the only intermediate unit; other units such as companies and educational institutions
are also significant within the complexity of multi-level socioeconomic
mobility changes. As future research continues in its attempt to complete
the puzzle of migration and transnational mobility, it is important to keep
in mind that we remain multidimensional individuals living in a world of
endless multidimensions.

Note

1. For example, see 'Wealthy Chinese Flock to the West'. *BBC* (28 July 2010).
   Available at http://www.bbc.co.uk/news/10760368. Accessed 28 February 2016.
      'Surge in Chinese House Buying Spurs Global Backlash'. *Financial Times*
   (25 February 2016). Available at http://www.ft.com/cms/s/0/fcc2d346-bcd3-
   11e4-9902-00144feab7de.html#axzz41SY0lGml. Accessed 28 February 2016.

Appendix

Participants	Education	Gender	Year of Birth	Age	Year of Arrival	Length of Stay (Year)	Place of Residence	Home Region in China	Occupation	Income Level	Marital Status	Visa Type
1. Tao	Master's	Female	1987	27	2010	4	Kent	Mid-west	Social media manager	35–45k	Married	Work
2. Zhipin	Bachelor's	Female	1981	33	2008	6	London	South	Accounts assistant	25–35k	Married	PR
3. Zhimin	Master's	Male	1983	31	2002	12	London	North east	Sales manager	15–25k	Single	UK passport
4. Bao	Master's	Female	1983	31	2007	7	Devon	East	Purchasing manager	15–25k	Single	Work
5. Yang	Master's	Male	1979	35	2002	12	London	East	Bank admin assistant	25–35k	Single	PR
6. Yizi[a]	Master's	Female	1983	31	2009	5	London	South	Advertising manager	35–45k	Single	Work
7. Zhaohui[a]	Bachelor's	Female	1991	23	2013	1	London	South	Master's student	n/a	Has a partner	Student
8. Jinhai	Master's	Female	1987	27	2010	4	London	East	Auditor	25–35k	Has a partner	Work
9. Demin	PhD	Male	1981	33	2003	11	London	East	Lecturer	45–55k	Married and parent	PR
10. Baowen	Master's	Female	1981	33	2005	9	Leeds	North East	Legal assistant (part-time)	15–25k	Married and parent	PR

Participants	Education	Gender	Year of Birth	Age	Year of Arrival	Length of Stay (Year)	Place of Residence	Home Region in China	Occupation	Income Level	Marital Status	Visa Type
11. Tian[a]	PhD	Female	1983	31	2005	9	Leicestershire	North	Lecturer	35–45k	Married	Work
12. Quan	Master's	Male	1988	26	2008	6	Hampshire	Mid-west	Electronic engineer	15–25k	Single	Work
13. Jin	Bachelor's	Female	1991	23	2013	1	Kent	Mid-west	Master's student	n/a	Single	Student
14. Ying	Master's	Female	1985	29	2001	13	London	East	Accounts assistant	25–35k	Married	PR
15. Liwen	Master's	Male	1984	30	2007	7	London	North	Telecommunications engineer	25–35k	Single	Work
16. Guozhi	Master's	Male	1988	26	2011	3	London	East	Funds analyst	35–45k	Has a partner	Work
17. Tengfei[a]	Master's	Male	1986	28	2011	3	Lancashire	North	PhD student	n/a	Has a partner	Student
18. Delun	Bachelor's	Male	1992	22	2014	0	London	Mid-west	Master's student	n/a	Has a partner	Student
19. Shan	PhD	Female	1982	32	2004	10	London	North	Post-doc researcher	35–45k	Married and parent	PR
20. Meilin	Master's	Female	1977	37	2001	13	London	East	Accountant (part-time)	Did not wish to tell	Married and parent	PR
21. Lan	Bachelor's	Male	1987	27	2012	2	Kent	North east	Master's student	n/a	Single	Student

	Education	Gender	Birth year	Age	Year	Years	County/City	Region	Occupation	Income	Marital status	Status
22. Bolin[a]	Master's	Female	1976	38	2001	13	Nottinghamshire	East	Export manager	15–25k	Married and parent	UK passport
23. Ran[a]	Master's	Male	1987	27	2008	6	London	Mid-west	Software engineer	35–45k	Married	Work
24. Beiyao[a]	PhD	Female	1984	30	2006	8	Wiltshire	North east	Process engineer	25–35k	Married and parent	Work
25. Kai	Master's	Male	1986	28	2002	12	London	East	Estate agent	15–25k	Single	Work
26. Jiayi	Master's	Female	1978	36	2007	7	Somerset	North east	Chinese medical doctor	25–35k	Married and parent	PR
27. Dahong	Master's	Female	1987	27	2008	6	London	South	Marketing analyst	25–35k	Single	Work
28. Qiaolin	Master's	Female	1978	36	1997	17	Devon	Mid-west	Purchasing manager	25–35k	Married and parent	PR
29. Gaomei	Master's	Female	1987	27	2010	4	Devon	North	Purchasing assistant	15–25k	Single	Work
30. Qianqian	Master's	Female	1987	27	2010	4	Devon	North	Purchasing assistant	15–25k	Has a partner	Work
31. Wenbin	Master's	Male	1978	36	2002	12	London	East	Entrepreneur	55k+	Single	UK passport
32. Chuanli	PhD	Male	1983	31	2011	3	Leicestershire	East	Research associate	25–35k	Single	Work
33. Feng	Bachelor's	Female	1980	34	2002	12	Manchester	South	Project IT manager	35–45k	Married and parent	PR

[a]Parents interviewed.
[b]Permanent resident permit.

Child's Name	Parents Interviewed	Age	Occupation	Education	Home Region in China
6. Yizi[a]	Mother	55	Teacher	University	South
7. Zhaohui[a]	Father	56	Semi-retired accountant	High school	South
11. Tian[a]	Father	57	Manager in state-owned company	University	North
17. Tengfei[a]	Father	58	Small grocery shop owner	High school	North
22. Bolin[a]	Father	68	Retired factory owner	High school	South east
	Mother	66	Retired factory owner	High school	South east
23. Ran[a]	Father	55	Head of state-owned factory turned consultant	High school	Mid-west
	Mother	51	Businesswoman	High school	Mid-west
24. Beiyao[a]	Mother	55	Semi-retired teacher	University	North east

References

Agree, E., Bissett, B., and Rendall, M. (2003). Simultaneous care for parents and care for children among mid-life British women and men. *Population Trends*, 112(Summer), pp. 29–35.

Anderson, B. and Blinder, S. (2017). Who Counts as a Migrant? Definitions and their Consequences. The Migration Observatory. Retrieved from http://www.migrationobservatory.ox.ac.uk/resources/briefings/who-counts-as-a-migrant-definitions-and-their-consequences/#kp1.

Archer, W. and Cheng, J. (2012). Tracking international graduate outcomes 2011. *BIS Research Paper, No. 62*. Department for Business Innovation & Skills. Retrieved from https://www.gov.uk/government/uploads/system/uploads/attach ment_data/file/32422/12-540-tracking-international-graduate-outcomes-2011.pdf.

Ball, S. (2003). *Class Strategies and the Education Market: The Middle Class and Social Advantage*. London: Routledge.

Bakken, B. (1993). Prejudice and danger: The only-child in China. *Childhood*, 1(1), pp. 46–61.

Baker, H. (1979). *Chinese Family and Kinship*. New York, NY: Columbia University Press.

Baldassar, L. (2007). Transnational families and the provision of moral and emotional support: the relationship between truth and distance. *Identities*, 14(4), pp. 385–409.

Banerjee, A. and Duflo, E. (2008). What is middle class about the middle classes around the world? *Journal of Economic Perspectives*, 22(2), pp. 3–28.

Bao, L. (2012). *Du Sheng Zi Nv Sheng Hua (Myth of Only-Child: Institution, Policy and Collective Psychology)*. Shanghai: Shanghai People's Press.

Barber, T. (2015). *Oriental Identities in Super-Diverse Britain: Young Vietnamese in London*. Basingstoke: Palgrave Macmillan.

Baumrind, D. (1991). The influence of parenting style on adolescent competence and substance use. *Journal of Early Adolescence,* 11(1), pp. 56–95.

Baumrind, D. (1971). Current patterns of parental authority. *Developmental Psychology*, 4(1, part 2), pp. 1–103.

BBC. (2011). Are Strict Chinese Mothers the Best? Retrieved from http://www.bbc.co.uk/news/magazine-12249215.

BBC. (2006). Language Schools Have Become Illegal Visa Factories. Retrieved from http://www.bbc.co.uk/pressoffice/pressreleases/stories/2006/06_june/28/language.shtml.

BBC. (2005). Language School Visa Scam. Retrieved from http://www.bbc.co.uk/pressoffice/pressreleases/stories/2006/06_june/28/language.shtml.

Becker, G. (1993a). The economic way of looking at life. *Coase-Sandor Working Paper Series in Law and Economics*. University of Chicago Law School. Retrieved from http://chicagounbound.uchicago.edu/cgi/viewcontent.cgi?article= 1509&context=law_and_economics.

Becker, G. (1993b). *A Treatise on the Family*. US: Harvard University Press.

Bennett, C. (2011). China's little emperors, The Guardian. Retrieved at https://www.theguardian.com/guardianweekly/story/0,12674,1383770,00.html.

Benton, G. and Gomez, E. (2011). *The Chinese in Britain, 1800–Present: Economy, Transnationalism, Identity*. Basingstoke: Palgrave Macmillan.

Bernstein, T. (1977). *Up to the Mountains and Down to the Villages: The Transfer of Youth from Urban to Rural China*. US: Yale University Press.

Bian, Y. (2002). Chinese social stratification and social mobility. *Annual Review of Sociology*, 28(1), pp. 91–116.

Biao, X. and Shen, W. (2009). International student migration and social stratification in China. *International Journal of Education Development*, 29(5), pp. 513–522.

Binah-Pollak, A. (2014). Discourses and practices of child rearing in China: The bio-power of parenting in Beijing. *China Information*, 28(1), pp. 27–45.

Birditt, K., Tighe, L., Fingerman, K., and Zarit, S. (2012). Intergenerational relationship quality across three generations. *The journals of gerontology. Series B, Psychological sciences and social sciences*, 67(5), pp. 627–638.

Bodycott, P. (2009). Choosing a higher education study abroad destination: What mainland Chinese parents and students rate as important. *Journal of Research in International Education*, 8(3), pp. 349–373.

Bodycott, P. and Lai, A. (2012). The influence and implications of Chinese culture in the decision to undertake cross-border higher education. *Journal of Studies in International Education,* 16(3), pp. 252–270.

Bourdieu, P. (1986). The forms of capital. In Richardson, J. ed. *Handbook of Theory and Research for the Sociology of Education*, 241–258. New York, NY: Greenwood Press.

Bryceson, D. and Vuorela, U. (2002). Transnational families in the twenty-first century. In Bryceson, D. and Vuorela, U. eds. *The Transnational Family: New European Frontiers and Global Networks*, 3–30. Oxford: Berg.

Bryman, A. (2008). *Social Research Methods*. New York, NY: Oxford University Press.

Carling, J. (2008). The human dynamics of migrant transnationalism. *Ethnic and Racial Studies*, 31(8), pp. 1452–1477.

Carlson, S. (2013). Becoming a mobile student – A processual perspective on German degree students. *Population, Space and Place*, 19(2), pp. 168–180.

Castles, S. and Miller, M. (2009). *The Age of Migration, 4th edition*. London: Palgrave Macmillan.

Cebolla-Boado, H., Hu, Y., and Soysal, Y. (2017). 'Why study abroad? Sorting of Chinese students across British universities.' *British Journal of Sociology of Education*. doi:10.1080/01425692.2017.1349649.

Chao, R. (2000). The parenting of immigrant Chinese and European American mothers: Relations between parenting styles, socialization goals, and parental practices. *Journal of Applied Developmental Psychology*, 21(2), pp. 233–248.

Chao, R. (1994). Beyond parental control and authoritarian parenting style: Understanding Chinese parenting through the cultural notion of training. *Child Development*, 65(4), pp. 1111–1119.

Chau, R. and Yu, S. (2001). Social exclusion of Chinese people in Britain. *Critical Social Policy*, 21(1), pp. 103–125.

Chen, X. (2003). The social impact of China's one-child policy. *Harvard Asia Pacific Review* (Summer), pp. 74–76.

Cheng, Y. (1994). *Education and Class: Chinese in Britain and the U.S.* Aldershot: Avebury.

CCG (Center for China & Globalization). (2017). *Report on Employment and Entrepreneurship of Chinese Returnees 2017*. Retrieved from http://www.ccg.org.cn/dianzizazhi/2017haiguibaogao.pdf.

CCTV (China Central Television Channel). (2014). Overseas Returnees Struggle to Find Jobs in China. Retrieved from http://english.cntv.cn/2014/05/12/VIDE1399849036955600.shtml.

China Daily. (2013). US Still Top Choice for Students. *China Daily*, 24 July. Retrieved from http://usa.chinadaily.com.cn/epaper/2013-07/24/content_16822768.htm.

China.org. (2015). 9-Year Compulsory Education. Retrieved from http://www.china.org.cn/english/education/184879.htm.

Choi, S. and Nieminen, T. (2013). Factors influencing the higher education of international students from Confucian East Asia. *Higher Education Research & Development*, 32(2), pp. 161–173.

Chou, R. (2010). Filial piety by contract? The emergence, implementation, and implications of the 'family support agreement' in China. *The Gerontologist*, 51(1), pp. 3–16.

Chow, N. (1991). Does filial piety exist under Chinese communism? *Journal of Aging and Social Policy*, 3(1–2), pp. 209–925.

Chow, S. and Chu, M. (2007). The impact of filial piety and parental involvement on academic achievement motivation in Chinese secondary school students. *Asian Journal of Counselling,* 14(1–2), pp. 91–124.

Classic of Filial Piety. (1988). *Sacred Books of the East 3: The Sacred Books of China: The Text of Confucianism*, Trans. Legge, J. Delhi: Motial Banarsidass.

Coleman, J. A. (2013). Researching whole people and whole lives. In Kinginger, C. ed. *Social and Cultural Aspects of Language Learning in Study Abroad*, 17–44. Amsterdam: John Benjamins.

Croll, E. (2006). The intergenerational contract in the changing Asian family. *Oxford Development Studies,* 34(4), pp. 473–491.

Crossley, N. (2012). Social class. In Grenfell, M. ed. *Pierre Bourdieu: Key Concepts, 2nd edition,* 85–97. Durham: Acumen.

Da, W. (2003). Transnational grandparenting: Child care arrangements among migrants from the People's Republic of China to Australia. *Journal of*

International Migration and Integration/Revue de l'integration et de la migration internationale, 4(1), pp. 79–103.

Dai, C. (2008). He Jingqiu: Jian Zheng 30 Nian Jian Bai Wan Xue Zi Liu Xue Da Chao (He Jianqiu: 30 Years of Study-Abroad Migration), *Zhong Guo Qing Nian Bao* (*China Youth*), 19 October. Retrieved from http://zqb.cyol.com/content/2008-10/19/content_2395061.htm (Chinese).

Dai, Y. and Dimond, M. (1998). Filial piety: A cross-cultural comparison and its implications for the well-being of older parents. *Journal of Gerontological Nursing*, 24(3), pp. 13–18.

Davis, A., Hirsch, D., and Padley, M. (2014). A minimum income standard for the UK in 2014. Joseph Rowntree Foundation Report. Retrieved from https://www.jrf.org.uk/report/minimum-income-standard-uk-2014.

Deutsch, F. (2006). Filial piety, patrilineality, and China's one-child policy. *Journal of Family Issues*, 27(3), pp. 366–89.

Donald, S. and Yi, Z. (2008). Richer than before – The cultivation of middle class taste: Education choices in urban China. In Goodman, D. ed. *The New Rich in China: Future Rulers, Present Lives,* 71–82. New York, NY: Routledge.

Ernst & Young (2014). *Zhong guo hai wai liu xue shi chang fen xi bao gao* (*China Overseas Study Market Analysis Report*). China: Ernst & Young Global Limited.

Falbo, T. and Poston, D. (1993). The academic, personality, and physical outcomes of only children in China. *Child Development*, 64(1), pp. 18–35.

Fang, Y. and Walker, A. (2015). "Full-time wife" and the change of gender order in the Chinese city. *The Journal of Chinese Sociology*, 2(4), pp. 1–19.

Farrell, D., Gersch, U., and Stephenson, E. (2006). The value of China's emerging middle class. *McKinsey Quarterly, 2006 Special Edition*, pp. 60–69.

Fei, X. (1992). *From the Soil – The Foundations of Chinese Society*. Berkeley, CA: University of California Press.

Feng, X. (1993). Pian jian yu xian ship: du sheng z inv jiao yu wen ti de diao cha yu feng xi (Prejudgement and reality: Investigation and analysis of educational issues among the only children). *She hui xue yan jiu* (*Sociological Study*), 1, 93–99.

Feng, Z., Zhan, H., Feng, X., Liu, C., Sun, M., and Mor, V. (2011). An industry in the making: The emergence of institutional elder care in urban China. *Journal of the American Geriatrics Society*, 59(4), pp. 738–744.

Finch, J. (1996). Inheritance and financial transfer in families. In Walker, A. ed. *The New Generational Contract: Intergenerational Relations, Old Age and Welfare*, 120–134. London: UCL Press.

Finch, J. (1989). *Family Obligations and Social Change*. US: Policy Press.

Finch, J. and Mason, J. (1993). *Negotiating Family Responsibilities*. London: Routledge.

Fischer, K. (2014). For Some Foreign Students, U.S. Education Is Losing Its Attraction. *The New York Times*, 25 May. Retrieved from http://www.nytimes.com/2014/05/26/world/asia/for-some-foreign-students-us-education-is-losing-its-attraction.html.

Fong, V. (2011). *Paradise Redefined: Transnational Chinese Students and the Quest for Flexible Citizenship in the Developed World*. Stanford, CA: Stanford University Press.

Fong, V. (2004). *Only Hope: Coming of Age Under China's One-Child Policy*. Stanford, CA: Stanford University Press.

Friedman, E. (1994). Reconstructing China's national identity: A southern alternative to Mao-era anti-imperialist nationalism. *The Journal of Asian Studies*, 53(1), pp. 67–91.

Gao, J. (2006). Migrant transnationality and its evolving nature: a case study of mainland Chinese migrants in Australia. *Journal of Chinese Overseas*, 2(2), pp. 193–219.

Gee, E. (1992). Only children as adult women: Life course events and timing. *Social Indicators Research*, 26(2), pp. 183–197.

Gen, H. and Zhang, L. (2015). "Fu nv neng din ban bian tian" de kao zheng (Retrieving the source of the slogan "Women hold up half the sky"), *Bei jing guan cha (Beijing Observation)* (3), pp. 74–75.

Goh, E. (2011). *China's One-Child Policy and Multiple Caregiving: Raising Little Suns in Xiamen*. Abingdon: Routledge.

Goh, E. (2006). Raising the precious single child in urban China – An intergenerational joint mission between parents and grandparents. *Journal of Intergenerational Relationships*, 4(3), pp. 7–28.

Goodman, D. (2008). Why China has no new middle class: Cadres, managers and entrepreneurs. In Goodman, D. ed. *The New Rich in China: Future Rulers, Present Lives,* 23–37. New York, NY: Routledge.

Göransson, K. (2009). *The Binding Tie: Chinese Intergenerational Relations in Modern Singapore*. Honolulu: University of Hawaii Press.

Goyette, K. and Xie, Y. (1999). Educational expectations of Asian American youths: Determinants and ethnic differences. *Sociology of Education*, 72(1), pp. 22–36.

Graham, H. (1983). Caring: A labour of love. In Finch, J. and Groves, D. eds. *A Labour of Love: Women, Work and Caring,* 13–30. London: RKP.

Granovetter M. (1992). Problems of explanation in economic sociology. In: Nohria N, Eccles R. eds. *Networks and Organizations: Structure, Form, and Action*, Harvard Business School Press: Boston, pp. 25–56.

Greenhalgh, S. (1985). Sexual stratification: the other side of "growth with equity" in East Asia. *Population & Development Review*, 11(2), pp. 265–314.

Greenhalgh, S. (2008). *Just One Child: Science and Policy in Deng's China*. US: University of California Press.

Guan, H. (1995). "Wen Hua Da Ge Min" Zhong Zhi Shi Qing Nian Shang shan Xia Xiang Yun Dong Shu Lun (The "sent-down movement" of the Cultural Revolution). *Dang Dai Zhong Guo Shi Yan Jiu (Study of Contemporary Chinese History)*, 5, pp. 68–74.

Guth, J. (2007). Triggering skilled migration: Factors influencing the mobility of early career scientists to Germany. *Focus Migration Policy Brief*, 6, pp. 1–7.

Hatton, C. (2013). New China Law Says Children 'Must Visit Parents'. BBC, 1 July. Retrieved from http://www.bbc.co.uk/news/world-asia-china-23124345.

Hidalgo, N., Siu, S., and Epstein, J. (2004). Research on families, schools, and communities: A multicultural perspective. In Banks, J. and Banks, C. eds. *Handbook of Research on Multicultural Education, 2nd edition*, 631–655. San Francisco, CA: Jossey-Bass.

Home Office. (2015). Apply to Join Family Living Permanently in the UK. Retrieved from https://www.gov.uk/join-family-in-uk.

Home Office. (2014). Immigration Statistics, January to March. Retrieved from https://www.gov.uk/government/publications/immigration-statistics-january-to-march-2014/immigration-statistics-january-to-march-2014.

Home Office. (2013). Immigration Statistics, January to March. Retrieved from https://www.gov.uk/government/publications/immigration-statistics-january-to-march-2013/immigration-statistics-january-to-march-2013.

Hong, L. (1987). Potential effects of the one-child policy on gender equality in the People's Republic of China. *Gender and Society*, 1(3), pp. 317–326.

Howden, D. and Zhou, Y. (2015). Why did China's population grow so quickly? *The Independent Review,* 20(2), pp. 227–248.

Hosking, P. (2015). Half of Pensioners Support Family. *The Times*, 29 April. Retrieved from http://www.thetimes.co.uk/tto/money/pensions/article4425459.ece.

Hu, Y. (2015). Gender and children's housework time in China: Examining behavior modeling in context. *Journal of Marriage and Family*, 77(5), pp. 1126–1143.

Hu, R. and Ye, N. (1991). *1988 Zhong Guo Jiu Da Cheng Shi Lao Nian Ren Zhuang Kuang Diao Cha* (*Survey of the Elderly in Nine Chinese Cities in 1988*). Tianjin: Tianjin Education Press.

Huang, J. (2010). Conceptualizing Chinese migration and Chinese overseas: The contribution of Wang Gungwu. *Journal of Chinese Overseas*, 6(1), pp. 1–21.

Huang, J. and Prochner, L. (2003). Chinese parenting styles and children's self-regulated learning. *Journal of Research in Childhood Education*, 18(3), pp. 227–238.

Huang, S. and Yeoh, B. (2005). Transnational families and their children's education: China's 'study mothers' in Singapore. *Global Networks*, 5(4), pp. 379–400.

Hussein, S. and Manthorpe, J. (2005). An international review of the long-term care workforce. *Journal of Aging and Social Policy*, 17(4), pp. 75–94.

Iannelli, C. and Huang, J. (2013). Trends in participation and attainment of Chinese students in UK higher education. *Studies in Higher Education*, 39(5), pp. 805–822.

Ikels, C. ed. (2004). *Filial Piety: Practice and Discourse in Contemporary East Asia*. Stanford, CA: Stanford University Press.

Ikels, C. (1990). Family caregivers and the elderly in China. In Biegel, D. and Blum, A. eds. *Aging and Caregiving: Theory and Practice*, 270–284. Newbury Park, CA: Sage.

James, N. (1992). Care = organisation + physical labour + emotional labour. *Sociology of Health and Illness,* 14(4), pp. 488–509.

Jiang, C. and Hancock, J. (2013). Absence makes the communication grow fonder: Geographic separation, interpersonal media, and intimacy in dating relationships. *Journal of Communication*, 63(3), pp. 556–577.

Jiao, S., Ji, G., and Jing, Q. (1996). Cognitive development of Chinese urban only children and children with siblings. *Child Development*, 67(2), pp. 387–395.

Kajanus, A. (2015). *Chinese Student Migration, Gender and Family*. Basingstoke: Palgrave Macmillan.

Keller, M., Edelstein, W., Krettenauer, T., Fu-xi, F., and Ge, F. (2005). Reasoning about moral obligations and interpersonal responsibilities in different cultural contexts. In Edelstein W. and Nunner-Winkler G. eds. *Morality in Context*, 317–337. Amsterdam: Elsevier.

Kim, J. (2010). 'Downed' and stuck in Singapore: Lower/middle class South Korean wild geese (Kirogi) children in Singapore. *Research in Sociology of Education*, 17, pp. 271–311.

Kitzman, K., Cohen, R., and Lockwood, R. (2002). Are only children missing out? Comparison of the peer-related social competence of only children and siblings. *Journal of Social and Personal Relationships*, 19(3), pp. 299–316.

Knowles, C. (2015). *Young Chinese Migrants in London, Runnymede*. Retrieved from http://www.gold.ac.uk/media/goldsmiths/departments/sociology/ Young_Chinese_Migrants_in_London.compressed.pdf.

Kuhn, P. (2008). *Chinese Among Others: Emigration in Modern Times*. Lanham: Rowman & Littlefield Publishers.

Kuijs, L. (2006). How will China's saving-investment balance evolve? *World Bank Policy Research Working Paper 3958*, July 2006. Retrieved from https://www. openknowledge.worldbank.org/handle/10986/8419.

Kuvshinov, D. (2011). Recent trends in the UK first-time buyer mortgage market. Paper presented at The Fifth IFC Conference: Initiatives to Address Data Gaps Revealed by the Financial Crisis, Basel, 25–26 August 2010, pp. 599–610. Bank for International Settlement. Retrieved from www.bis.org/list/ifcbulletins/index.htm.

Lee, K. (2010). Gender, care work, and the complexity of family membership in Japan. *Gender & Society*, 24(5), pp. 647–671.

Leung, J. and Shek, D. (2011). "All I can do for my child" – Development of the Chinese parental sacrifice for child's education scale. *International Journal on Disability and Human Development*, 10(3), pp. 201–208.

Levitt, P. and Glick Schiller, N. (2004). Conceptualizing simultaneity: A transnational social field perspective on society. *International Migration Review*, 38(3), pp. 1002–1039.

Levitt, P. and Sørensen, N. (2004). The transnational turn in migration studies. *Global Migration Perspectives*, 6, Geneva: Global Commission on International Migration.

Lewis, J. and Meredith, B. eds. (1988). *Daughters Who Care*. London: Routledge.

Lewis, L. (2013). Ambition and Angst: Inside China's Middle Class. *The Times*, 5 March. Retrieved from http://www.thetimes.co.uk/tto/life/article3705469.ece. Accessed 3 March 2016.

Ley, D. (2010). *Millionaire Migrants: Trans-Pacific Lifelines*. MA: John Wiley & Sons.

Li, Chunling. (2010). Characterizing China's middle class: Heterogeneous composition and multiple identities. In Li, C. ed. *China's Emerging Middle Class: Beyond Economic Transformation*, 135–156. Washington, D.C.: Brookings Institution Press.

Li, Cheng. (2010). Introduction: The rise of the middle class in the middle kingdom. In Li, C. ed. *China's Emerging Middle Class: Beyond Economic Transformation*, 3–31. Washington, D.C.: Brookings Institution Press.

Li, H. (2010). Higher education in China: Complement or competition to US universities? In Clotfelter, C. T. ed. *American Universities in a Global Market*, 269–304. Chicago, IL: University of Chicago Press.

Li, Q. (2005). Zhong Guo Cheng Shi Pin Kun Ceng Wen Ti (Poverty in Chinese cities). *Fu Zhou Da Xue Xue Pao (Journal of Fuzhou University)*, 19(1), pp. 21–28.

Liang, Z. and Tan, K. (1997). Shan xi shen yi chen xian "wan hun wan yu jia jian ge" sheng yu zheng ce shi shi xiao guo de ren kou xue fen xi (A demographic analysis of the result of the birth control policy implementation in Yi chen xian, Shan xi Province), *Zhong Guo Ren Kou Ke Xue (Chinese Journal of Population Science)*, 1997(5), pp. 1–10.

Lie, M. (2010). Across the oceans: Childcare and grandparenting in UK Chinese and Bangladeshi households. *Journal of Ethnic and Migration Studies*, 36(9), pp. 1425–1443.

Lin, J. (1988). The household responsibility system in China's agricultural reform: A theoretical and empirical study. *Economic Development & Cultural Change*, 36(3), pp. 199–224.

Lin, J. and Sun, X. (2010). Higher education and China's middle class. In Li, C. ed. *China's Emerging Middle Class: Beyond Economic Transformation*, 217–244. Washington, D.C.: Brookings Institution Press.

Liu, F. (2008a). Constructing the autonomous middle class self in today's China: The case of young-adult only-children university students. *Journal of Youth Studies*, 11(2), pp. 193–212.

Liu, F. (2008b). Negotiating the filial self: Young-adult only-children and intergenerational relationships in China. *Young,* 16(4), pp. 409–430.

Liu, G. (2006). *The Right to Leave and Return and Chinese Migration Law*. Leiden: Martinus Nijhoff Publishers.

Liu, H. (2011). An emerging China and diasporic Chinese: Historicity, state, and international relations. *Journal of Contemporary China*, 20(72), pp. 813–832.

Liu-Farrer, G. (2016). Migration as class-based consumption: The emigration of the rich in contemporary China. *The China Quarterly*, 226(June), pp. 499–518.

Lo, M. and Liu, Y. (2009). Quality of life among older grandparent caregivers: A pilot study. *Journal of Advanced Nursing*, 65(7), pp. 1475–1484.

Löckenhoff, C., Chan, W., McCrae, R., De, F, Jussim, L., De Bolle, M., et al. (2014). Gender stereotypes of personality: Universal and accurate? *Journal of Cross-Cultural Psychology*, 45(5), pp. 675–694.

Luk, W. (2008). *Chinatown in Britain: Diffusions and Concentrations of the British New Wave Chinese Immigration.* Le Sueur, MN: Cambria.

Ma, G. and Yi, W. (2010). China's high saving rate: Myth and reality. *International Economics,* 122, pp. 5–39.

Ma, Y., Wang, Z., Sheng, X., and Shinozaki, M. (1994). *A Study on the Life and Consciousness of Contemporary Urban Family in China: A Research in Beijing with Comparison among Bangkok, Seoul and Fukuoka.* Kitakyushu: Kitakyushu Forum on Asian Women.

MacCormack, G. (2002). Filial piety and the pre-T'ang law. *Fundamina: A Journal of Legal History,* 8, pp. 137–164.

Massey, D. S., Arango, J., Hugo, G., Kouaouci, A., Pellegrino, A., and Taylor, J. (1998). *Worlds in Motion: Understanding International Migration at the End of the Millennium.* New York, NY: Oxford University Press.

Mazzarol, T. and Soutar, G. (2002). Push–pull factors influencing student destination choice. *International Journal of Education Management,* 16(2), pp. 82–90.

Melik, J. (2012). China: The Paradox of Foreign Education. *BBC,* 2 August. Retrieved from http://www.bbc.co.uk/news/business-19076873.

Milwertz, C. (1997). *Accepting Population Control: Urban Chinese Women and the One-Child Family Policy.* Surrey: Curzon Press.

Ministry of Education of PRC. (2015). Zhong Guo Shi Shi Quan Min Jiao Yu Gai Kuang (Report on Chinese National Education). Retrieved from http://www.moe.gov.cn/s78/A23/jkw_left/moe_866/tnull_13252.html.

Modigliani, F. and Cao, S. L. (2004). The Chinese saving puzzle and the life-cycle hypothesis. *Journal of Economic Literature,* 42(1), pp. 145–170.

Mosneaga, A. and Winther, L. (2013). Emerging talents? International students before and after their career start in Denmark. *Population, Space and Place,* 19(2), pp. 181–195.

National Bureau of Statistics of the PRC. (2015). Statistics of Study Abroad Population and Returned Population (1978–2014). Retrieved from http://data.stats.gov.cn.

National Bureau of Statistics of the PRC. (2011). 2010 Nian Di Liu Ci Quan Guo Ren Kou Pu Cha Shu Ju Gong Bao (Date Release of the 6th Census [2010] [No.1]). Retrieved from http://www.stats.gov.cn/tjsj/tjgb/rkpcgb/qgrkpcgb/201104/t20110428_30327.html.

Nania, S. and Green S. (2004). *Deus ex M.A. China: Are Mainland Chinese Students Saving Britain's Universities?* The Royal Institution of International Affairs. Retrieved from https://www.chathamhouse.org/sites/files/chathamhouse/public/Research/Asia/bnjul04.pdf.

Nedelcu, M. (2012). 'Netizenship' and migrants' online mobilization: Transnational participation and collective action in the digital era. In Isabelle, R. and Saita, E. eds. *Mediating Cultural Diversity in a Globalized Public Space,* 34–52. Basingstoke: Palgrave Macmillan.

OECD. (2011). Lessons from PISA for the United States, Strong Performers and Successful Reformers in Education. Paris: OECD Publishing.

OECD. (2013). *World Migration in Figures*. Retrieved from http://www.oecd.org/els/mig/World-Migration-in-Figures.pdf.

Ong, A. (2003). Techno-migrants in the network economy. In Beck, U., Sznaider, N., and Winter, R. eds. *Global America: The Cultural Consequences of Globalization*, 153–173. Liverpool: Liverpool University Press.

Ong, A. (1999). *Flexible Citizenship: The Cultural Logics of Transnationality*. Durham, North Carolina: Duke University Press.

ONS. (2006). *Foreign Labour in the United Kingdom: current patterns and trends*, Office for National Statistics.

ONS. (2013a). Immigration Patterns of Non-UK Born Populations in England and Wales in 2011. Office for National Statistics, UK.

ONS. (2013b). Migration Statistics Quarterly Report, November 2013. Office for National Statistics, UK.

ONS. (2012). 2011 Census: Key Statistics for England and Wales, March 2011. Office for National Statistics, UK.

Pan, Y. (2002). An examination of the goals of the rustication program in the People's Republic of China. *Journal of Contemporary China,* 11(31), pp. 361–379.

Parreñas, R. (2005). Long distance intimacy: Class, gender and intergenerational relations between mothers and children in Filipino transnational families. *Global Networks*, 5(4), pp. 317–336.

Parreñas, R. (2001). *Servants of Globalization: Women, Migration and Domestic Work*. Stanford, CA: Stanford University Press.

Park, K. S., Phua, V., McNally, J., and Sun, R. (2005). Diversity and structure of intergenerational relationships: Elderly parent–adult child relations in Korea. *Journal of Cross-Cultural Gerontology*, 20(4), pp. 285–305.

Parker, D. and Song, M. (2007). Inclusion, participation and emergence of British Chinese website. *Journal of Ethnic and Migration Studies*, 33(7), pp. 1043–1061.

Parker, D. (1995). *Through Different Eyes: The Cultural Identities of Young Chinese People in Britain,* England: Avebury.

Polit, D. and Falbo, T. (1987). Only Children and Personality Development: A Quantitative Review. *Journal of Marriage and Family*, Vol. 49, No. 2 (May, 1987), pp. 309–325.

Porter, C., Hart, C., Yang, C., Robinson, C., Olsen, C., Zeng, Q., Olsen, J., and Jin, A. (2005). A comparative study of child temperament and parenting in Beijing, China, and the Western United States. *International Journal of Behavioral Development,* 29(6), pp. 541–551.

Poston, D. and Duan, C. (2000). The current and projected distribution of the elderly and eldercare in the People's Republic of China. *Journal of Family Issues*, 21(6), pp. 714–732.

Prince, R. (2010). David Cameron: Net Immigration Will Be Capped at Tens of Thousands. *The Telegraph*, January 10. Retrieved from http://www.telegraph.co.uk/news/politics/6961675/David-Cameron-net-immigration-will-be-capped-at-tens-of-thousands.html.

Qian, J. (2009). Shou Pi Fu Mei Fang Wen Xue Zhe Shi Zen Yang Cheng Xing De? (How was the first group of US visiting scholars arranged?). *Ren Min Ri Bao Hai Wai Ban* (*People's Daily Overseas Version*), 9 January, p. 6. Retrieved from http://paper.people.com.cn/rmrbhwb/html/2009-01/09/content_173081.htm (Chinese).

Qu, X. (2010). Zhong Guo Yang Lao Bao Xian Zhu Du De Yan Bian, Fa Zhan Yu Si Kao (Evolvement, development and ponder [*sic*] of pension system in China), *She Hui Ke Xue Guan Li Yu Pin Lun* (*Social Science Management and Review*), 3. Retrieved from http://iple.cass.cn/upload/2012/02/d20120206122641010.pdf (Chinese).

Quoss, B. and Zhao, W. (1995). Parenting styles and children's satisfaction with parenting in China and the United States. *Journal of Comparative Family Studies*, 26(2), pp. 265–280.

Ravenstein, E. (1889). The laws of migration. *Journal of the Royal Statistical Society*, LII, pp. 241–301.

Ravenstein, E. (1885). The laws of migration. *Journal of the Royal Statistical Society*, XLVIII(Part 2), pp. 167–227.

Royal College of Nursing. (2010). Care Home under Pressure: An England Report. Retrieved from https://www2.rcn.org.uk/__data/assets/pdf_file/0006/314547/Policy_Report-Care_Homes_under_pressure_final_web.pdf.

Reeves, R. and Howard, K. (2013). *The Glass Floor: Education, Downward Mobility, and Opportunity Hoarding*. Center on Children and Families at Brookings. Retrieved from http://www.brookings.edu/~/media/research/files/papers/2013/11/glass%20floor%20downward%20mobility%20equality%20opportunity%20hoarding%20reeves%20howard/glass%20floor%20downward%20mobility%20equality%20opportunity%20hoarding%20reeves%20howard.pdf.

Robertson, S. (2011). Student switchers and the regulation of residency: The interface of the individual and Australia's immigration regime. *Population, Space and Place*, 17(1), pp. 103–115.

Schans, D. and de Valk, H. (2011). Filial obligations among immigrants and native Dutch: A comparison of perceptions and behaviour among ethnic groups and generations. In Kraler, A., Kofman, E., Kohli, M., and Schmoll, C. eds. *Gender, Generations and the Family in International Migration*, 99–120. Amsterdam: Amsterdam University Press.

Shelter. (2013). 'Generation Rent' Locked Out of Property Market – Shelter England. Retrieved from https://england.shelter.org.uk/news/june_2013/generation_rent_locked_out_of_property_market.

Singh, S., Robertson, S., and Cabraal, A. (2012). Transnational family money: Remittances, gifts and inheritance. *Journal of Intercultural Studies*, 33(5), pp. 475–492.

Skeldon, R. (2007). The Chinese overseas: The end of exceptionalism? In Thuno, M. ed. *Beyond Chinatown, New Chinese Migration and the Global Expansion of China*, 32–48. Copenhagen: Nias Press.

Skeldon, R. (1996). Migration from China. *Journal of International Affairs,* 49(2), pp. 434–456.

Solomon, D. (2012). *The Contribution of Family Financing to the First-Time Buyer (FTB) Market: A Model-Based Analysis.* Centre for Business and Economic Research. Retrieved from https://cebr.com/reports/bank-of-mum-and-dad-for-ftb/.

Song, L., Li, S., and Feldman, M. W. (2012). Out-migration of young adults and gender division of intergenerational support in rural China. *Research on Aging,* 34(4), pp. 399–424.

Song, M. (1999). *Helping Out: Children's Labor in Ethnic Business.* Philadelphia, PA: Temple University Press.

Stark, O. (1991). *The Migration of Labor.* Cambridge: Basil Blackwell.

Stark, O. (1984). Migration decision making: A review article. *Journal of Development Economics,* 14, pp. 251–259.

Sun, K. (2014). Reconfigured reciprocity: How aging Taiwanese immigrants transform cultural logics of elder care. *Journal of Marriage and Family,* 76(4), pp. 875–889.

Sun, Y., Wang, C., and Wang, F. (2015). Zhong Guo Cheng Xian Ju Min Sheng Huo Man Yi Du Dai Ji Cha Yi Yan Jiu (Generational difference of life satisfaction among urban and rural residents). *Diao Yan Shi Jie. (The World of Survey and Research),* 8, pp. 9–14.

Sung, K. (2001). Family support for the elderly in Korea: Continuity, change, future directions, and cross-cultural concerns. *Journal of Aging and Social Policy,* 12(4), pp. 65–79.

Teo, S. (2007). Vancouver's newest Chinese diaspora: settlers or "immigrant prisoners"? *GeoJournal,* 68, pp. 211–222.

The Guardian. (1993). Over the Counter, the Chinese in Britain. *The Guardian,* 7 July.

The State Council of PRC. (2012). Zhong Hua Ren Min Gong He Guo Zhu Xi Lin (Di Qi Shi Er Hao) (Order of the President of the People's Republic of China [No. 72]). Retrieved from http://www.gov.cn/flfg/2012-12/28/content_2305570.htm (Chinese).

The Times. (2012). Eagle Dad in New Stunt to Make a Man of Son, 4. *The Times* [Online], 30 August. Retrieved from http://www.thetimes.co.uk/tto/news/world/asia/article3522919.ece.

The Migration Observatory. (2015). International Students and the Net Migration Target: Should Students Be Taken Out? Retrieved from http://www.migrationobservatory.ox.ac.uk/resources/commentaries/international-students-and-the-net-migration-target-should-students-be-taken-out/.

Tobin, J., Wu, D., and Davidson, D. (1989). *Preschool in Three Cultures.* New Haven, CT: Yale University Press.

Tomba, L. (2004). Creating an urban middle class: Social engineering in Beijing. *The China Journal,* 51, pp. 1–26.

Tsang, A., Irving, J., Alaggia, R., Chau, S., and Benjamin, M. (2003). Negotiating ethnic identity in Canada: The case of the "satellite children". *Youth and Society,* 34(3), pp. 358–384.

Tse, J. and Waters, J. (2013). Transnational youth transitions: Becoming adults between Vancouver and Hong Kong. *Global Networks,* 13(4), pp. 535–550.

Tsong, Y. and Liu, Y. (2009). Parachute kids and astronaut families. In Tewari, N. and Alvarez, A. N. eds. *Asian American Psychology: Current Perspectives,* 365–380. New York, NY: Taylor & Francis.

Tsui, M. (2005). Family income, home environment, parenting, and mathematics achievement of children in China and the United States. *Education and Urban Society,* *37*(3), pp. 336–355.

Tu, M. (2016). Chinese one-child families in the age of migration: Middle class transnational mobility, ageing parents, and the changing role of filial piety. *The Journal of Chinese Sociology,* 3(15), pp. 1–17.

Tu, M. (2017). The transnational one-child generation: Family relationships and overseas aspiration between China and the UK. *Children's Geographies.* doi: 10.1080/14733285.2017.1393499.

Unger, J. (1980). Bending the school ladder: The failure of Chinese educational reform in the 1960s. *Comparative Education Review,* 24(2), pp. 221–237.

Universities UK. (2014). The funding environment for universities 2014: International students in higher education: The UK and its competition. Retrieved from http://www.universitiesuk.ac.uk/highereducation/Documents/2014/InternationalStudentsInHigherEducation.pdf.

Universities UK. (2013). The UK's Relationship with China: Universities. Retrieved from http://www.universitiesuk.ac.uk/highereducation/Pages/UKsRelationshipChinaUniversities.aspx#.UwDBes6V34o.

Vertovec, S. (2009). *Transnationalism.* New York, NY: Routledge.

Walder, A. (1989). Social change in post-revolution China. *Annual Review of Sociology,* 15, pp. 405–424.

Walker, A. ed. (1996). *The New Generational Contract: Intergenerational Relations, Old Age and Welfare.* London: UCL Press.

Wang, D. (2010). Intergenerational transmission of family property and family management in urban China. *The China Quarterly,* 204, pp. 960–979.

Wang, G. (2007). Liuxue and Yimin: From study to migranthood. In Thuno M. ed. *Beyond Chinatown, New Chinese Migration and the Global Expansion of China.* Copenhagen: Nias Press.

Wang, H. and Guo, J. eds. (2012). *Guo Ji Ren Cai Lan Pi Shu: Zhong Guo Hai Gui Fa Zhan Bao Gao* (*Blue Book of Global Talent: Annual Report on the Development of Chinese Returnees*), No. 1. China: Social Science Academic Press. Retrieved from http://www.ccg.org.cn/Research/View.aspx?Id=449 (Chinese).

Wang, H. and Miao, L. eds. (2013). *Guo Ji Ren Cai Lan Pi Shu: Zhong Guo Hai Gui Fa Zhan Bao Gao* (*Blue Book of Global Talent: Annual Report on the Development of Chinese Returnees*), No. 2. China: Social Science Academic Press. Retrieved from http://www.ccg.org.cn/Research/View.aspx?Id=511 (Chinese).

Wang, Z. (2003). Gender, employment and women's resistance. In Perry, E. and Selden, M. eds. *Chinese Society: Change, Conflict and Resistance,* 162–186. New York, NY: Routledge.

Wang, Z. and Tian, X. (2015). Zhong Guo Yang Lao Ti Zhi Jie Gou Zhuan Xin Si Kao (Rethinking the reformation of the Chinese pension system). *Xing Zheng Guan Li Gai Ge* (*Administration Reform*), 5. Retrieved from http://kyhz.nsa.gov.cn/xzxy_kygl/pf/xzxywz/yksInfoDetail.htm?infoid=2544 (Chinese).

Waters, J. (2012). Geographies of international education: Mobilities and the reproduction of social (dis)advantage. *Geography Compass*, 6(3), pp. 123–136.

Waters, J. (2011). Time and transnationalism: A longitudinal study of immigration, endurance and settlement in Canada. *Journal of Ethnic and Migration Studies*, 37(7), pp. 1119–1135.

Waters, J. (2006). Geographies of cultural capital: Education, international migration and family strategies between Hong Kong and Canada. *Transactions of the Institute of British Geographers*, 31(2), pp. 179–192.

Waters, J. (2005). Transnational family strategies and education in the contemporary Chinese diaspora. *Global Networks,* 5(2), pp. 359–378.

Waters, J. (2002). Flexible families? 'Astronaut' households and the experiences of lone mothers in Vancouver, British Columbia. *Social and Cultural Geography*, 3(2), pp. 117–134.

Waters, J. (2003). Flexible citizens? transnationalism and citizenship amongst economic immigrants in vancouver. *Canadian Geographer*, 47(3), pp. 219–234.

Watson, J. (1977). The Chinese: Hong Kong villagers in the British catering trade. In Watson, J. ed. *Between Two Cultures: Migrant and Minorities in Britain,* 181–213. Oxford: Basil Blackwell.

Watson, R. (2014). *Student Visa System Fraud Exposed in BBC Investigation,* BBC. Retrieved from http://www.bbc.co.uk/news/uk-26024375.

Whyte, M. (2012). China's post-socialist inequality. *Current History*, 2012 (September), pp. 229–234.

Wolf, M. (1984). Marriage, family, and the state in contemporary China. *Pacific Affairs*, 57(2), pp. 213–236.

Whyte, M. (2004). Filial obligations in Chinese families: Paradoxes of modernization. In Ikels, C. ed. *Filial Piety: Practice and Discourse in contemporary East Asia,* 106–127. Stanford, CA: Stanford University.

World Bank. (2015). School Enrolment, Secondary, Private (% of Total Secondary). Retrieved from http://data.worldbank.org/indicator/SE.SEC.PRIV.ZS.

World Bank. (2015). Urban Population (% of Total). Retrieved from http://data.worldbank.org/indicator/SP.URB.TOTL.IN.ZS?page=1.

World Bank. (2006). Gender Gaps in China: Facts and Figures. Retrieved from http://siteresources.worldbank.org/INTEAPREGTOPGENDER/Resources/Gender-Gaps-Figures&Facts.pdf.

Wu, B., Mao, Z., and Xu, Q. (2008). Institutional care for elders in rural China. *Journal of Aging and Social Policy,* 20(2), pp. 218–239.

Wu, X. (2006). Jumping into the sea: self-employment in labor markets transition, and social stratification. *Sociological Studies*, 6, pp. 120–146.

Wu, X. and Li, L. (2012). Family size and maternal health: Evidence from the one-child policy in China. *Journal of Population Economy*, 25, pp. 1341–1364.

Wu, X. and Treiman, D. (2004). The household registration system and social stratification in China: 1955–1996. *Demography*, 41(2), pp. 363–384.

Xinhua News. (2007). Haigui Became Haidai: It May Not All Be Bad. *Xinhua News*, 5 June. Retrieved from http://news.xinhuanet.com/comments/2007-06/05/content_6198655.htm (Chinese).

Xinhua News. (2004). Deng Xiaoping: Most Successful Returned Overseas Student. *Xinhua News*, 16 August. Retrieved from http://www.opindia.com/2018/03/china-arrests-women-married-to-men-from-gilgit-baltistan-pakistan-govt-silent/.

Xinhua News. (2003). Overseas Degree Holder Face Rejections: Why Did Haigui Become Haidai? *Xinhua News*, 25 December. Retrieved from http://education.news.cn/2003-12/25/content_1247140.htm (Chinese).

Yang, D. (2006). Gao Deng Jiao Yu Ru Xue Ji Hui: Kua Da Zhi Zhong de Jie Ceng Cha Ju, (Access to higher education: widening social class disparities). *Tsinghua Journal of Education*, 27(1), pp. 19–25.

Yang, G. (2011). *The Power of the Internet in China*. US: Columbia University Press.

Yeung, W. J. J. (2013). Higher education expansion and social stratification in China. *Chinese Sociological Review*, 45(4), pp. 54–80.

You, Y. (2007). A deep reflection on the "key school system" in basic education in China. *Frontiers of Education in China,* 2(2), pp. 229–239.

Yu, C. (2012). Nong Min "Yang Er Fang Lao" Guan Nian De Dai Ji cha Yi Ji Zhuan Bian Qu Xiang (Change trend and difference between generations of farmers' Concept of "Raising Sons for Old Age"). *Ren Kou Xue Kan (Population Journal)*, 6, pp. 40–50.

Zhan, H., Feng, X., and Luo, B. (2008). Placing elderly parents in institutions in urban China: A reinterpretation of filial piety. *Research on Aging*, 30(5), pp. 543–571.

Zhan, H. and Montgomery, R. (2003). Gender and elder care in China: The influence of filial piety and structural constraints. *Gender and Society,* 17(2), pp. 209–229.

Zhang, Q. (2012). China's Elder-Care Woes. *Shanghai Daily*, 26 June. Retrieved from https://nursing.duke.edu/sites/default/files/centers/ogachi/chinas_eldercare_woes_feature_shanghai_daily_06262012.pdf.

Zhou, H., Mo, D., Luo, R., Yue, A., and Rozelle, S. (2016). Are children with siblings really more vulnerable than only children in health, cognition and non-cognitive outcomes? Evidence from a multi-province dataset in China. *China and World Economy, 24*(3), pp. 3–17.

Zhou, M. (1998). "Parachute kids" in Southern California: The educational experience of Chinese children in transnational families. *Educational Policy,* 12(6), pp. 682–704.

Zhou, W. (2013). *How Does a Traumatic Experience During Youth Affect Life Later? The Long-Term Impact of the Send-Down Program during the Chinese Cultural Revolution*. Retrieved from http://www.dal.ca/content/dam/dalhousie/pdf/faculty/science/economics/RePEc/dal/wparch/paper_ZhouAug15.pdf.

Zhu, H. and Lou, S. (2011). Development and reform of higher education in China. Cambridge: Candos Publishing.

Zissimopoulos, J. and Smith, J. (2010). Unequal giving: Monetary gifts to children across countries and over time. *Discussion Paper No. 4698*. Institute for the Study of Labor (IZA). Retrieved from http://ftp.iza.org/dp4698.pdf.

Zweig, D. and Han, D. (2011). "Sea turtles" or "seaweed?" The employment of overseas returnees in China. In Kuptsch, C. ed. *The Internationalization of Labour Markets,* 88–104. Geneva: International Institute for Labour Studies.

Index